Fate's Take-Out Slide

ALSO BY GEORGE GENOVESE
WITH DAN TAYLOR

A Scout's Report: My 70 Years in Baseball
(McFarland, 2015)

Fate's Take-Out Slide

*A Baseball Scout Recalls
Can't-Miss Prospects Who Did*

GEORGE GENOVESE
with DAN TAYLOR

McFarland & Company, Inc., Publishers
Jefferson, North Carolina

LIBRARY OF CONGRESS CATALOGUING-IN-PUBLICATION DATA

Names: Genovese, George, author. | Taylor, Dan (Daniel Edwin), author.
Title: Fate's take-out slide : a baseball scout recalls can't-miss prospects who did / George Genovese with Dan Taylor.
Description: Jefferson, North Carolina : McFarland & Company, Inc., Publishers, 2017. | Includes index.
Identifiers: LCCN 2017040304 | ISBN 9781476670102 (softcover : acid free paper) ∞
Subjects: LCSH: Baseball players—United States—History. | Baseball players—United States—Biography. | Baseball—United States—History.
Classification: LCC GV865.A1 G45 2017 | DDC 796.357—dc23
LC record available at https://lccn.loc.gov/2017040304

BRITISH LIBRARY CATALOGUING DATA ARE AVAILABLE

ISBN (print) 978-1-4766-7010-2
ISBN (ebook) 978-1-4766-2977-3

© 2017 Estate of George Genovese. All rights reserved

No part of this book may be reproduced or transmitted in any form or by any means, electronic or mechanical, including photocopying or recording, or by any information storage and retrieval system, without permission in writing from the publisher.

Front cover: Paul Pettit preparing for his first workout with the Pittsburgh Pirates (Pettit collection)

Printed in the United States of America

McFarland & Company, Inc., Publishers
　Box 611, Jefferson, North Carolina 28640
　　www.mcfarlandpub.com

Acknowledgments

On behalf of George Genovese, thanks are due a great many people for their support and assistance. Words cannot begin to express appreciation enough to my wonderful wife, Eve, for her encouragement, patience, and diligent editing. The family of George Genovese, his daughter Kathleen Haworth, granddaughters Rose and Holly Haworth, son-in-law David Haworth, and niece LeeAnne Marino, were tremendously supportive and invaluably helpful, for which I am grateful. Few things in life can top the motivation, insights, and guidance provided by great friends to whom I am indebted: John Van Ornum, Tom Watt, and Artie Harris.

Many thanks for the assistance and direction from the staff of the microfilm section at the Carnegie Library in Pittsburgh, Pennsylvania; Baseball-Reference.com; Joan Jasper and the staff of the San Francisco Public Library; the staff of the Historical Documents Section of the Los Angeles Public Library; the New Orleans Public Library; the Richmond Memorial Library in Batavia, New York; the Ohio History Connection; Carol Massey of the Edith Garland DuPré Library at the University of Louisiana, Lafayette; Maria Martinez and the staff of the Phoenix Public Library; the Lakeland Public Library; the Fresno County Public Library; Jonathan Waltmire and the staff of the Annie R. Mitchell History Room at the Tulare County Library; the Lancaster branch of the County of Los Angeles Public Library; and the *Chicago Tribune, Collegiate Baseball, Honolulu Star-Bulletin, The Sporting News, The Stanford Daily,* and *The New York Times.*

So many have shared wonderful insights, tremendous information and great stories for which I thank Phil Belmonte, Bob Bennett, Richard Beverage, Bob Bishop, Augusto Cárdenas, Tyrone Culver, Dick Davey, Joe Dodder, Bill Dougherty, Paul Doyle, Harry Dunlop, Arlo Engel, Wayne Graczyk, Eric Hardgrave, Gail Henley, Jin Hisa, Jay Jaffe, Hank Jones,

Acknowledgments

Juan Marichal, Dave Meier, Gar Myers, Ron Necciai, Mel Nelson, Bruce Nichols, Buzz Nitschke, Richard Noe, Joe Nolan, Irv Noren, Chris Patrick, Ronnie Paul, Paul Pettit, Thad Reece, Jesse Reid, Gary Ryerson, Art Santo Domingo, Art Shallock, Al Strane, Bert Strane, Brent Strom, Derek Tatsuno, George Theodore, Tim Theissen, Frank Thomas, Daniel VanDeMortel, and Keith Williams.

And finally, to George Michael Genovese. Thank you. Your friendship will be forever cherished, your confidence embraced and your pearls of wisdom carried daily. Truly you are Baseball's Best There EVER Was.

Table of Contents

Acknowledgments — v

Introduction — 1

1. Tinseltown's Tale — 5
2. Samson and Delilah with Diamonds — 28
3. Painted by the Numbers — 46
4. Lessons from the College of Baseball — 73
5. Greatness Shackled — 97
6. One Glorious Night — 111
7. The Hot Debate — 128
8. The Whole Package — 141
9. Cracked by the Whip — 155
10. The Man Among Boys — 167
11. Aloha Means "Goodbye" — 177
12. The Blue Moon — 187
13. Upping the Ante — 198

Index — 211

Introduction

Baseball is a great game. It's done a lot for me. But I sometimes wonder what might have happened if I had not gone to Bucky Harris and told him I wanted to go back to Hollywood. It was probably a mistake. I'd finally made it to the big leagues. I was playing for Washington. The girl I planned to marry was out in California, and I missed her. I'd taken a pay cut to go from the Pacific Coast League to the big leagues. Can you believe that? It's true! Most of all, I wasn't getting to play, and I felt that I should have been. So, one month into the 1950 season between games of a doubleheader in Boston, I went to the manager's office and told Bucky Harris I wanted to go back to Hollywood. It was the last day I ever spent in the big leagues. Did I make a mistake? Would I have become the shortstop there in time if I had been patient? I've thought about that a lot over the years. That's the side of baseball that the fans rarely hear about. Not just *what* might have been, but *why* did it or didn't it?

When I came to the Giants, Jack Schwarz, the director of scouting and the farm system, used to tell the story of how close the club came to not getting one of their all-time greats. A scout in the South had bussed several players to the Giants' spring training complex for a tryout. After a pretty quick workout, it became clear that these boys couldn't play. When Jack got back to his office, the phone rang. It was the scout telling him that he hadn't been able to send one of the boys over with the others and that he was putting him on the bus from Alabama right then. Jack said that thinking about how bad those other boys had been, he almost told the scout to forget it. Something made him stop. He's glad he did. The Giants have to be glad he did because the next day that other boy showed up, and when he got into the batting cage, he began tearing the cover off the ball and the Giants signed him! The player was Willie McCovey.

As a scout, you see flashes of talent that your experience says might be a glimpse of future greatness. It takes a lot of ingredients to develop that talent into greatness. Sometimes it can be as simple as the right guy liking a player or the wrong guy not liking a player.

During the 34 years that I worked for the Giants, I learned a lot from Jack Schwarz and from Carl Hubbell, who worked alongside of him. "Hub" was one of the all-time greats. He saved the Giants franchise. During the Depression, every time he pitched in the Polo Grounds, he packed that ballpark. Hub pitched in the big leagues for the Giants for 16 years. He was the National League Most Valuable Player twice. For five consecutive years in the 1930s, he won 20 games. In 1947 he was voted into the baseball Hall of Fame for a career that almost never happened.

Before he came to the Giants, Carl went to spring training with Detroit. Ty Cobb was the manager, and he didn't like him. The most Carl ever got to do was pitch a little batting practice before he was sent to the minor leagues. A couple of years later, Hub was pitching in the Texas League when Horace Stoneham's attorney happened to see him. He told Mr. Stoneham he ought to take a look at this left-handed pitcher, and when the Giants did, they bought his contract. In all the years he owned the Giants, Mr. Stoneham held Carl in the highest regard.

Because of what he had been through, Carl had a saying: "There never was a horse that couldn't be rode or a rider who couldn't be throw'd." When he said it about a player, Jack, Mr. Stoneham, and I always knew what Hub meant—never say "never."

A gift is something that should never be taken for granted. When I came to the Giants, there were minor-league managers and some scouts who were careless about their evaluations. I had to fight to prevent guys like Jose Cardenal, Minervino Rojas, Jesus Alou, and a lot of others from being released. Because he didn't hit much in his first couple of years in the farm system, a lot of our guys wrote off Randy Hundley. After we traded him, he became an All-Star with the Cubs. Players sometimes make mistakes, too. Jack Clark didn't get along with his high school coach and quit the team in his junior year. If one of his friends and a new assistant coach hadn't talked him into coming back out for his senior season, who knows what might have become of Jack? He played 18 years in the big leagues and was in the All-Star Game four times.

Just like one person's opinion can make or break a career, misfortune has been known to rob men of greatness. Hugh Alexander was a great scout. Before that, he had the makings of an even greater ballplayer. He signed with Cleveland out of high school in 1936 and in his first season in the minors batted .348. Hugh could really run. He had been a sprint champion in track and field in high school. But Hugh wasn't just some speedster. He could hit for power. In his first season in organized ball, he hit 28 home runs. In his second year, in class C ball, he had hit 30 home runs in 79 games when Cleveland brought him up to the big leagues. The owner of the ballclub said Hugh was going to be a big part of the rebuilding of the team.

Back in those days, ballplayers didn't make a lot of money. They'd go back home in the offseason and work another job for five months. Hugh took a job working in the oil fields in Oklahoma. One day there was a terrible accident, and Hugh's left hand was injured so badly it had to be amputated. His career was done. The Cleveland general manager liked Hugh and gave him a job as a scout, something he did for the next 60 years. He signed a lot of very good ballplayers, too.

Rick Reichardt was the player responsible for bringing in the draft. He was a five-tool ballplayer from the University of Wisconsin. In 1964 the Angels outbid everybody to get him by giving him a $205,000 signing bonus. So many teams were upset by such a large bonus that they voted to create the draft.

Reichardt could run, and he could hit for power. He got off to a good start. During his second season, he didn't feel well one night. He had his roommate take him to the hospital. The doctors found he had a kidney problem, and they had to remove his kidney. After that he didn't see as well at night. They say he also had some stamina problems. He wasn't the same ballplayer.

We have seen tragedies rob the game of great young players. Nick Adenhart was a very good young pitcher who had begun to establish himself with the Angels when he was killed in a car crash. The St. Louis Cardinals projected Oscar Tavares to be a future star. He had hit a big home run in the 2014 playoffs against the Dodgers then just a few days later was killed in a car accident in the Dominican Republic. He was just 22 years old.

Over the years, I've thought about my decision to tell Bucky Harris I wanted to go back to Hollywood. I regretted it. Who knows, if I had been patient I might have gotten the shortstop job. Could I have stayed in the big leagues for a few years? Maybe. I guess things worked out, though. The next year I *was* back at Hollywood. After that season, Branch Rickey bought my contract for the Pirates, and he made me a manager. Mr. Rickey gave me some scouting assignments, and I guess that ultimately led to my becoming a scout with the Giants.

Success and failure can be as close as the length of a gnat's wing. For every Maury Wills, whose speed changed the game, there is a Howie Jennings, who might have achieved as much or more if it wasn't for a bad decision. For every Sandy Koufax, whose name became synonymous with pitching greatness, there is a Paul Pettit, who may have been every bit as good were it not for a flawed idea. For every Juan Marichal, who used a unique pitching style and great talent to reach Cooperstown, there is a Nestor Chavez, whose date with brilliance was taken by tragedy. On the following pages, Dan Taylor and I share with you the stories of Jennings, Pettit, Chavez, and other players from my 70 years in baseball. These are players that I managed, played with, played against, or scouted. Every one of them should have achieved greatness were it not for fate or misfortune. Oh, and by the way, I married the girl, and we were married for 47 years. Yes, I'd say it all worked out.

1

TINSELTOWN'S TALE

It was Hollywood that first brought to mainstream America the woeful tale of a rising star whose climb to greatness was fatefully intersected by tragedy. This story that captivated a motion picture producer and one of its biggest production houses was a baseball version of Icarus, the high flyer who catastrophically plunged from the heights after a flirtation with brilliance—Monty Stratton. Moviegoers would be touched by the remarkable story of the former Chicago White Sox' pitcher's quest to come back from terrible tragedy. In the minds of ballplayers and baseball fans, however, the true Monty Stratton story was one of "what could have been."

Late in the 1948 season, my contract was bought by the Hollywood Stars. It wasn't long after I joined the ballclub that I got exposed to Hollywood. I liked to go out to the park in the morning and get in a training session. One day in the fall, I came up out of the dugout, and our field was filled with people. A big camera was near the baseline. There were a lot of people sitting in the stands. One of them was the actress June Allyson. There were producers, a director and his assistants, makeup people. It was quite a production. The actor Jimmy Stewart was out on the pitcher's mound in a baseball uniform. He was trying to pitch with a stiff left leg to mimic the subject of the picture. They were filming *The Stratton Story* **about the life of Monty Stratton.**

On a late morning during the spring of 1928, Monty Stratton's concentration was broken by clamoring voices. The 15-year-old had been consumed with the activity that dominated his life since his father had succumbed to pneumonia a year earlier—working the family's 104-acre farm in Celeste, Texas, 65 miles northeast of Dallas. Sweat poured from the tall, lanky teenager's brow as he used all of his might to steady the plow that was being pulled by two 1,400-pound horses. Their father's death had heaped strenuous responsibilities on Stratton and his six brothers. Chopping cotton, harvesting grain, and tending livestock took priority over school and made Monty scarce at Wagner High School. His teachers understood the family's plight and that Monty would only be in class when there were lulls in the requirements on the farm.

His classmates understood the Stratton family's plight as well. But on this particular afternoon, several of Monty's school pals felt there was a priority much higher than anything that could be pressing on a farm—a baseball game.

The boys had trekked to the Stratton farm on a mission. Their high school team was to play a fierce rival from a neighboring town that afternoon. They felt Stratton could be their ace in the hole. "You have to pitch for us," one of the boys pleaded. "You're so tall, your size will scare 'em stiff!" It was a plea Monty Stratton couldn't refuse.

After returning the horses to the barn, Stratton grabbed his mitt and set out for the school with his pals. Unknowingly, Monty Stratton embarked upon a journey that would change the course of his life.

Before that afternoon, Monty Stratton had never pitched before. Outfield had always been his position during the sandlot or school games. Once on the mound, however, a fierce, unhittable fastball and a sharp bending curve launched from his 6-foot-5-inch frame, and both helped Wagner High to handily vanquish their rival. Stratton's pitching performance spawned a marvel-charged storytelling that reached three men of baseball influence. Independent ballclubs were rife throughout Texas and always in search of talent. By the following spring, Monty Stratton was able to help his mother make ends meet by pitching on Sundays for one of those independent clubs.

While Stratton's pitching skills were raw, the velocity of his fastball was eye-popping. The teen was practically unhittable, and it wasn't long before his skills were in even greater demand. Within two years, the right-handed pitcher was toiling for three different Texas semipro teams. It was one of those games during the summer of 1932 that vaulted Monty Stratton into the professional ranks and ultimately onto the radar of the Chicago White Sox.

A team from the small northeast Texas border down of Leonard had traveled to Celeste and meekly succumbed to Stratton. The Leonard players went home and spread tales of Stratton's talents. One of the men that heard them was a former minor-league ballplayer, Jude Tate, who, it so happened, kept an eye peeled for talent for the Van Alsten club in the Red River League. Almost a year to the day after he first heard about Stratton, Tate happened to walk into a ballpark in Greenville, Texas, where Stratton was pitching. Tate was impressed, and once the game was over, he convinced Stratton to sign with the Van Alsten club.

Stories of Stratton's exploits with Van Alsten continued to spread. When they reached Ray Largent, who scouted Texas for the Chicago White Sox, he became determined to see Stratton for himself. Once he had, Largent was so impressed that he arranged for the young sensation to join the Galveston Bucs of the Texas League.

There, he was used in relief. The higher level of competition didn't faze him. By early May, Stratton had reeled off a string of 18 consecutive scoreless innings. Scouts from several major-league clubs flocked to Galveston to evaluate Stratton's skills. When Largent learned of the budding interest, he reminded Roy Koehler, the Bucs' general manager, of his club's arrangement with the White Sox. The deal called for the White Sox to provide the Bucs with players in exchange for first crack at any of the Bucs' prospects that they wished to buy. Largent made the owner of the White Sox, J. Louis Comiskey, aware of the interest that rival clubs were showing in Stratton. Largent painted a glowing picture of the pitcher's skills to Jimmy Dykes, the White Sox manager. Six weeks into the 1934 season, the White Sox bought Stratton's contract for $1,200.

Two days later Stratton stepped off the train in Chicago. The Texas farm boy found himself in a new and daunting world that was filled with hustle and bustle and teeming with the sort of offerings and culture not found anywhere near Celeste, Texas. Never before had Stratton seen buildings so tall, so many cars on the streets, so many people in one place. In restaurants his Texas drawl caused double takes. When it was partnered with the use of words such as "reckon" and "shucks," it brought grins and the occasional snickers from the locals. The enormity of the White Sox ballpark, Comiskey Park, was overwhelming. The first time Stratton stepped from the dugout, he gawked at the vision of the 52,000 seats that wrapped the playing field in two distinct decks.

Jimmy Dykes had no illusions at what he was getting. Largent had painted a succinct picture of a raw talent brimming with potential. Still, Dykes didn't hesitate to hand Stratton a uniform and suit him up. The Chicago White Sox were awful. They were mired in last place in the American League and had been for much of the preceding decade. The pitching staff was old and had seen better days. What the Chicago White Sox desperately needed was new blood.

June began with a visit from the Detroit Tigers. Mickey Cochrane's club was in third place, just a game and a half out of first. The disparity between pennant contender and cellar dweller showed on the field. In the top of the sixth inning, the Tigers hammered the ball all around Comiskey Park, scoring four times to increase their lead on the White Sox to 10–0. A paltry crowd groaned its displeasure. Dykes had seen enough. He called time, went to the pitcher's mound, and instructed the umpire to bring in the relief pitcher from the bullpen, Monty Stratton.

Hank Greenberg, a wily veteran, took advantage of Stratton's slow delivery and promptly stole second base. The rookie then gathered himself and got Jo-Jo White to hit a fly ball to left field that became the final out of the inning.

In the seventh inning, Stratton used his curveball and a newly developed underhand sinker to induce groundouts and retire the Tigers without a hit. By the eighth inning the Tigers had assembled an idea of how his pitches broke and on what counts he threw which pitch in his arsenal. A trio of All-Stars—Goose Goslin, Mickey Cochrane, and Charlie Gehringer—smashed hits off of Stratton. Jimmy Dykes and Muddy Ruel, the White Sox' catcher, shouted encouragement that helped the pitcher keep his composure. Resorting to his sinker, Stratton minimized the damage by getting a double-play ball that was followed by a ground-ball out to end the inning. Dykes stuck with his rookie in the ninth inning, and while Detroit managed to extend its lead to 12 runs, the tall Texan had outperformed the seasoned veterans who had been on the mound prior to his entry.

Following the game both Dykes and Comiskey acknowledged that they saw good things from Stratton. "He needs more experience," Dykes told sportswriters after the game. A week later Stratton was sent to the minor leagues and joined the Omaha Packers.

Monty Stratton carried much more than a suitcase on his journey to Omaha. He took with him valuable advice and encouragement. Dykes and his coaches were the encouragers. From Muddy Ruel, Stratton learned that he had to use his glove to better cover the baseball, lest opposing hitters see his finger grip on the ball and gain an idea of what pitch Stratton was about to throw. Ted Lyons, the three-time, 20-game winner and the ace of the White Sox' pitching staff, offered ideas on how to study and make mental notes about the strengths and weaknesses of opposing hitters.

Once in Omaha, Stratton put the advice to work. Pitching for a bad ballclub in the hitter-happy Class C Western League, Stratton managed eight wins over the final two and a half months of the season. His was the third-best wins tally on the team. Away from the diamond, Stratton savored his $2,400 salary. He enjoyed the spoils that came with being a professional ballplayer. Stratton ate better than ever before. The three- and four-course restaurant meals piled on weight, and soon Stratton weighed 30 pounds more than when he had arrived. Also, that summer in Omaha, Stratton met an attractive 18-year-old, Ethel Milberger. The pitcher began courting the girl, and in time the two would marry.

Through the winter months, Jimmy Dykes wondered whether Monty Stratton was ready to be part of the 1935 White Sox' pitching staff. Weeks before spring training was to conclude at Brookside Park in Pasadena, California, Stratton complained of a severe charley horse. The injury kept the young prospect unable to pitch and left Dykes with no choice but to send Stratton to the minor leagues.

Once recovered, Stratton performed in a way that made his advocates proud. He enjoyed a breakthrough season. The White Sox had assigned Stratton to the St. Paul Saints of the Class AA American Association. It was a league that combined young prospects like him with seasoned veterans, many with major-league experience. Undaunted, the tall, talented Texan coursed his way through the league's hitters much as he tilled soil on the farm. He won his first nine starts without a defeat. On June 14, in a tension-filled game against the Milwaukee Brewers, Stratton brought a halt to Eddie Marshall's league-record 43-game hitting streak. Three weeks later Stratton was chosen to be the starting pitcher in the league's all-star game. "He is the most promising young pitcher I've seen in this league in ten years," gushed the Cleveland Indians' general manager, Billy Evans, after he had watched Stratton toss three hitless, scoreless innings in the all-star game. By the end of the season, Stratton had amassed 17 wins, which was the third-best total in the league. His success brought a summons to join the White Sox for the final month of the season.

Jimmy Dykes made Stratton and Ted Lyons roommates on the road. Ted was a real good guy. He was from Louisiana but played college ball in Texas. In his day, he was one of the best pitchers in baseball, but by this time he was near the end of his career. Ted and Monty hit it off. They became great friends, and Ted was a real mentor to Monty. He taught him a lot.

Five days after joining the ballclub in New York, Stratton was rewarded with his first big-league start. It came against the mighty Yankees. His opponent was in a fight with Detroit for the American League pennant while Chicago held down fourth place and sought a first-division finish for the first time since 1920.

In the bottom of the first inning, the Yankees got two runners on base before Stratton retired Ben Chapman, Lou Gehrig, and George Selkirk with relative ease. It was with that ease that Stratton sailed into the fourth inning in a scoreless tie. After Gehrig singled, Bill Dickey hit a screaming line drive past Stratton and into center field to put the Yankees on the scoreboard. Blondy Ryan added a second run to the tally with a sacrifice fly before Stratton quelled the uprising.

The Yankees had little success against Stratton's side-arm fastball, sharp breaking curve, and underhand changeup in the fifth and sixth innings. They added a third run in the seventh on Chapman's single. In the eighth inning, Stratton showed signs of fatigue. Blondy Ryan brought two runners home with a triple. Despite the five-run deficit, Dykes' faith in Stratton didn't waiver. The White Sox strung together a rally in the ninth. They scored twice and had runners at second and third when Jackie Hayes flied out to right field to end the game. The 5–2 loss was Stratton's first decision as a major leaguer.

The loss sent the White Sox into a tailspin. Early season rainouts had caused a manager's nightmare—11 September doubleheaders to make up the games that had been postponed. The White Sox tired. They had lost seven of their last nine games when they arrived in Philadelphia, where in three days they would play seven games, six in doubleheaders against the last-place Athletics. On the first day in Philadelphia, Dykes gave Stratton his second big-league start. The young Texan was shaky from the get-go. Stratton gave up a double, a single, and a walk to fall behind, 1–0, in the bottom of the first.

Monty Stratton then displayed an uncanny ability to ignore trouble, redouble his focus, and work his way out of a jam. A bunt, a comebacker, and a groundball earned three outs to put down the Athletics' opening-inning rally. Over the next two innings, a line drive by Jimmie Foxx was the only ball the Athletics hit hard. In the fourth and sixth innings, the Athletics again scored, only to have Stratton induce weak groundouts and strikeouts that prevented more trouble. Stratton left for a pinch-hitter in the eighth, and though Chicago lost, 4–3, the young hurler did not figure on the decision.

Five days later Stratton pitched eight stellar innings in Washington only to have the game stretch 14 innings before the White Sox were able to pull out a 3–1 win. By now Jimmy Dykes was beginning to believe that Monty Stratton was everything he was reputed to be, a strong-armed pitcher with the kind of talent that could one day make him the ace of the White Sox' pitching staff. The game that established the young right-hander as a starter that his manager could count on was Stratton's fourth big-league start, a September 22 game in Cleveland. As was becoming customary, Stratton got into trouble in the first inning. The Indians scored twice, but those would be the only two runs they would score the entire ballgame. In the second, fourth, fifth, sixth, and seventh innings, Stratton retired the side in order. He was touched for hits in the eighth and ninth but kept the home team off the scoreboard. Following the final out, Chicago's catcher, Merv Shea, shook Stratton's hand then handed him the game ball to celebrate the Texan's first big-league victory, a 9–2 triumph.

Celebrating dotted Stratton's final start of the 1935 season. In the second game of their September 28 doubleheader in Comiskey Park, the Detroit Tigers needed to win to clinch the American League pennant and a spot in the World Series. The prize was a powerful incentive, and the Tigers used it to pummel Stratton en route to an 8–3 win.

While Dykes was pleased with the pitcher's burgeoning success, he was not pleased with Stratton's expanded waistline. The manager frowned at the belly that Stratton's Omaha eating habits had produced and sent Monty home with instructions to lose weight in the offseason.

Winter work on the farm helped to shed 20 pounds. When the following spring arrived, the expectations for success were high for Monty Stratton. During chats with reporters, Dykes used terms such as "polished product" and "marked improvement" to describe Stratton's spring-training performances. The Chicago Cubs' manager, Charlie Grimm, told Dykes that "the Sox had located a real pitcher," in Stratton. After watching Stratton throttle an opponent, one sportswriter labeled the hurler "a rare find." On the eve of Opening Day, a large article in *The Sporting News* trumpeted six top rookies to watch in 1936. Among the group was Monty Stratton and a young New York Yankees outfielder by the name of Joe DiMaggio.

Stratton fulfilled the expectations during the first month of the season. Dykes handed him the ball to start the second game of the season, and Stratton responded by overwhelming the St. Louis Browns. It was not long into the season that his results took a nosedive. In succession, the burgeoning standout was battered by the Tigers and Red Sox, failed to escape the sixth inning against the Yankees, then gave up four early runs at home and lost to Boston again. Dykes was convinced something was wrong. It was only after a checkup by the team doctor that Stratton confessed he'd concealed a painful sore throat. The doctor diagnosed tonsillitis and eased the pain with medication. Stratton received the all-clear to resume working out, but one afternoon, just as he stepped from the Comiskey Park dugout, the pitcher doubled over in extreme pain. Rushed to a hospital, Stratton was quickly prepared for surgery, and his appendix was removed. It would be a month before he would be able to pitch again.

As a return to action neared, Stratton's bad break turned into even worse luck. His balky tonsils began to act up again. The team's doctor said there was no other remedy but surgery. Another trip to the operating room added yet another month to Stratton's time on the sidelines. There were just six weeks left in the season when Monty Stratton buttoned up a White Sox flannel emblazoned with the number 25 and returned to the team. Dykes gave him the ball in relief against the Athletics. Stratton was rusty, and Philadelphia scored on him to win the game.

It was three weeks later on September 2 that Stratton showed flashes of the talent that had drawn lofty preseason praise. Dykes started the right-hander in the second game of a doubleheader against Cleveland. As was becoming customary, Stratton struggled in the first inning. Earl Averill clobbered a long home run to stake the Indians to a 2–0 lead. From that point on, however, Monty Stratton became practically unhittable. He pitched into the ninth before tiring and was replaced. Chicago won, 6–3.

Monty Stratton was clearly rounding into form and his performance stoked the White Sox fires. Five days after beating the Indians, Stratton took a no-hitter into the fifth inning against Philadelphia. Pinky Higgins led off the inning with a single to break up the no-hit bid. Stratton calmly shook it off and held the Athletics at bay over the final four innings. The suddenly surging White Sox won, 17–2, to climb into second place.

On the final day of the season, Monty Stratton had fans on the edge of their seats. His side-arm fastball, downward breaking curveball, and underhand changeup held the St. Louis Browns hitless for five innings. Chicago took a 4–0 lead to the top of the sixth, where Stratton retired the first two batters on routine groundballs. Needing only to retire Lyn Lary to put another no-hit inning into the scorebooks, Stratton uncorked a pitch that the Browns' shortstop pounced on. The crack of the bat from contact with the pitch echoed then was followed an instant later by groans from White Sox fans as the ball landed on the green grass of left field for the first base hit off Stratton that afternoon. Stratton got the final out on a meek tapper back at him then strode toward the White Sox dugout to loud applause from an enthusiastic Comiskey Park crowd.

By the time the seventh inning had begun, Chicago now sat on an 8–0 lead. Black clouds, however, amassed both literally and figuratively over and around the ballpark. A storm rolled into Chicago and darkened the city's southern skies, threatening rain. Stratton retired the first two batters when calamity struck. Back-to-back singles followed by a walk loaded the bases. Tom Carey singled to bring home the Browns' first run and end Stratton's shutout. Ed Coleman pinch-hit and belted a double that cleared the bases and made the score 8–4. Lyn Lary singled Coleman home with the Browns' fifth run. Seeing his pitcher tire, Dykes called time out and replaced Stratton with Clint Brown. St. Louis added one more run to close the gap to two before Brown was able to secure the final out of the inning. It was then that the skies opened up. Rain pelted the stands and puddled up on the playing field, which left the umpires with no choice but to call the game. With the 8–6 win, the White Sox had a pair of ascensions to celebrate. Their third-place finish represented the first time they had finished in the first division in 16 years. The late-season pitching performances by Monty Stratton clearly confirmed his status as one of the brightest young pitching talents in the American League.

When the 1937 season began, Stratton picked right up where he had left off at the end of the 1936 season. On the second day of the season, the tall right-handed pitcher took a four-hit shutout into the ninth inning against St. Louis and beat the Browns, 6–1. A week later he succeeded in pitching a shutout against the Browns, tossing no-hit ball into the fifth inning and allowing half of the eight hits St. Louis managed only after tiring during the final two innings.

On May 5, Stratton took a two-hit shutout into the sixth inning against Philadelphia, where a misplayed ball turned into a double and was followed by a run-scoring Athletics single. Still holding a 4–1 lead, Stratton dispatched the Athletics with ease in the seventh. Bad luck would turn the eighth inning into misadventure. With two outs, successive errors by Luke Appling and Boze Berger opened the floodgates to a Philadelphia rally. By the time Jimmy Dykes removed Stratton from the game, Philadelphia had scored six times and would go on to win, 7–6.

Stratton shook off the misfortune and pitched seven innings of scoreless three-hit baseball to beat the Yankees in his next turn. Five days later, he crafted his second shutout of the season when he held the Cleveland Indians to just three hits in a complete game victory. On May 21, Stratton's 25th birthday, Dykes sent him to the mound in Philadelphia. Stratton's control wasn't sharp. In each of the first five innings, the Athletics managed to put at least two runners on via either walks or singles, but each time Stratton escaped with little damage. The White Sox took a 2–1 lead into the bottom of the sixth inning. In that inning Philadelphia got to Stratton once again. With two outs and the tying run on third base, Stratton looked to all to have escaped more damage. He got Billy Werber to hit a groundball to Tony Piet at third base. Piet's throw across the diamond, however, sailed wildly past first base. The very next hitter, Wally Moses, clubbed a home run that sent Philadelphia to a 4–3 victory, spoiling Stratton's celebration.

To fans and opponents, Stratton's demeanor was the very picture of both calm and confidence. The truth was entirely different. Arch Ward, the *Chicago Tribune*'s savvy columnist, shared the secret with his readers. Ward wrote that the pitcher "forgoes dinner after he works a game. The nervous strain robs him of all desire for food."

The month of June saw Stratton reel off five wins, two of which came during a ten-game Chicago win streak that saw the White Sox soar from sixth into a first-place tie with the Yankees. The White Sox ended June with another win streak, this one seven games. Stratton initiated the second streak by blanking Philadelphia, 2–0, on a three-hit shutout in which he didn't walk a man. The streak concluded when Stratton beat the mighty Tigers in a game in which he took a no-hitter into the seventh inning and finished with a complete game three-hit win—his ninth of the season.

Accolades poured. Writers hailed the new pitching ace of the White Sox. But the biggest of the accolades came from Joe McCarthy, manager of the New York Yankees. At the end of June, McCarthy selected Stratton to pitch in the All-Star Game. The White Sox ace was to join Lefty Gomez, Lefty Grove, Mel Harder, Tommy Bridges, and Wes Farrell on the six-man American League pitching staff for the annual parade of stars in Washington, D.C. Six years after pitching his first game at the urging of high school pals, Monty Stratton was regarded as one of the best pitchers in baseball.

On July 4, in his final start before the All-Star Game, Stratton set out for his tenth win of the season. The achievement would give him the most wins in the American League. The White Sox staked their ace to a five-run early lead, which allowed Stratton to pitch relaxed against the Browns in St. Louis. In the sixth inning, Stratton laced a single to center field. While trying to score on a single by Mike Kreevich, Stratton slid into home plate then grabbed his hand in pain. Worry rippled through the White Sox dugout. The team's trainer gingerly looked at the hand and worried aloud that a bone might have been fractured. Stratton was driven to the hospital, where X-rays were negative. The team doctor prescribed a week's rest, and Dykes had to call McCarthy with the news that Stratton would not be traveling to Washington for the All-Star Game.

The White Sox resumed the second half of the season with another series against St. Louis. In the series finale Dykes tabbed Stratton to pitch and blew a big sigh of relief when Stratton blanked the Browns for six innings. In the top of the seventh, the Browns broke through and scored three times to tie the game. One half-inning later the outcome was decided. Standing at the plate, wagging a bat, Monty Stratton put a mighty swing into the offering by the Browns' pitcher, Lou Koupal. The ball sailed over the fence and into the left-field stands for a home run that made Chicago victorious, 4–3.

Stratton rose to even higher prominence during the season's second half. He pitched shutouts to beat the Red Sox and Athletics. When Lou Gehrig and Joe DiMaggio roughed him up in a high-scoring game in New York, Stratton maintained his composure, battled the mighty Yankees, and was rewarded when his teammates scored in the ninth to win, 7–6.

Thanks in part to Stratton's pitching, the White Sox spent the entire month of July in second place. When they arrived in New York on August 5 for four games with the American League front runners, the White Sox were 20 games above .500 and five games out of first place. Exuberance evaporated from the White Sox clubhouse after the Yankees scored 22 runs and steamrolled their way to wins in each of the first three games.

Stratton drew the start for game four of the series. He was keen to halt his team's slide. Through the first three innings, Stratton was perfect. Chicago led, 3–0, and all nine Yankees batters had been retired, most of them meekly on ground-ball outs. When Stratton took the mound for the bottom of the fourth inning, things soon drastically changed. His pinpoint accuracy was gone, so too was the overpowering velocity of his fastball. Frankie Crosetti led off the inning with a single. Joe DiMaggio walked. Bill Dickey was ordered walked intentionally to load the bases. Stratton then plunked Jake Powell with a pitch that brought Crosetti home with a Yankees run. The tenacious hurler managed to pitch his way out of further trouble, but more came his way an inning later.

With two runners on, Dykes recognized that something was amiss with his standout, and he removed Stratton from the game. The Yankees erupted and went on to tally 13 runs in a 13–8 romp. The loss was devastating to the White Sox. It dropped them nine games behind New York. They traveled next to Boston, where their losing streak grew to seven, and they fell into third place. Worse, injury had once again struck Monty Stratton. After the loss to the Yankees, Stratton complained of losing all strength in his right arm. It was diagnosed as fatigue. Two weeks' rest was prescribed. Without him the White Sox fell further and further out of the pennant race.

On August 29 the hapless Philadelphia Athletics arrived in Chicago. Dykes decided the time was right to send his pitching ace back to the mound, but the high spirits at Stratton's return would very quickly turn to regret. From the game's opening pitch, the Athletics hammered everything Monty Stratton offered. Wally Moses opened the game with a double, and seven batters later—following two doubles, two singles, three stolen bases, and two walks—Dykes reached the limit of his patience and yanked Stratton from the game. Philadelphia went on to set an American League record by scoring 12 runs in that first inning. The White Sox were crushed both literally, 16–0, and figuratively. After the game Stratton told the sportswriters that his arm felt fine. He conceded, however, that he had been afraid to cut loose. The determined pitcher vowed that he would ask Dykes for another start the following week and promised the outcome would be better. Despite Stratton's wish, Dykes held him out. The manager did not use his pitching ace again for a month. During a game with Cleveland, Stratton was instructed to warm up in the bullpen. Bob Feller was shutting down the White Sox. In the eighth inning with Cleveland leading, 4–0, Dykes sent Stratton out to pitch. He surrendered a single to the leadoff batter, but two ensuing fly-ball outs and a strikeout made for a smooth return to action and proved to his manager that Stratton had sufficiently recovered.

Three days later the White Sox concluded the 1937 season with a doubleheader in St. Louis. Dykes tabbed Stratton to start the second game. His stuff was rusty, and his control was not particularly good, but Stratton battled. The young hurler helped his cause with two hits at the plate. The White Sox closed the campaign with a 7–2 win. The win assured the White Sox of a third-place finish in the American League, three games behind Detroit and 19 games behind the first-place Yankees. It was their best season since 1920.

As for Stratton, despite losing six weeks to his arm injury, he had amassed 15 wins, the sixth-best total in the American League. His 2.40 earned run average was second best to the 2.33 mark of the Yankees' Lefty Gomez. Stratton's 15–5 record and .750 winning percentage was third best among the top 12 pitchers in the league.

J. Louis Comiskey had taken a liking to his new star pitcher. The owner of the ballclub held Stratton's work ethic, humility, and good character in high regard. In November Stratton received evidence of that esteem. He opened a letter from the White Sox' owner that contained his contract for the 1938 season. Comiskey offered a $6,000 raise. Stratton summoned a bit of courage and sent a letter back to Comiskey that asked for $2,000 more.

That was just not something young players did. The owners were real tightfisted men, and if you got on their bad side, it could ruin your career. There were a lot of ballplayers who saw their careers ruined by getting on the wrong side of an owner.

When Comiskey received Stratton's reply he smiled, shook his head, and instructed his secretary to send the pitcher another contract, this one with a revised salary of $12,000, the third-highest salary on the ballclub. Days later, an even greater gift blessed the Stratton household. Ethel gave birth to the couple's first child, a boy whom they named Monty Jr.

The sunny outlook that accompanies the rolling out of bats and balls to begin spring training was short-lived for the White Sox in 1938. For six years the team had made Pasadena, California, their spring training home. The sunshine that brightened Brookside Park, across the street from the Rose Bowl, was replaced in February 1938 by torrential rain. Not long after the players arrived, Southern California was hit with its worst rain storms in 50 years. The second of two major storms hit late at night on March 1 and continued for almost two days. When it blew out of the region, it had dumped more than 10 inches of rain, destroyed more than 5,000 buildings, and left 800 cars stranded. The White Sox were among the stranded, unable to escape to alternate training options in Arizona or Texas. For four days, the players, their coaches, and manager could do nothing but sit around their hotel and write letters home or play cards.

Once the weather improved and drills began, rain was replaced by injury as their nemesis. On the same day, the team's star shortstop, Luke Appling, broke his right leg in two places, and their star pitcher was injured, too. Stratton's was a peculiar biceps injury. Appling was declared out for three months while Stratton was day-to-day. As the days passed there was little progress. Concern over Stratton's arm grew. By the time the team arrived in Chicago to begin the 1938 season, their mound ace still could not pitch.

Without Appling and Stratton, the team got off to a poor start. By the third week of the season, the White Sox had a losing record and sat in fifth place in the eight-team American League standings. It was a month into the season before Stratton got into his first game. Dykes brought him out of the bullpen, and he worked a successful ninth inning against Cleveland. Over the next five weeks, Dykes worked his ace back into top form, alternating Stratton between occasional one-inning relief appearances and starts. The results were mixed: an uncharacteristic nine-walk outing against the Tigers one week and a flawless relief stint against the Red Sox the next.

The White Sox were hovering just above last place when the Yankees came to Chicago in the middle of June. Attendance was suffering. Few were spinning the turnstiles to watch the lowly club play. After seeing his team drop the first two games of the series, Dykes handed the ball to Stratton to pitch the last game of the set. The sparse crowd left Comiskey Park buzzing that afternoon. They had witnessed Stratton in stellar form. He pitched the distance and scattered only four hits against the mighty Yankees. Luck, however, was not entirely on the Texan's side. Twice he had become flustered after errors by teammates' prolonged innings. Walks and hit batters set the table for Monte Pearson, Lou Gehrig, and Tommy Henricks to make three of the Yankees' four hits produce runs. Pearson's two-out double in the second inning scored two of them. Gehrig's home run in the sixth inning added one more run, and Henricks' ninth-inning triple led to the fourth of five Yankee runs.

Despite the result, Chicago's seventh consecutive loss at home, Stratton's performance had brought a ray of hope to the White Sox clubhouse. He remained a starting pitcher for the rest of the season and in six weeks had notched 10 wins. In his lone loss during that stretch, Stratton slammed a home run against the Tigers, but his hitting prowess failed to help the White Sox outscore their opponent.

On August 20 Stratton struck out nine to beat the Yankees and earn his 15th win of the season. Seven days later he hooked up with Cleveland's 19-year-old fireballing sensation, Bob Feller. With the phenom mowing his way through Chicago's batting order, Stratton's effort was hampered by walks and fielding miscues. In an especially frustrating third inning, Cleveland's Ken Keltner hit a ball at Luke Appling that looked certain to be the final out. Appling, however, mishandled it and Keltner reached first base. Flustered, Stratton walked the next two batters, then with the bases loaded, Lyn Lary smashed a ball at Marv Owen, the White Sox' third baseman. Owen wasn't able to field it cleanly, and two runners scampered home to score. Jeff Heath clubbed a home run in the seventh inning as Cleveland sent Stratton to his ninth loss of the season, 6–1.

When the team finished its season, players packed up trunks and suitcases and boarded trains or hopped in cars for the journey home. All around the departing players was a city awash in baseball euphoria. The city's jubilation was for the crosstown Cubs, who had won the National League pennant and were preparing to meet the Yankees in the World Series.

Stratton embarked upon a winter in Texas with Ethel and Monty Jr. Despite his injuries, there was much to be pleased about the 1938 season. His win total ranked sixth among all American League pitchers. While the 15–9 won-lost record was not produced with the same overpowering performances that he had enjoyed in 1937, Stratton received consolation. When the tabulating concluded, he had received four percent of the vote for American League Most Valuable Player. But for the seventh consecutive year, the award went to a hitter—Boston's Jimmie Foxx, who won it for the third time in his career after hitting 50 home runs, driving in 175, and batting .349 for the Red Sox.

Monty and Ethel spent the Thanksgiving holiday at his mother's farm and planned a Sunday afternoon party to celebrate their son's first birthday. On that morning the weather was cold and crisp but not deterrent to Monty's plan to go outdoors and do some shooting. He strapped on his leather holster then set out onto the 104-acre farm, where he had been raised. A prized .32 revolver slapped against his right hip as he trudged over furrows, through scrub, and mire. After close to 30 minutes, Stratton had ventured a half mile from his mother's house. Suddenly, a rabbit jumped from the brush. Stratton whipped his pistol from the holster and fired a shot at the bounding animal. He watched for a sign his shot had hit the mark but pursed his lips as the rabbit's churning legs propelled the creature from his range. Stratton's eyes scanned the terrain for more targets while he walked along a thicket. As he stuffed the gun back into the holster, a loud shot rang out. The sound echoed against the calm November sky. Frightened birds flushed from nearby trees. Monty Stratton lay crumpled on the ground in pain and gravely wounded.

Blood poured from a wound near his right hip. Excruciating pain seared through Stratton's right leg. He fought to regain composure. Cries for help went unheard. He realized no one knew where he was and that he was too far from the farmhouse to attract attention. Slowly Stratton began to dig his elbows into the earthen sludge. First the left, then the right, and back again. Each thrust slowly dragged his injured body on an agonizing trek for help.

As clear thinking replaced the initial shock, ideas darted through Stratton's mind. He made a plan to try to reach the road to the farmhouse. Perhaps someone might travel by and happen upon him. It was the wounded baseball star's best chance for swift help.

It had been only a simple jostle, but one that happened with the safety off. The jarring caused the gun to discharge. From point-blank range, the .32 slug had pierced Stratton's right leg. It entered just below the hip, traveled down the leg, and lodged behind his knee. Now Stratton was in a race for his life. Every second seemed an eternity. Once he finally reached the road, he began to yell. Louder and louder he cried for help, all the while digging his elbows into the earth to pull his body an inch at a time closer to his mother's farmhouse. Five hundred yards from the house he hollered again, and still nobody came. Breathing deeply and bleeding profusely, Stratton continued to pull his body over the dusty ground. Two hundred yards from the farmhouse he cried out again. This time he waved his cap and hoped someone might see him. An instant later he heard clatter. Tilting his head up, Stratton saw the backdoor of the farmhouse thrust open. Ethel had heard him. She ran down the road to her wounded husband. A loud shriek flew from her lungs when she saw what had happened. Ethel swiftly turned and ran to get their car.

Monty Stratton lay weakened from the loss of blood when Ethel strained to load him into the car. They set out for the nearest hospital but on arrival were sent immediately to St. Paul Hospital in Dallas, which they were told was better equipped to treat him.

When doctors first saw Stratton, they knew they were in a race with time. Blood loss put his life in peril. Stratton's older brothers, Hardin and Roland, raced to the hospital. Not long after they arrived, their shirt sleeves were rolled up, and their blood surged through tubes. As soon as doctors were able, Monte Stratton was given a transfusion then taken to an operating room. A surgeon removed the bullet but found that the femoral artery had been severed. He tied the artery to stop the blood loss. The hope was that circulation would return.

Almost instantly after Stratton had arrived at the hospital, phone calls and cables sent word of the tragedy to family members, friends, and teammates. Harry Grabiner, the White Sox' vice president, gasped on being told the news. He slammed down the telephone then gave one of the team's scouts in Texas orders to go to the hospital and phone with any updates on Stratton's condition. Grabiner then phoned St. Paul's Hospital and offered to fly the "finest specialists from Chicago" if it would help to save Monty Stratton's life. He was assured his pitcher's care was in the finest hands. Reporters called and caught Grabiner in despair. "Baseball is secondary now," he told them. "Our concern is about his health. We are all hoping nothing more serious develops." From New York to Los Angeles, newspapers flew off the presses carrying astonishment. On street corners of every major city, newspaper hawkers cried out the startling news. "Stratton Wounded in Hunting Mishap," trumpeted the *New York Times*. "Stratton Seriously Wounded in Accident," heralded the *Los Angeles Times*. White Sox fans who grabbed the *Chicago Tribune* saw bold letters that pronounced, "Stratton Sox Pitcher Shot; May Lose Leg."

Throughout the night, Ethel Stratton clutched her baby and sat in a chair by her husband's bedside. Nurses made frequent checks of Stratton's right leg, each time looking for favorable signs. By morning the worst fears were realized. It was Dr. Arthur Thomasson who sat down alongside Ethel Stratton and broke the bad news. "The leg is beginning to turn black," he calmly explained. "Collateral circulation has failed to set up. Gangrene is beginning to set in. I am afraid an amputation is imperative."

It was just after four o'clock in the afternoon when Stratton was placed under anesthesia. Three doctors gathered in the operating room. The procedure was short. At five o'clock word flashed to Chicago that Stratton had lost his leg. The limb was amputated just above the knee. Twenty minutes later, a weak Monty Stratton was back in his room. Dr. Thomasson told Ethel Stratton that her husband's condition was satisfactory, and he did not expect any complications. "Your husband," he assured her, "should recover."

Teammates reacted to the news with shock and anguish. Ted Lyons wept. Billy Webb, who had been Stratton's manager at Galveston and recently joined the White Sox' coaching staff, was shattered. Jimmy Dykes flew across the country to visit. Stratton said weakly to his manager, "I'm alive, have my wife, son, relatives, and more friends than I ever dreamed I have." When the Chicago Cubs trainer, Andy Lotshaw, heard about the tragedy, he shook his head and groused to a reporter, "The only shooting a baseball player should do is in a dice game."

I was in high school when his accident happened. The news was in all the papers. It was a terrible thing, but I don't think most people realized just how good Monty Stratton was and how truly tragic his accident was.

Just over a week after the operation, J. Louis Comiskey phoned the Strattons with a promise—a lifetime job with the White Sox. Comiskey added that the Chicago Cubs had agreed to play the White Sox in an exhibition game on April 17. For the first time ever in baseball, all of the money collected from the game would go to Monty Stratton. Jimmy Dykes said he wanted Stratton to be on his coaching staff and was taken aback when Stratton expressed appreciation then added, "I'm going to pitch again."

Two weeks after the operation, several sportswriters around the country were surprised to receive handwritten notes in the mail from Stratton. An editor at *The Sporting News* opened an envelope and welled up when he read, "Please accept my thanks for remembering me in so nice a way." Throughout the winter, cables, cards, and letters poured into Stratton's Greenville home with postmarks from every state in the union. At Christmas he was overwhelmed by bags that contained 815 letters.

During the usually raucous Chicago Baseball Writers Banquet in January, a note from Stratton was read. It conveyed gratitude to both Comiskey and Phillip K. Wrigley, owner of the Cubs, for their plans to stage a benefit game in his honor. "I feel fine and am looking forward to accomplishing many things when I get my artificial limb," Stratton wrote. "I do not intend to let it handicap me to any great extent." Specialists fitted Stratton for an artificial leg in January. In the first few days after the fitting, he would stand in his living room and practice steadying himself and regaining his balance. In February Stratton began to take daily walks. Evenings he would stand at one end of the living room and fling a baseball across the room into an easy chair. One day, Ethel scolded Monty for damaging the chair. When she suggested they throw outside, Monty grumbled, "You're not much of a catcher." Ethel shot back, "Well, you're not much of a pitcher—yet."

Their games of catch became a daily activity. Stratton tinkered with his pitching motion. His biggest challenge was to develop a means to pivot on the artificial limb. Once perfected, he began to cut loose. His pitches whistled into Ethel's mitt with greater and greater velocity until one day a fastball struck the leather so hard that it knocked her backwards onto her rear end. Both gawked at one another with amazement and an unspoken realization that Stratton had regained much of his pre-amputation skills.

While his Chicago White Sox teammates were arriving in Pasadena for spring training, Stratton was experimenting on a pitcher's mound in Texas. He didn't pitch many balls. Just enough to experience both frustration and optimism. While almost every newspaper article written about Stratton during the winter of 1938–39 included a line about his career being over, deep down Monty held out hope of pitching again one day. He increased the amount of pitches that he threw each day. Ray Largent, the scout who had signed him, drove over from his home in McKinney for a visit one afternoon. He watched silently as Stratton fired ball after ball while trying to balance his delivery on the artificial leg. When Largent glanced at Ethel Stratton, she said, "He looks as good as ever. Except he's not so graceful." Largent grinned but the next morning phoned Comiskey and said, "He won't pitch this year," then paused to add, "if ever."

Opening Day was approaching when Stratton kissed Ethel and ran his fingers through Monty Jr.'s hair then climbed into his car and drove out of Greenville. He was anxious to get to Chicago, so anxious that he drove the 680 miles to Omaha in one day. Reporters who learned he was staying the night in their city scrambled to speak to the former All-Star. Some were surprised when he said he wanted to pitch again. "If it can be done, I'll do it," he vowed.

On April 14 the press was summoned to J. Louis Comiskey's office to witness Stratton in a White Sox uniform pose with the team owner and

1. Tinseltown's Tale

manager and announce that he had signed a coaching contract with the team. An almost giddy welcome waited in the clubhouse, where broad smiles painted the faces of the White Sox players when their former teammate entered. Ted Lyons was especially happy to see his old roommate. "The gamest guy in the world," Lyons beamed to a sportswriter.

Once the season began, Stratton plunged into his coaching responsibilities. He enthusiastically welcomed Dykes' idea to pitch batting practice and would do so almost every day throughout the season. Stratton was also assigned to coach first base. On Opening Day Stratton had to beg off the duty after three innings when he was overtaken with fatigue and discomfort from the standing.

Rain dampened the excitement of Stratton's benefit game. A storm left the field so wet that the umpires said the teams couldn't play. Comiskey and Wrigley looked over their schedules and agreed their teams would meet again when both had a day off on May 1. When the day came, Comiskey Park was abuzz. Several dozen newsreel cameramen from outlets all around the country jostled at the ballpark's entrance to capture the enthusiasm and flavor of the day. Comiskey Park's ushers refused to take pay for working the game. Telegraph operators passed the hat and made a cash donation to the Stratton fund. The Lydy Parking Company turned over all of the money their attendants collected to the fund. Ticket takers were made busy collecting stubs from the more than 25,000 fans who streamed into Comiskey Park. Former White Sox standout, Ray Schalk, who managed the Indianapolis Indians, diverted the team from its road trip to St. Paul to attend the game. Though he was battling a sore arm, Dizzy Dean insisted to the Cubs' manager, Charlie Grimm, that he wanted to pitch in the game.

During batting practice, many of the sportswriters scrutinized Stratton's throwing motion as he pitched. Glances were exchanged and nods and shrugs made at suggestions that Stratton struggled with his balance. Most agreed that the idea of Stratton pitching again wasn't the problem, it was fielding. Several writers wondered aloud how he would ever manage to field bunts.

An hour before the game was to begin, Monty was introduced and limped to home plate. Several individuals and groups gathered for presentations. A committee that had staged a testimonial dinner for the former Cubs' catcher, Gabby Hartnett, gave him a check for $407.20. Another committee presented Stratton with a watch. Stratton then was left speechless when his former teammate, Tony Piet, came to home plate and handed him the keys to a new automobile.

A loud roar went up from the crowd when Stratton tossed the ceremonial first pitch, and two hours later the White Sox celebrated a 4–1 win while the Cubs hustled to catch a train for Philadelphia.

Days later when the gate receipts and donated funds were tallied, Harry Grabinger proudly announced that Stratton would receive $29,845. When asked his plans, Stratton said he would build a new home on his own farm and invest the remainder for retirement.

His former teammates marveled at Monty's sense of humor and upbeat demeanor. The White Sox dugout would break out in uproarious laughter when Stratton would holler at an opposing pitcher who was struggling, "Look out, or you'll be wearing a wooden leg like mine!"

Throughout the summer, Stratton used his batting practice stints to hone his pitching skills. With each batting practice session that Stratton threw, his pitching skills improved. By the middle of the summer, players remarked that his pitches seemed almost as good as they were before the injury.

Stratton began to prod Dykes for a chance to pitch in a game. The manager resisted. By July the two had made an agreement. If the White Sox had nailed down third place when they opened the final three-game series of the season, Jimmy Dykes would pitch Stratton in one of the final three games in St. Louis.

The issue there was money. Where a team finished in the standings meant a certain amount of prize money for all the players on the ballclub. There was a big difference between third- and fourth-place money, and remember, America was just coming out of the Depression. That money meant a lot to the ballplayers. Dykes didn't want to experiment with Stratton in a game that had money on the line.

On September 17 the White Sox arrived on the east coast for a series with the Red Sox and Yankees. They owned third place, a game and a half ahead of the Cleveland Indians. By the time the White Sox left New York, they had lost four straight games. They fell into fourth place and trailed Cleveland by a half game. When the White Sox boarded their train for St. Louis, Monty Stratton had been informed he would not be activated. The team lost two of their final three games and finished in fourth place.

Stratton remained a White Sox coach for the next two seasons, pitching batting practice each day and coaching first base. Just before Christmas during the winter of 1941, Stratton learned that the Lubbock Hubbers of the West Texas-New Mexico League needed a manager. He sent the owner a letter expressing interest and got the job. Ten days into the season he quit. He couldn't take the bus rides, and the stress of managing had caused him to lose 15 pounds.

For the next two years Stratton concentrated on farming. He worked his own acreage and helped neighbors who were shorthanded because of World War II. He drew the figure of a man on the side of his barn and occasionally flung fastballs and curves in its direction. Monty Jr., who was now four, and the family dog, Happy, were enlisted as retrievers.

In 1944 Ethel Stratton prodded Monty to get back in the game. He resisted. So, she assembled several local players from Greenville and pushed Monty into pitching for the team. The former White Sox ace pitched the team into the semifinals of the state semipro tournament. A year later a coach phoned to ask Monty if he would recommend a pitcher for an important game in a semipro tournament in Houston. Stratton said he couldn't think of anyone. Ethel Stratton wrote the coach a letter to suggest Monty. The coach enthusiastically added Monty to his team and marveled as he held the opposition to just two hits and drove in his team's only two runs.

Art Willingham, the business manager of the Sherman Twins in the East Texas League, heard about Stratton's performance. He contacted Monty with the offer of a contract to return to professional baseball for the 1946 season. It offered the chance to pitch for a Class C club, and Stratton eagerly snatched the opportunity. Any apprehension that Stratton was up for the challenge evaporated on April 30. In his first game with the club, Stratton pitched a one-hitter. The East Texas League was Class C, in the lower levels of the minor leagues. Still, the competition included more than a dozen former big-leaguers just home from the war. Throughout the summer, Stratton made 27 starts for the Twins. Never were there fewer than 2,500 fans in the stands when he pitched. They saw Stratton win 18 times while losing only eight.

In Hollywood, Douglas Morrow was looking for inspiration. He had been asked to write a screenplay about rehabilitation. Morrow thought the project should focus on an actual-life story. As he pondered possibilities, Monty Stratton came to mind. Morrow looked into what the former White Sox standout was doing and was flabbergasted to learn that Stratton was pitching and doing well in Texas.

The two men met and reached a deal to make a movie based on Stratton's life. Metro Pictures agreed to make the movie and set aside a budget of $1,771,000. Van Johnson and Ronald Regan desperately sought to play the starring role but couldn't because of contractual ties to other studios. The role went to Jimmy Stewart. June Allyson was cast as Ethel Stratton.

Once the project moved into full production mode, Monty and Ethel

Stratton moved to California. Monty was to be an advisor and help promote the film. Within days of arriving, Stratton joined cast and crew for filming at Gilmore Field.

Stratton was an advisor on the film. He was at the ballpark for all the filming sessions, and I'd get together with him. We'd talk about the picture and talk a lot of baseball. I really enjoyed my conversations with him. He was such a good guy, a really good guy.

During the spring of 1949, the cast along with Stratton traveled to Chicago and Greenville, Texas, for advance screenings. Metro circled June 2 on the calendar for the full launch but not before hosting a gala anniversary party to celebrate the release of the film on June 1 at the Egyptian Theatre.

In June of 1949 they held a premier for the film, and our ballclub was made the featured guests. We all had to go down there in suits and ties, and they had us up on stage. It was quite an evening.

Hollywood had come off a string of poor sports movies, but *The Stratton Story* turned the trend around. Edwin Schalbert of the *Los Angeles Times* lauded the film. Celebrated Hollywood columnist Hedda Hopper called the picture, "as American as apple pie," and praised Stewart's portrayal of Stratton as an "outstanding performance." *The Stratton Story* earned more than $4,000,000 at the box office, and in March of 1950 Douglas Morrow's idea and faith in Stratton was rewarded when he received the Academy Award for Best Motion Picture Story.

Once the advising and promotional appearances had concluded, the Strattons packed up and returned to the farm in Greenville. As the spring of 1950 approached, the Greenville Majors in the Class B Big State League offered a contract. Though he was now 38 years old, Stratton didn't hesitate to accept the offer. When asked about it, he told an interviewer, "Spring comes around and the grass gets green. I dunno, baseball gets into your blood, I guess." The season was Monty Stratton's last in professional baseball. Three years later he barnstormed and pitched single games with several teams before hanging up the spikes and glove for good at the age of 41.

When most people think of Monty Stratton, they think of his comeback, which was remarkable. You have to wonder how good he might have been if he hadn't had the accident. With a little luck, he might have won 20 games in 1937 and again in 1938. Maybe he'd would have been like Lefty Gomez and Bob Feller, one of the best pitchers in the American League.

Maybe he would have followed his teammate, Ted Lyons, into the Hall of Fame. Who knows. He had a lot of talent. He loved the game. It makes you wonder just how good he might have been.

For decades Stratton's teammates and manager were left to wonder what might have been. Their belief was perhaps best capsulized by the president of the White Sox, Grace Comiskey, when she said to J.G. Taylor Spink of *The Sporting News*, "He would have been one of the greatest pitchers in American League history."

2

SAMSON AND DELILAH WITH DIAMONDS

Two fans marveled at the browning, autograph-covered baseball. The ball was a treasure from a time gone by, a marvelous time in the history of Southern California baseball. Across the sphere's horsehide were scrawled the names of future big-league standouts: Irv Noren, Willie Ramsdell, and Art Shallock.

To the novice fan, one signature meant nothing. To the onlooker who knew the 1949 Hollywood Stars well, the autograph represented the best player on the team—someone who should have become a big-league star yet didn't—Jim Baxes.

Nobody expected much out of us in 1949. After all, we had finished near the bottom of the Pacific Coast League in '48, and it had been several years since Hollywood was a pennant contender. The papers weren't giving us much of a chance, but in spring training you could see that we had the makings of a pretty good ballclub. Irv Noren had been the MVP in the Texas League. He had some power and played a very good center field. Frankie Kelleher and Chuck Stevens had power. Gene Handley was a good second baseman. But the best-looking ballplayer in spring training was a guy who joined our ballclub almost by accident: Jim Baxes.

Beneath the pines that dwarfed the wooden outfield fence at San Fernando Park, the perennial Pacific Coast League also-rans prepared for the 1949 season. A feeling of frustration had engulfed the ballclub during a dismal summer of 1948, the sort that spurred management to make dramatic offseason changes that were designed to both appease and impress. The management of the Hollywood Stars hadn't worked to please just any

2. Samson and Delilah with Diamonds   29

fans. The most ardent followers of the Pacific Coast League club *were* Hollywood stars. It was a ballclub cloaked in celebrity.

The movie stars came out to the ballpark every night. Groucho Marx and his family had box seats right next to our bat rack. Ronald Reagan and Clark Gable were at almost every game. George Raft was usually sitting down near left field gambling, and he was betting against us! Gary Cooper and Mickey Rooney came out. It was really something.

Stars of motion pictures and the recording industry weren't just fans; several owned a stake in the club. Bob Cobb, owner of the famed Brown Derby restaurant, was the team's vice president, and he ran the operation. Other members of the ownership group were film star Barbara Stanwyck, iconic movie director Cecil B. DeMille, singing cowboy Gene Autry, and actor William Frawley.

After his team finished sixth in the eight-team Pacific Coast League with 104 losses, Cobb vowed change. In November he made the team's radio announcer the manager. Fred Haney wasn't just some radio voice, though. He had played seven seasons in the big leagues then later managed the St. Louis Browns from 1939 through the first 44 games of the 1941 season. The diminutive, personable Haney returned home to Los Angeles, bought and ran a liquor store, then got into broadcasting. It was as the radio voice of the Hollywood Stars that Haney developed a large following with utterances like his standard sign-off line at the end of each game, "This is Fred Haney, rounding third and heading for home."

To try to improve the Stars, Haney and Cobb set out to utilize their contacts in baseball to get better players. Calls by Haney reeled in two solid starting pitchers, Glen Moulder from the White Sox and Jack Salveson from the Browns. Cobb tapped an old friend, Branch Rickey, and arranged a tie-up with his Brooklyn Dodgers that brought Irv Noren to play center field, Herb Gorman to handle right field, Mike Sandlock to catch, and Art Shallock for the pitching staff. But the newcomer who would have the greatest impact on the improvement of the 1949 Hollywood Stars was a player they landed purely by accident.

During the winter Branch Rickey, Jr., who ran the Dodgers' farm system, had an idea to save money. He asked Haney and Cobb if a few young minor-league players that lived on the West Coast could train with Hollywood. Rickey explained that this would spare the Dodgers the cost of flying them across country to Brooklyn's spring training base in Vero Beach, Florida. Haney agreed, never thinking it would bring the Stars one of their best players. It didn't take the Hollywood manager long to be overwhelmed by Jim Baxes.

Right away, Baxes was one of our best ballplayers. He had a great arm, he ran well, and he could hit for power. We had a lot of veterans on our ballclub, even a few guys who had played in the big leagues, but it was only a few days into spring training when you could see Baxes had talent. There was no way Fred Haney was giving him back to the Dodgers.

Born Dimitros Speros Baxes to Greek immigrants, Baxes had done little, if anything, to distinguish himself as a prospect during his first two seasons in professional baseball. He hit .257 in Class C ball straight out of high school, then .249 at Class B ball before getting a five-game taste of the top tier of minor-league ball, where Baxes had just a .182 batting average playing for Class AAA St. Paul.

His results in the pro game were not what had been projected when Jim Baxes had been the 1946 City Player of the Year at San Francisco's Mission High School. No less an authority than the Hall of Fame outfielder, Ty Cobb, had proclaimed the young infielder a future star after watching him play. Brooklyn clinched his signature on a contract after Baxes shone in the 1946 National High School all-star game in New York. Playing against the best players from around the country, Baxes had three hits and received the Lou Gehrig Award as the game's Most Valuable Player.

Glasses made Baxes look more student than ballplayer. A chiseled physique on a 6-foot-1-inch, 190-pound frame, however, prompted teammates to tag him with a one-word nickname, "Adonis."

Hollywood was in the most talented of all the minor leagues. The Pacific Coast League was a Class AAA league, the highest level of minor league. Many people called it the "third major league," and in 1945 club owners had voted to try to become just that. The league was filled with former big-leaguers and prospects who were knocking at the door to get to the major leagues.

During spring training, Baxes bunked with several other rookies above a bar near the park where the Stars trained in San Fernando. Celebrities liked to drop in and buy drinks and meals for the young players and talk a little baseball.

It wasn't long into spring training when Fred Haney had a problem: Where to play Baxes? The 21-year-old had only played second base in his pro career. That position, however, belonged to Gene Handley, the slick-fielding former Philadelphia standout. "He couldn't beat out a polished player like Handley," Haney admitted to a sportswriter. The young player's strong throwing arm gave Haney an idea. He tried Baxes at third base, and

2. Samson and Delilah with Diamonds

soon fierce competition for the starting job was raging between the rookie and Hollywood's incumbent third baseman, Don Ross. It was a duel that would quickly be resolved once the exhibition games began. That's when Baxes went on a hitting tear. His three hits, including a two-run single, helped Hollywood beat Portland, 4–2. Against the Los Angeles Police Department, Baxes went 3-for-4 in an 8–7 Hollywood win. It wasn't long before Haney began to experiment with Ross at first base, a clear sign that Baxes had won the job.

He got off to a big start. Baxes was hitting everything. Nobody knew anything about him when spring training began, but now Fred Haney and Bob Cobb told Mr. Rickey they wanted to keep him with Hollywood. Mr. Rickey agreed, and he assigned Baxes' contract to Hollywood.

It was in Al Wolfe's March 9 column in the *Los Angeles Times* that fans were first exposed to "the sensation of the spring." While Haney kept his true thoughts close to the vest and downplayed the rookie's exploits, Wolfe wrote that Baxes "looked positively terrific." The manager, however, claimed to be seeking someone with more experience to handle the position. Haney was playing coy. He didn't want Baxes to slack off. By the time opening day arrived, the Hollywood manager ceased his game of verbal poker and acknowledged Baxes as his starting third baseman.

Jim Baxes was hailed as the greatest prospect in the Brooklyn Dodgers' farm system. Months later the third baseman was inescapably in Branch Rickey's doghouse. (Mark Macrae collection)

The schedule maker had Hollywood open the season on the road, first in San Diego, then Sacramento. Fans would have to make do with Jack Sherman's verbal descriptions on KLAC radio before they had a chance to see their team in person. From those first-week radio imageries, fans built affection for a new favorite, Jim Baxes.

The new third baseman played a key role in helping Hollywood win four of its first five games. Branch Rickey surprised Haney by flying to Sacramento to see the Stars first hand. With the Dodgers' general manager watching, Baxes hammered out three hits, including a two-run home run in a ten-inning loss to the Sacramento Solons. The very next night Baxes homered in the second inning as Hollywood won, 5–3. Continuing the torrid hitting, Baxes concluded the road trip with four hits and found himself with a new experience on his return to Southern California: a fan club.

A crowd that exceeded 8,000 brought an exuberance that bordered on electricity to Gilmore Field for the Stars' home opener. Those fans roared with delight when Jim Baxes belted two hits and helped Hollywood defeat San Francisco, 5–0. The next night Hollywood won again, its fifth in a row, 1–0, and squeezed alongside San Diego into a tie for first place in the Pacific Coast League. The excitement grew to near hysteria two nights later, when Jim Baxes crushed a 400-foot home run to highlight a 7–4 win over San Francisco that pushed Hollywood into sole possession of first place.

Baxes really took to playing third base. He was quick. He had good instincts, and he had a great arm. I don't know if it was because he wasn't sure of himself or wasn't sure of making that long throw across the diamond, but he'd tap the ball into his glove two or three times, take a little crow hop. He'd make you nervous that he was going to get the ball there in time to get the runner. But he could fire the ball across the diamond in a hurry, and he always got it there a step ahead of the other guy.

The regard for Baxes heightened within both the Brooklyn Dodgers and Hollywood Stars front offices. Convinced that Baxes was not a flash in the pan, Haney released Don Ross. The Hollywood manager ceased being subtle and amplified the praise that was wafting from fans and sportswriters. "In another two years, Baxes could be another [Pie] Traynor," Haney told reporters, comparing the rookie to a Hall of Fame player. "He's big, yet quick as a cat. I've never seen a better arm on an infielder, and Jim hits a long ball—as long as anybody on our ballclub."

Regard for Baxes swelled too at McKeever Place and Montgomery Street in the Flatbush section of Brooklyn, where the Dodgers' offices were located. "We wouldn't sell him for anything," a Dodgers executive told a sportswriter. "Not for sale," was Branch Rickey's answer to any club that inquired about the availability of the young third baseman.

It didn't take long for Hollywood's fans and the local sportswriters to grow enamored with the young third baseman. Nicknames were penned by the press and pinned on the young slugger by enthusiastic fans: "The Big Greek," "The Greek Adonis," and "The Grecian Gladiator," to name a few. Bob Cobb pounced on the local excitement over Baxes. He sought to exploit that Baxes was the only player of Greek ancestry in the Pacific Coast League. Plans were made for a Jim Baxes Night at Gilmore Field. Photographers posed the budding standout with a local Greek Orthodox priest and two members of the Greek community for pictures that would appear in the local newspapers to promote the event.

Requests for appearances by Baxes poured into the Stars office from schools and organizations around Southern California. Baxes found his free time filling up. He was kept busy with trophy presentations at schools and talks to business luncheons. Interest in Baxes extended beyond the sports page. Columnists in the society and gossip pages seized upon the interest in Baxes by adding tidbits about the shining star. But one column caught the attention of every player in the Hollywood clubhouse and filled the room with laughter. "Feminine hearts flutter and often pound at Gilmore when the Grecian strong boy strides to the plate," the *Los Angeles Times* columnist wrote. "But Dimitrios has no time for romance." The paper was passed around the room beneath the stands at Gilmore Field to howls of laughter. Baxes' teammates knew the idea was far from the truth.

On a road trip to San Diego early in the season, Baxes had wandered into a Greek restaurant not far from the ballpark. He almost instantly was smitten with the 16-year-old daughter of the restaurant's owner. She was infatuated with the admiring ballplayer. Among many of his teammates it was no secret that in the weeks after their meeting in San Diego, Baxes would meet up with the girl, and the two would slip across the border for motel-room trysts in Tijuana, where the age of consent was six years younger than in California. Whenever the Stars played in San Diego, the girl's parents would be in the stands, beaming. They made no secret to friends and restaurant customers that they hoped the talented ballplayer might become their son-in-law.

The Stars' winning ways electrified their fan base. Large crowds both pleased Cobb and caused him headaches. In mid–May an overflow turnout forced management to rope off the outfield warning track to accommodate all of the fans who had turned up for the game. It was not long after that the phenomenon became a repeat occurrence at Gilmore Field. By mid-season, preliminary planning would begin to expand the seating capacity of Gilmore Field. In addition to the capacity of Gilmore Field, another problem vexed Cobb and his fellow owners. The Pacific Coast League's schedule maker had the Stars playing on the road more than at home during the first two months of the season. The Pacific Coast League played a unique schedule. Every team played one seven-game series a week. Sunday games were always doubleheaders, and Mondays were offdays. A road trip lasted two weeks, or two seven-game series. Each time the Stars would excite their fans with a series win or sweep, the team was off to the airport and flying away to the San Francisco Bay Area or Pacific Northwest, not to return for two weeks.

At the height of their mid–May fervor, the schedule sent the Stars to the Pacific Northwest. The Portland Beavers were enduring a woeful start and struggling to climb out of the cellar. To the Stars' chagrin, the Beavers were no pushover. They taxed Hollywood with a pair of 12-inning fights to begin the series. Jim Baxes played a starring role in both, with a tie-breaking single in the first game and three hits the next night. Once Hollywood had dispatched the Beavers, they arrived in Seattle to rampant rumors that the struggling Rainiers were about to fire their manager. The Stars won five of their seven games from the Rainiers. Baxes highlighted two of the wins, one with a long home run and the other with a multi-hit game.

We were playing good baseball. Irv Noren was hitting for high average, showing good power and playing a great center field. He was establishing himself as one of the best players in the league. Frankie Kelleher, our left fielder, was among the home-run leaders. Herb Gorman, our right fielder, was a real RBI man. Gene Handley was as good a second baseman as there was anywhere. Our pitching staff was throwing good games. The guy who really made things happen was Baxes.

Fred Haney's ballclub returned from the Pacific Northwest firmly entrenched in first place. Seven games with Portland leading up to the Memorial Day weekend awaited. Big crowds were expected. A pregame fashion show emceed by the comedian Georgie Jessel helped bring more than 6,000 fans into the park on a Tuesday night. Exuberant fans weren't the only ones to press through the turnstiles that night. Roy Hamey, the Pittsburgh Pirates' general manager, and Del Webb, owner of the New York Yankees, turned up to study the talent on the field.

Art Shallock drew the start, and the left-handed pitcher mowed down Portland's lineup in order through the first three innings. At the end of the third inning while walking off the field, a fan in the stands caught Shallock's eye. Seated directly behind the Stars dugout was a stunning woman with Nordic blond hair. The pitcher noted her natural beauty. In the dugout Shallock turned to a teammate and nodded in the direction of the woman, "That's a great-looking girl!" A broad grin creased the teammate's face. "Forget it," he chuckled. "She's here for 'Adonis'!" Another teammate heard the conversation and added, "She was out here damned near every night before the road trip."

The woman was Barbara Payton, a 21-year-old striking beauty who was under contract to Universal and had just finished costarring with Lloyd Bridges in her first movie, *Trapped*. Barely a year earlier Payton had caught the eye of an agent when she stepped from the swimming pool at the Roosevelt Hotel. "You look like Lana Turner," the man said, "but you got her beat in the body. Can you act?" In her first year in Hollywood, Payton had been a source for gossip. She had been rumored to have had an affair with Bob Hope and flings with Howard Hughes and George Raft. As Stars teammates talked about the beauty behind their dugout, one noted, "She's really taken a liking to Jim."

On the field Baxes' play fueled growing acclaim. His batting average rose to over .300. Polling was being done for the Pacific Coast League all-star game in Seattle in July, and Baxes, along with Irv Noren, was being called a sure bet to make the south team.

Baxes' activities away from the ballpark were almost as much of a topic of conversation among his teammates as his success on the field. Talk was rife in the locker room about the first-year player's involvement with Barbara Payton. A reserve player shared a story with teammates of an altercation Baxes told him about that had occurred while out late one night with the actress. The couple was stopped at a light while in Payton's car. A car full of mouthy, twenty-something guys pulled up alongside, and the driver made a crude comment. Baxes stepped from the car and pummeled the driver of the other car before he and Payton sped off.

If his teammates had concerns that Payton might be a distracting influence to Baxes, the third baseman's play quelled whatever worries were held. By July Jim Baxes was being heralded as the best third baseman in the Pacific Coast League. One *Los Angeles Times* columnist raved that the rookie "now looks like the best hot-corner prospect in baseball." While in his home town of San Francisco for a series against the Seals, Baxes learned that he had been selected to play in the Pacific Coast League all-star game. With family and friends in the stands at Seals Stadium, Baxes celebrated the news by hammering out three hits to highlight a Hollywood victory.

When the league took its midseason break for the all-star game, Hollywood sat in first place, nine games atop second-place Sacramento. Baxes traveled to Seattle, where, playing with the best players in the Pacific Coast League, he clubbed three hits and helped the south defeat the north, 5–3.

Following the all-star break Southern California's Greek community paid tribute to Hollywood's all-star. On a night in his honor, the 20-year-old was given a bevy of gifts from Greek American admirers. Cobb added a generous check to recognize Baxes' selection to the all-star game. The next night Baxes began a home-run tear that would end only after he had hit four in three nights to up his season tally to 19. His three-run home run capped a sweep of the Los Angeles Angels. Baxes remained red hot with a game-winning home run in the first game of a Sunday doubleheader then hit two more home runs in the second game to seal a sweep. When the Portland Beavers rolled into town, they caught the brunt of Baxes' hot streak. The third baseman doubled home two runs in a 4–0 Hollywood win, then ripped five hits in a Sunday doubleheader sweep.

While the play of their star third baseman brought joy to the Stars front office and the team's fans, it would also soon create anxiousness. Ardent baseball followers noted that the Brooklyn Dodgers were embroiled in a tenacious pennant chase. If there was a weak link in the Dodgers lineup, it was the play of their third baseman, Billy Cox. The embryonic stage of the uneasiness involved this notice. Rumors that it was Baxes who offered a solution to the Dodgers' predicament shifted unease into concern. During the first week of August, the arrival of Branch Rickey, Jr., at Gilmore Field exploded that concern into out-and-out worry.

In the days that followed the Rickey visit, Haney tried his best to calm matters. "No, I'm not worried about the Dodgers cutting us up just when we're battling for a pennant, too," he told the press. Rickey Senior phoned to assure both Cobb and Haney they had nothing to fear. The Dodgers' boss promised he would not call up any Hollywood players. Cobb, however, was leery. He recalled the same sort of promise being made by the Cleveland Indians owner, Bill Veeck, to his counterpart in San Diego. In that case, just a few weeks later Veeck reversed himself and called the Padres' star first baseman, Luke Easter, to the big leagues.

With six weeks left in the season, Haney had his own pennant chase concerns to contend with. Among the biggest was a tiring pitching staff and a hurt and weary third baseman. Baxes had played every inning of every game going back to the first exhibition game in February. His foot and hand hurt. He confided to his manager that he was tired. Haney promised he would give Baxes some time off, but with the team faltering, he never did.

We got hit with a bunch of injuries late in the season. Stevens went down, Handley got hurt, and Johnny O'Neill couldn't play. Art Shallock was out. Even our batboy was gone. He got knocked unconscious by a foul ball and had to spend a couple of days in the hospital. I wasn't immune. During a Sunday doubleheader with San Diego, I tried to score from third on a sacrifice fly to right field. I was running full speed with my head down and never saw that Dee Moore, the Padres' catcher, had come up the line several feet and planted himself. The collision sent me flying. I slammed against the backstop wall and was knocked cold. It took me out of the lineup for a couple of weeks. With so many key players out injured, we fell into a slump, and about that time Oakland got hot and ate away at our lead.

Depleted by the injuries, Hollywood lost eight of 11 games. Five of those losses were inflicted by second-place Oakland. Hollywood's once-big lead shrank to just three games with 20 games to play. On Sunday, September 5, Haney's worries became a crisis. His team was locked in a pitching duel with Sacramento in the first game of a doubleheader. Willie Ramsdell had held the Solons to one hit, an eighth-inning home run. The Stars, however, had managed just three. One of their hits had been Frankie Kelleher's 25th home run. In the bottom of the ninth Kelleher walked. Haney signaled for Baxes to lay down a bunt to try to get Kelleher to second base. Baxes complied and pushed a bunt toward third base before sprinting to first. When he reached the bag, the muscular Hollywood standout collided with Sacramento's second baseman, Freddie Marsh. Shrieks and gasps rose from the stands at the sight of Baxes somersaulting then landing heavily to the ground. The 10,432 fans who had cheered when the bunt was initially dropped fell silent as Haney, teammates, and the team's physician raced from the dugout toward the fallen player.

Baxes was on the grass in a lot of pain. He complained to our team doctor of pain in his stomach, and he said he felt like something tore when he took his fall. The doctor ordered Baxes taken right away to Park View Hospital for X-rays, and he told Fred Haney that Baxes may have a broken rib and torn muscles. It might mean Baxes could be through for the rest of the season.

Though the Stars swept the doubleheader, many were glum when they left Gilmore Field for home. Adding Baxes to all of the other injured players who were out of the lineup would mean a decidedly weakened batting order that could affect the pennant race. The next afternoon Haney and many of the Stars players were surprised to see Baxes walk into the locker room at Gilmore Field. X-rays had failed to find any broken bones, and further evaluations did not find any muscle tears. Baxes was sore and stiff but insisted on suiting up. Haney reminded Baxes that he was the manager, and it was *he* who made out the lineup card. Baxes' name wasn't going to be on it for a couple of days. A couple of days wound up being five before Haney called on Baxes again. He eased his star back into action with a pinch-hit appearance during a doubleheader sweep of San Diego.

When we got to the last couple of weeks of the season, pennant fever really took hold. We had a few hundred fans come to send us off at the airport when we flew up to San Francisco. The mayor announced that when we returned it would be Baseball Week in Los Angeles. An overflow crowd was expected for one of our last games. It was all pretty exciting.

Baxes returned to the starting lineup for the series in San Francisco and played with a renewed energy. He celebrated his return with two hits against his hometown team then slammed an eighth-inning home run that helped Hollywood beat the Seals, 8–6. Baxes closed out the series with two hits in a 10–3 win on Sunday.

When the Stars returned home it was announced that Irv Noren had been voted the Pacific Coast League's Most Valuable Player by a panel of 20 sportswriters who covered the league. Baxes received a vote and an accolade from Al Wolfe in his column in the *Los Angeles Times,* writing that "he improved by such gigantic leaps and bounds that he is now called the greatest prospect in the Brooklyn farm system. Baseball people wouldn't be surprised if he were to wind up one of the brightest stars in the Major Leagues."

Hollywood needed just three wins to clinch the Pacific Coast League pennant, and Baxes delivered timely hits in the first and third games of the series with Seattle to extend Hollywood's win streak to five. The wins put the Stars to within one win of their first pennant in 19 years. On Thursday night, September 4, Gilmore Field surged with a rare level of electricity. More than 8,000 fans came to see the end of a drought. Once the final out was made and the Stars had defeated Seattle, 7–4, confetti filled the air, and players streamed onto the field and followed their manager as he trotted to center field, where a hastily-made pennant was hoisted up the Gilmore Field flagpole. Hollywood had closed out its championship regular season with 109 wins, the most in the club's history. They won the Pacific Coast League by five games over Oakland.

A $35,000 purse awaited the winner of the Governor's Cup playoff series, and the Stars won four of five games from Sacramento to advance to the finals. San Diego surprised many by beating Oakland to earn the right to oppose Hollywood for the Pacific Coast League postseason championship. Even more surprising, Hollywood stumbled and lost the first two games of the title series. Before fluster could slump into despair, Hollywood's fans received relief. In the third game of the series, Jim Baxes provided heroics with a home run that sparked an 8–6 Hollywood win. The next night Baxes had three hits, and Hollywood evened the series at two wins apiece with a 7–4 triumph.

On a chilly Saturday night in Gilmore Field with momentum up for grabs, Baxes rapped out two more hits to put Hollywood in command of the series. Hollywood swelled that momentum with a 7–0 shellacking of the Padres to enter game six brimming with confidence. They then closed out the series with an 8–4 triumph.

In the manager's office Cobb and Haney toasted their success with a scotch and soda. "This has been my most happy year in baseball," Haney gushed. Back in Brooklyn, Branch Rickey had accepted Washington's offer of $50,000 for Irv Noren's contract and continued to tell inquirers that Jim Baxes was not for sale.

Baxes had decided to spend the winter in Southern California. Barbara Payton convinced him to try to get into the motion picture industry. Little did he know that another effort on his behalf by Payton would change the course of his career. Not long after Branch Rickey had mailed out contracts for the 1950 season, his telephone rang. The caller identified herself as Barbara Payton. The actress said she was calling on behalf of Jim Baxes and chastised the Dodgers' president for the salary offer he had made to the player. Payton demanded a significant raise for Baxes—$10,000, which was double the pay for major-league rookies. When the woman told Rickey where Baxes should play during the upcoming season, the executive was taken aback. "I'm not talking to you," Rickey thundered, "I'm only talking to the ballplayer," then slammed down the phone.

In an instant, the comet that drew awe as it streaked through the Pacific Coast League went dark. Jim Baxes' place in the Brooklyn Dodgers organization went from a lofty perch reserved for an exalted phenom to the dark purgatory that was Branch Rickey's inescapable doghouse. When spring training began, Baxes did not report. Rickey called the demand "exorbitant." For weeks the two men held to their positions. Their war of wills continued long into spring training before Baxes ultimately gave in. Rickey dispatched Baxes to the Dodgers' farm club in St. Paul, Minnesota. He explained to the press that he wanted Baxes to reacquaint himself with playing second base.

A lot of people bought Mr. Rickey's explanation that he wanted Baxes to play second base. He told the press that he considered Gene Handley the best second baseman in the Pacific Coast League. Baxes wasn't going to beat him out, so that's why Jim was sent to St. Paul. The real reason Baxes was sent to St. Paul was that Mr. Rickey wanted to get him away from that actress [Barbara Payton]. Mr. Rickey wanted to break Jim and that actress up.

Baxes got off to a terrible start with St. Paul. After playing in 13 games, the shining rookie star of the 1949 Pacific Coast League season was hitting a paltry .132. Barbara Payton, on the other hand, was a star on the rise. Though she had lost out on a role in the *Asphalt Jungle* to a newcomer named Marilyn Monroe, her disappointment was brief. Weeks later Payton was hired to star opposite James Cagney in *Kiss Tomorrow Goodbye*. She had signed a seven-year contract with a studio that would pay her $5,000 per week. By the spring of 1950 Payton was engrossed in filming. Her acting wasn't all that filled the gossip columns. She had fallen head over heels for the actor Franchone Tote.

"Baxes Returns to Hollywood!" screamed the large headline in the May 13, 1950, edition of the *Los Angeles Times*. Former teammates wondered about the timing of the move. Was it motivated by news in the gossip columns about Barbara Payton, that she was occupied with a new film and a new love interest? Or was it, as Branch Rickey explained, that he'd given up on the idea of Baxes being Brooklyn's future second baseman and sent him back to Hollywood to play third?

Unfortunately, the arrival would be one of the few headlines penned about the player during the 1950 season. Baxes struggled. He developed a long swing, a penchant for trying to hit home runs, and a frustrating tendency for striking out. Baxes struck out more times than all but two players in the entire Pacific Coast League. The player whose fielding had enthralled Fred Haney in 1949 made more errors in 1950 than almost anyone else on the Hollywood ballclub. Late in the season, the astute *Los Angeles Times* columnist Braven Dyer wrote, "Batting a puny .232, Baxes is of little value as an everyday player."

A lot of us on the club wondered if his glasses weren't a problem. Baxes wore small, round glasses with a rim. A lot of guys liked to hit with the largest glasses they could find. They didn't want rims affecting their vision. Guys brought it up with Baxes, but he wouldn't change.

Baxes toppled from a perch at the top of baseball's most heralded prospects. It was a fall that was both swift and harsh. Once the 1951 season was underway, not only was Jim Baxes no longer considered a prospect, he wasn't a ballplayer. Uncle Sam had come calling, and Baxes was drafted into the Army. It would keep him out of professional baseball for two years.

By the time Baxes returned from his military commitment, there had been changes within the Dodgers organization. Branch Rickey was gone, off to run the Pittsburgh Pirates. E.J. "Buzzie" Bavasi now called the shots as general manager. There were also young third-base prospects whom the Dodgers held in higher regard. They manned the position at the Dodgers' top farm clubs, which pushed Baxes down to Class AA and the Texas League. It wasn't long, however, before the once-heralded prospect attempted to regain that reputation. Playing for Ft. Worth in an exhibition game against the Chicago White Sox, Baxes homered twice. On opening night of the Texas League season, Baxes homered twice again, and after three weeks of the 1953 season, he had belted nine home runs. On May 16 Bavasi and the Dodgers' chief scout, Andy High, traveled to Texas to watch Baxes play in person. With two outs in the bottom of the ninth inning, Baxes sent a blast screaming over the left-field fence for a game-winning home run. Bavasi and High left the ballpark impressed. But any ideas they might have had to promote the returned Army veteran were quashed the following night. On a close play at third base, Baxes was bowled over by an opposing baserunner. He suffered an injured thigh and spent much of the next three weeks on the dugout bench recovering.

For the next five seasons Baxes bounced among Dodgers farm clubs. Impressive home-run tallies coupled with high strikeout totals and low batting averages defined his reputation. But in the spring of 1959, Baxes received a break. The Dodgers invited him to spring training, but there were no expectations. Junior Gilliam was their third baseman. Dick Gray and Bob Lillis were in a fight to be his backup. During the final week of spring training, a hard-hit groundball took a bad hop and smacked Gilliam just above the left eyebrow, opening a large cut. Walter Alston, the Dodgers' manager, sent Baxes in as his replacement. By the end of the afternoon, the battle for one of the final spots on the ballclub had drastically changed. Baxes singled and doubled off the Braves' Bob Buhl and the next day slammed a triple in an exhibition game against the Phillies.

When the Dodgers broke camp and headed for Chicago to begin the season, Baxes had not only made the ballclub but was Alston's third baseman. "I'm confident I can cut it," he said to a newspaper reporter. "I think I've improved a lot these last couple of years." The usual brightness and glee that accompanies the start of a new baseball season was instead replaced by glum and discouragement in Chicago. A snowstorm hit the city. As the Dodgers rode their bus from the hotel to Wrigley Field, Jim Baxes gazed out the window at a city painted in a way he had never seen in his native San Francisco. "What's that white stuff?" he asked a teammate. What it was, was a large enough collection of snow to force postponement of the game.

The next afternoon Baxes buttoned up a gray Dodgers road jersey with the large number 29 on the back. He carried his bats into the dugout and noticed that Alston had penciled his name in the eighth spot in the Dodgers batting order. In the sixth inning, the onetime phenom slashed his first big-league hit, a single to center field. The next afternoon Baxes swatted two more hits to help the Dodgers to their first win of the season.

After the two weekend games in Chicago, a tremendous enthusiasm greeted the Dodgers in their new home city. The club had moved west from Brooklyn a year earlier, and Los Angeles had embraced its new heroes. Sixty-one thousand fans roared their adoration as the Dodgers took on the St Louis Cardinals under the bright lights of the Los Angeles Coliseum. It was an adulation far greater than what Baxes had experienced ten years before, during the Hollywood Stars' pennant-winning season. Baxes was remembered and cheered when he came to bat. He reached base once during the home opener when he was hit by a pitch, but the next day he showed a glimpse of the skills that had made him so popular with Hollywood in 1949. In the bottom of the third inning, Baxes stroked a single off the Cardinals' veteran left-hander, Larry Jackson. Four innings later a rookie pitcher was summoned from the St. Louis bullpen to make his major-league debut. Jim Baxes would be the first batter that the rookie faced. When Bob Gibson fired his first pitch in the major leagues, Baxes thrust a muscular swing into the ball. It whistled high into the air and soared over the 42-foot-high screen in left field and landed in the seats for a home run to cap a 5–0 Dodgers win. The next night Baxes homered again, a three-run blast to help the Dodgers defeat St. Louis, 7–6.

During the second week of the 1959 baseball season, Jim Baxes was sent reeling. Junior Gilliam had recovered from his injury and was handed his job back. Baxes was relegated to the bench, where he stewed. The Dodgers embarked upon a 17-game road trip, and although Gilliam struggled, Alston showed the respect managers often give to veteran players and let him play himself back into shape. In Cincinnati Alston put Baxes back in the lineup, and the rookie took full advantage. He singled twice, and in the eighth inning managed to put a ball in play that drove home a run. The next day, however, Baxes was not in the lineup. Dick Gray played third base and hit a long home run while playing stellar in the field.

2. Samson and Delilah with Diamonds

The road trip wrapped up in San Francisco, where Baxes had the opportunity to reunite with family and friends. After an extra-inning win over the Giants on Saturday afternoon, May 9, Baxes traveled across the bay for dinner at the home of his brother Andy in Oakland. During the meal, the phone rang. It was the Dodgers calling for Jim. The team's traveling secretary bore news that Baxes was being sent to the minor leagues. He had to hurry to the airport to catch a flight for Spokane. Wrought with anger, Baxes barked, "I'm not going!" then slammed down the phone. Frustrated and angry, Baxes returned to Southern California. When Bavasi finally reached him, the player argued that the move wasn't fair. He pleaded his case, pointing out that he had been hitting .303, had hit two home runs in the eight games he got into, played steady defense at third base, and deserved to play in the major leagues. Baxes insisted that he would quit unless Bavasi traded him to another big-league club. For two weeks Baxes played golf and worked at his brother-in-law's sheet metal company. Pleas from the business manager and manager of the Spokane club were rebuffed. Whenever Bavasi phoned, Baxes would repeat his demand to be traded. Finally, on May 22, the standoff ended and Bavasi gave in. "You're going to Cleveland," he said in their final conversation.

The very next night Baxes suited up for the Indians, and in the seventh inning, his new manager, Joe Gordon, sent him to the plate to pinch-hit. Baxes introduced himself to his teammates with a home run off the Tigers' ace pitcher, Jim Bunning. Gordon wrote Baxes' name on his lineup card the next night, and the newcomer responded with two hits then replicated the feat again the night after.

When Baxes joined the ballclub, the Indians were in a fierce fight for first place with the Chicago White Sox. Both Gordon and the team's general manager, Frank Lane, had been particularly frustrated by poor play at third base. Days before Baxes had been acquired, Lane had traded for Granny Hamner. Then days after, he traded for Willie Jones. Hamner and Jones contested the job during a stretch in which the Indians lost 13 of 16 games and fell into third place. On June 28 Gordon wrote Baxes into his starting lineup for a game against the Boston Red Sox. In the bottom of the second inning, Baxes drove a ball over the left-field fence for a home run, the only run of the game as Cleveland celebrated regaining first place. Three days later, Willie Jones was traded to Cincinnati.

On the Fourth of July, Baxes provided fireworks with his bat by belting an 11th-inning home run in a 12–9 win over Detroit. When he hit a key home run two nights later, his teammates had tagged him with the nickname "Hercules."

Throughout July, Gordon juggled his infield, playing whoever was hot. Baxes alternated with George Strickland at third base, and then when Billy Martin slumped, he was moved to second base. It was a position Baxes hadn't played in more than ten years, and his play reflected it. Gordon was criticized. "Baxes scares pitchers," the manager answered. "He swings a strong bat. Besides, he does a satisfactory job in the field." During a loss to the Yankees, Baxes botched a pair of potential double plays. Lane fumed from his box seat. "Awful! That's a crime!" It wasn't long before Martin was back at second base and Baxes was on the bench.

The pennant pursuit remained fierce entering August. Cleveland trailed the White Sox by one game. Five nights into the month, Billy Martin was struck by a pitch below the left ear. Several bones were broken. He required surgery and would miss the remaining eight weeks of the season. Second base belonged to Jim Baxes for the rest of the season.

Baxes played a key role in Cleveland's furious chase for the pennant. He homered to highlight a win over the Athletics. The next day he ripped two doubles. Against the Senators, Baxes hit a three-run home run, and the following night his two-run home run helped Cleveland to a 5–4 win. August ended with four games against the White Sox. The Indians had won eight games in a row and held second place, just two games behind Chicago. A World Series–like atmosphere took the town. More than 70,000 fans turned out for the opener and 66,000 for the finale. Baxes went hitless in the series. Cleveland lost all four games and fell five and half games behind Chicago in the standings.

The very next weekend the two clubs met again. Baxes homered in the Friday night series opener, and the Indians went on to win two of the three games in the series. Throughout September the Indians were unable to make up any more ground, and they finished the season in second place.

In 77 games with the Indians, Baxes hit 15 home runs and drove in 38. Of concern to Lane as he looked ahead to the 1960 season was that Baxes had batted just .239 and made 15 errors. During the winter Baxes was among several big-league players invited to baseball banquets around the Southern California area. In November he received his contract for the 1960 season and immediately balked at the salary offer. He returned the contract to Lane with a letter demanding more money. Almost immediately, the Cleveland general manager began shopping Baxes. He found no takers. When Buzzy Bavasi phoned to inquire about Lane's interest in a trade involving Billy Martin, he was offered Baxes instead and said no. Finally, on February 15, with spring training about to begin and Baxes holding firm to his demand for more money, Frank Lane sold the infielder's contract to San Diego of the Pacific Coast League. Jim Baxes never played another game in the major leagues.

He had a lot of ability. He should have been in the big leagues back when he had that big year with Hollywood, but that girl had a ring in his nose. She really ruined his career.

3

Painted by the Numbers

The gathering of Pacific Coast League alumni attracted both millennials and octogenarians, the curious and the ardent as well as collectors and historians. Scanning the room, a former ballplayer recognized one of the alums, a tall man with gray hair, a mustache, and glasses. Filled with mischief, the former ballplayer needled the alum about the signing bonus he had received. More than 65 years later, the alum, Paul Pettit, was still defined by the dollars.

Paul Pettit was tremendous. I was playing for Hollywood in 1949, and you couldn't pick up a paper without reading about him. Remember, the Dodgers hadn't moved west yet, so the high schools got a lot of attention in those days. Well, Pettit was something special. It seemed like every time I read the paper, I was reading that he'd thrown another no-hitter, so I went out to watch him play. He had a great fastball and a very good curveball. Paul was a very good athlete. He could hit, he had power, and he could run, too. It's unfortunate that when people talk about Paul, they talk about the money because he was a very good ballplayer, a real good ballplayer and a real good person, too.

They came, both the curious and the convinced, the doubting and the devoted. Skeptics and supporters made a regular pilgrimage to a corner of the high school campus in the tiny Southern California town of Lomita, California. They were lured by an intensity of praise for a pitcher that hadn't reached the ears of scouts and baseball executives in decades.

Conviction spawned exuberance. Curiosity fed urge. Not since H. E. Covert lit a cigar, tossed the match toward what he thought was a water discharge pipe, and was blown over by the subsequent explosion had so many come to Lomita to see a phenomenon. In Covert's case the explosive discovery of natural gas and oil brought an influx of job seekers. The phenomenon of the spring of 1949 involved a pitcher whom scouts were calling the best they had ever seen, a boy with a searing fastball that made opposing hitters look silly and call its hurler a man among boys.

Several days each week during March, April, and May, crowds that reached the unheard-of number for high school baseball of a thousand or more would squeeze into the stands at Narbonne High School. Administrators at the school had to use bleachers from the football field to accommodate the turnout. Mixed among the students, teachers, parents, and townsfolk were men in black suits, white shirts, and thin black ties. Fedoras, a bowler or two, and an occasional Irish flat cap would shade their thinning scalps from the bright Southern California sun. To the knowing, their garb—brown, and in some cases, reddened skin, leathery in texture, with weatherworn cracks across necks, brows, and cheeks—was a clue to the men's profession and the years it had them in the sun. The defining evidence, however, was a single bulging cheek, bloated by a wad of dark brown tobacco leaves. The men were baseball scouts. They represented the Tigers, Pirates, Cardinals, Dodgers, Giants, and Browns, among others. They came to Lomita and followed the town's high school baseball team when it went to nearby towns so that they could watch the school's star player—the best schoolboy pitcher in the country, Paul Pettit.

Paul Pettit was raised in a Lomita-area housing project. His father, George, was a quiet man who worked as a watchman. Pettit's mother was a nurse, a caring woman. Their son grew to be bigger than most of his classmates, 6 feet 2 inches tall and jut-jawed, with a thick head of dark hair that he combed back, except for a disobedient tuft that liked to flop to the left. He was quick to flash a grin, filled with humility that pleased his mother, and a strong work ethic that made his father proud.

In the eighth grade, Pettit struck up a friendship with a classmate, Darrold "Gar" Myers. The two had a thirst for baseball in a town where few baseball opportunities existed. During the spring of 1946, Myers saw a notice in the local newspaper that grabbed his attention. A semipro team sponsored by Standard Oil was holding tryouts in a neighboring town. Myers hopped on his bicycle and went to check it out. What he discovered was a team run by a scout for the St. Louis Browns, Art Swartz. Many of the best high school players in Southern California had seen the same newspaper notice and had come to try out. The afternoon was competitive but rewarding. Myers made the team. Before heading for home the teen approached the scout. "I have a friend," Myers said and told the scout about Pettit. "Bring him on by," Swartz replied. So it was that Paul Pettit came to step into a realm of greater scrutiny, acclaim, and reward than any amateur player ever had before.

The following weekend Pettit turned up to try out for Swartz's team. The scout paid particular attention when Pettit threw. He saw a left-handed slinger who threw hard but flung a hittable fastball and a flat curve toward home plate. The negatives were not dissuasive. In Paul Pettit, Art Swartz saw his own son. Only three years earlier, Sherwin "Bud" Swartz had been a average left-handed pitcher at University High School in Los Angeles when his father suggested changes. Art Swartz raised Bud's arm angle and adjusted the tempo of his delivery. The changes brought significant improvement. Bud Swartz went unbeaten in his senior year of high school. He pitched University High to the city championship then went straight from high school to pitch in the major leagues.

Art Swartz had similar ideas for Paul Pettit. He instructed the boy to raise his arm angle from a side-arm slot to one with a more over-the-top arc. He had Pettit shift his body weight onto his left leg at the height of his windup rather than stay balanced and simply push off the rubber with his left foot. Swartz then instructed Pettit to pause for an instant as he lifted his right knee before beginning his stride. Finally, Pettit was recommended to drive his right elbow toward home plate as his body followed and the pitching arm came through. Results from the change were instantaneous and dramatic—a searing four-seam fastball with backspin that moved away from a right-handed hitter and rose as it approached home plate.

Maybe the most celebrated amateur player in baseball history, Paul Pettit prepares for his first workout with the Pittsburgh Pirates. (Pettit collection)

In one of the first games Pettit would pitch for the scout's team, the Signal Oilers, Swartz himself tugged on the catcher's gear and went behind the plate. He was eager to evaluate Pettit from the unique vantage point. It all made the 15-year-old pitcher nervous. Pettit, shaking like a leaf, struggled to find the strike zone. He threw 12 straight balls and walked the first three batters that he faced. With the bases loaded and nobody out, Swartz called time-out. He walked to the pitcher's mound and told Pettit to concentrate on simply hitting the catcher's mitt. The teen locked his gaze onto that spot and struck the next three batters out.

At the end of the summer, Swartz lost Standard Oil's sponsorship and was forced to disband his ballclub. This sent Pettit and Myers in search of a new team, and in time they found the Hermosa Beach Seals. The Seals were run by a former minor-league catcher and manager, Fred Millican, who was a part-time scout for the Pacific Coast League's Hollywood Stars. The man was almost immediately awed by his new pitcher. Millican tutored Pettit on strategy. He explained the best pitch to throw on particular ball and strike counts, discussed game strategy and the appropriate tactics to employ. Millican was so impressed with the pitcher that he penned a letter to a fellow Hollywood Stars scout, Rosey Gilhausen, with news of his discovery.

Rosey was quite a character. Almost every high school coach in the Los Angeles area knew him. He'd played a little minor-league ball before the war, then after the war he went to work for Northrup Aircraft and scouted part-time for the Hollywood Stars. If Rosey thought you loved the game and could play, there was almost nothing he wouldn't do for you. He had a good eye for talent, and he liked giving kids an opportunity to play.

At first meeting, Pettit and Myers took a liking to Gilhausen. They would ride their bicycles to his home and listen to his baseball stories. The scout took the boys to Gilmore Field to watch Hollywood Stars games and meet the management of the ballclub. In the executive lounge at the stadium, the teens were introduced to the movie star, George Raft. The brush with celebrity left them starstruck and more than a little awestruck at the gorgeous woman on the actor's arm.

In the spring of 1948, Gilhausen arranged for Pettit and Myers to play summer ball for a semipro team in Hollister, California—325 miles north, near the central California coast. The opportunity came with a summer job. By day Pettit was jigging, filling 100-pound sacks with garlic bulbs. The work built strength in his fingers. Myers was an apricot grinder. By night, their sole focus was baseball.

The league was made up of teams from surrounding farming communities—King City, Salinas, and Monterey—and filled with players who had professional experience, mostly from the Pacific Coast League. Despite being the youngest and least-experienced player in the league, Paul Pettit shone.

Success brought reward. With each win Pettit earned greater acclaim in the small town. He rarely had to pay when he stopped at a hot dog stand or a diner for lunch. When it was Pettit's turn to pitch, area farmers who followed the team didn't bat an eye at placing $1,000 wagers with friends who followed the opposition.

The summer was near idyllic. The baseball was fun. Pettit had money in his pocket. He was pitching well. There were no scouts to prod him after games with questions. A couple of weeks before Pettit was to pack and return to Lomita, a scout from San Jose happened by the ballpark in Hollister. Impressed by the left-handed pitcher who was warming up to start the game, he asked a couple of fans if they knew the boy's name. Their answer left the man momentarily startled. He had heard rumors about a sensational Southern California pitcher by the name of Paul Pettit, and now he had stumbled upon the legend in person. The scout scrambled to a telephone. By the time Pettit pitched again, anonymity was gone. Almost every scout in Central and Northern California knew he was in the league and filled the stands to watch him pitch.

When winter faded into the spring of 1949, tranquility was no longer part of Paul Pettit's life. A simplistic game had been enveloped by complexity. The 17-year-old lived life in a fish bowl. Generous praise had grown to legend. Reporters wanted interviews. Fans wanted autographs. Scouts curried favor with Pettit's father and mother in the hope it would lure the pitcher to their team once it came to decision time. Paul Pettit was simply the best amateur pitcher in America.

On the field the pitcher continued to improve. Myers noted that Pettit had "perfect balance" and control that was "exceptionally good." Pettit developed a slow, looping curve and had perfected a window-shade changeup. The slow pitch deviated so much from the velocity of his fastball that more than once an observer was heard to crack that his pitch should be made illegal. Together with Myers, his catcher, Pettit worked to take advantage of the late rise his fastball enjoyed. "If you keep the ball down, keep it at the knees, these guys will think it's going to be a ball," Myers pointed out one day. "They won't swing. With that late hop we'll get a strike call every time!"

Pettit opened league play by pitching a two-hit shutout to beat San Pedro High, 3–0. He struck out 11 in seven innings to beat Torrance High. By the time Narbonne had blown through league play, Pettit had fired six no-hitters, three of them in succession. "There hasn't been a schoolboy pitcher around like this for a long, long time," Brooklyn Dodgers president, Branch Rickey, crowed. He called Pettit "right out of this world."

Prior to a game one afternoon, Babe Herman, a scout for the Pittsburgh Pirates, stood quietly behind the chain-link fence and watched Pettit warm up. Herman was an astute student of pitchers. His judgment came from a playing career in the late 1920s, where he twice finished second in the National League batting race while playing for Brooklyn. As Pettit waited for a return throw from his catcher, Herman broke the silence. "Son, you're getting a lot of attention. If you don't get a bonus offer of $90,000, something's wrong." Pettit was momentarily taken aback by the praise. He knew that pro ball would soon beckon but until that moment had no idea of his value on the market.

The intensity on Pettit grew to unheard-of levels. Scouts wanted to measure his skills against stronger competition and arranged games for his high school team so they could watch Pettit pitch against semipro clubs and even college teams.

I felt they were putting too much pressure on the boy. He was pitching too much. These men were setting up sometimes three games a week on top of his high school games. The arm can only take so much, and it worried me that Paul might get hurt.

In late May scouts turned out in droves for the Dorsey High Tournament. It was one of the more popular events in Southern California. Games were played on four adjoining fields. This gave scouts the unique opportunity to see several prospects at a time. Whenever Pettit pitched, however, three of the diamonds were largely ignored. The bleachers at the field where Pettit was performing would be packed.

On the afternoon in which Pettit pitched his first game in the tournament, more than 2,500 fans squeezed into the stands to witness the phenom perform. Pettit pitched a two-hit shutout and beat University High, 5–1. Later that same day he tossed another two-hitter and belted a two-run home run to help Narbonne defeat Washington High, 2–0.

Through the spring, Pettit and his teammates breezed through their league rivals. Pettit's performances were staggering. In an extra-inning game against Banning High, he struck out 27 over 12 innings. In a seven-inning game, he struck out 19.

With two games left in the season, Pettit was given a break from pitching and a start in center field. Early in the game Pettit pulled off a play that not only left observers in awe but his body damaged. Narbonne's opponent had a runner on second base when the batter cracked a sinking line drive toward right center field. On the sound of contact Pettit turned to his left and sprinted in pursuit of the ball. Convinced he could make the catch, Pettit lunged, extended his right arm, and grabbed the ball inches above the grass. Adrenalin pumping, Pettit rose to his knees. The runner had tagged up from second base and was dashing toward third. Pettit twisted his upper torso to the left and unleashed a powerful throw. The ball scorched through the air and reached the third baseman's mitt just in time to tag the startled runner out. Behind the plate, Myers stood in awe. "Ah, man!" he hollered at what he called "one of the greatest throws [he'd] ever seen." In the bleachers, cheers rose from students and fans, while a smile filled George Pettit's face.

Three days later Paul Pettit took the mound to pitch Narbonne's final regular-season game. It was not long into the game before Gar Myers knew that something was wrong. The velocity of Pettit's fastball was off. The ball didn't have its usual late rise, and what's more, Pettit couldn't keep the ball down in the strike zone. Instead, his pitches were high and tended to sail. In the dugout between innings the catcher raised the matter with his pitcher. "Paul, you're throwing different. You're not pausing. You're throwing faster. Your ball is sailing." Pettit shrugged off the observation. Myers pondered. He was certain that Pettit was holding his left shoulder in, protecting it. He thought about the remarkable catch two days earlier and the long, hard throw Pettit had made from the knees. Gar Myers wondered quietly if Paul had hurt his arm.

I was there that day. You could see Paul didn't have his usual stuff. His fastball didn't have the same zip, and there wasn't that late life to it. I felt pretty certain Paul had gotten hurt somehow. My first thought was about all the extra pitching those scouts had made him do. They'd asked too much of him. They'd injured him.

Once Narbonne High had completed its baseball season and earned the city title, the work of the scouts shifted. Their evaluations had been made and reports were filed. The 16 major-league organizations now focused their efforts on signing the players that their scouts had recommended. Baseball rules prohibited amateur players from signing contracts until their high school graduation ceremony had concluded. As mid–June approached, scouts once again descended upon Lomita. They snapped up four of Pettit's teammates. Chuck Schildmeyer signed with the Philadelphia Phillies. Les Phillips and Kyle Bowers both signed with Pittsburgh. The Brooklyn Dodgers outhustled Pittsburgh and the Detroit Tigers for Gar Myers. While his teammates celebrated their good fortune, the most

3. Painted by the Numbers 53

celebrated high school player in America had to wait. Paul Pettit would not graduate for another six months.

Major-league teams may have had to cool their heels until late January, but another interested party did not. In an office on Sunset Boulevard in Hollywood, a man was concocting a unique plan that would send shockwaves through major-league baseball. Frederick Stephani was a movie producer who had made a name for himself in 1936 with the hit *Flash Gordon*. He wanted to make sports films, but the big names of the day—Ben Hogan, Ralph Kiner, and Pancho Gonzalez—commanded far too much money for the use of their name and likeness. On the advice of a colleague, Stephani sought out an up-and-comer who seemed destined to make it big. There was one such candidate whose name was regularly in all the papers: Paul Pettit.

In late August a telegram arrived at the Pettit home. It was from Stephani, who asked to meet. Stephani explained his idea to Pettit and his parents—films about Pettit's career. The first would be *The Life of a Rookie*. The teen was taken aback. "I've never acted," he said. Stephani proposed an exclusive personal services contract. He offered Pettit $60,000. Remembering the advice of Babe Herman, Pettit turned it down. A few days later Stephani contacted the Pettits again and this time extended a higher offer. Pettit rejected it. It would be late November before the Pettits would hear once more from Stephani. His third offer rose to $85,000. This time the Pettits agreed. The arrangement covered ten years for Paul's services as an athlete and actor. The producer further explained that he would sell Pettit's contract to the highest-bidding major-league club and retain Paul's film rights.

The agreement fell under the laws and policies of the motion picture industry, specifically the Coogan child labor law. Moneys were to go into a court-sanctioned trust account. Pettit's father was appointed conservator, and the ballplayer would receive $200 per month until his 21st birthday.

When news of the contract reached executives of major-league ballclubs, many were convinced they smelled a rat. Stephani was accused of acting as a front to help a club circumvent signing rules. "I have no connection to baseball," Stephani, a German immigrant, protested to reporters. "I have never even played baseball."

Two weeks after the contract was agreed to, the day arrived that every major-league club had circled on their calendar—Friday, January 27, 1950, the day Paul Pettit received his high school diploma. While the 18-year-old celebrated, Stephani fielded calls from several major-league organizations inquiring about the contract. The film producer told reporters that one club had made "a very fine offer," while six others had expressed interest in obtaining Pettit. The producer set the following Monday as a deadline for offers to be received.

Over the weekend fierce bidding broke out. Several of the bidding clubs exceeded $75,000 with their offers. The press speculated the New York Yankees and Brooklyn Dodgers to be frontrunners. Not long after Stephani's deadline had passed, Pettit was summoned to a meeting at a downtown Los Angeles law office. When Paul and his father entered the office, they were surprised to find reporters and photographers waiting in the outer lobby. Stephani greeted the Pettits and ushered them inside the lawyer's private office, where several men were waiting. Stephani introduced Roy Hamey, general manager of the Pittsburgh Pirates, who in turn introduced Tom Downey, the Pirates' area scout. "Paul, we've bought your contract from Mr. Stephani," Hamey beamed. "Not so fast," George Pettit snapped. "We want $100,000!" The demand left the men from Pittsburgh flustered. Stephani suggested Hamey and Downey join him in a private, adjoining room. The trio left. For several anxious moments Paul and George Pettit sat quietly. Their silence was broken when the door to the private suite opened. "You have a deal," Hamey said with a smile.

Never before had an amateur player been paid so much to sign a professional contract. The agreement made Paul Pettit the first player in professional baseball history to receive a six-figure signing bonus. His deal shattered the bonus record of $75,000 that the Detroit Tigers had given to a high school catcher, Frank House, in 1949.

Stephani waved the waiting photographers into the office to capture Pettit's signing. The coveted pitcher sat behind a desk, pen in hand and contract copies spread out over the desktop. Flashbulbs burst as the photographers shouted for Pettit's father, Stephani, Hamey, and Downey to lean in behind Paul and watch the celebrated occasion. Reporters barked questions. "Did the bonus total $100,000?" "Call it that, and you'd be close enough," Hamey answered coyly. Al Wolf of the *Los Angeles Times* scribbled notes as Downey said he'd been watching Pettit since "he was knee high to a grasshopper." Hamey elaborated, "Our scouts have watched him closely for a long time, rate him very highly, and believe he has a chance to become an outstanding pitcher in the majors."

The money put unfair expectations on Paul. The Pirates hadn't fielded a winner in several years. Since the war they'd been in or near last place three out of the four years. The fans were looking for something to give them hope, and giving Paul all that money made some people think he could come in and help the Pirates turn things around right away.

3. Painted by the Numbers

The largess of the signing bonus astonished baseball fans and players alike. Hall of Fame pitcher Grover Cleveland Alexander told a sportswriter, "Why, that's more than I got in my 20 years in the big leagues." Sportswriters explained the signing bonus with quotes from scouts who called Pettit "the greatest prospect they'd ever seen." Behind the scenes, in boardrooms and ballpark offices, incredulous team owners and executives reacted with anger. The St. Louis Cardinals demanded that the commissioner investigate both the contract and circumstances that led to the agreement. Fred Slaigh, their team president, argued that the Stephani contract circumvented the high school graduation rule. "The transaction is an outrageous evasion!" he blasted. The Yankees made veiled accusations of a conspiracy to give a club an edge. "If a major-league club was behind this, something drastic must be done," their general manager, George Weiss, said to reporters. Accusatory fingers pointed to Bing Crosby. The popular crooner-actor was part owner of the Pirates. There were men in baseball who were certain that Crosby or an associate had orchestrated the arrangement with Stephani for the Pirates' gain. "Definitely not," Roy Hamey snapped. Quietly, there were murmurs in Southern California that another actor, Joe E. Brown, was actually the one behind the scheme with Stephani, though nobody had proof.

The commissioner, "Happy" Chandler, dispatched his own investigator, who reported that everything was on the up-and-up. Not convinced, the *New York Daily Herald* launched its own investigation. After several weeks of interviewing and sifting, the newspaper's sports editor, Bob Cooke, wrote that he had irrefutable proof that the movie contract was a scheme hatched by the Pirates with Stephani six months before Pettit's graduation to get around signing rules and successfully land Pettit. "Ridiculous," Stephani barked at a reporter. The *Daily News*' reporting drew little response and no action from the baseball commissioner's office.

By Valentine's Day the Stephani controversy was largely forgotten, thanks to Pittsburgh's newspapers, which unleashed the enthusiasm of the city's long-suffering fans by printing photographs of the heralded phenom in a Pirates uniform for the first time. The pictures came from a pre-spring training orientation camp for rookies, the sort of event that rarely if ever got publicity. Only this time baseball's first $100,000 bonus player was one of the participants.

The sight of the camp, Perris Park in San Bernardino, California, had all the trappings of a Hollywood premier. Reporters and photographers milled about. Perhaps the biggest Pirates fan of all, Bing Crosby, came to see the prized pitcher for himself. Photographers brought the pair together and had Pettit lean behind Crosby's shoulder, mouth agape, as if singing a chord. "He's much more handsome than Bob Hope," Crosby wisecracked. "Maybe he'll turn out to be quite an actor at that!"

Pettit's first workout brought a crush of the curious, which was comprised of fans, baseball enthusiasts, and coaches from area high schools and colleges. It was the coaches who became alarmed by some of what they witnessed. "Gosh-darn boy has ten different coaches telling him all sorts of things they think he's doing wrong," Pete Beiden of Fresno State told a player. "They've got the boy all fouled up."

Once the prospect camp concluded, the major-league Pirates arrived to start spring training. Only one participant in the rookie camp remained behind—Paul Pettit, who joined up with the major leaguers. A little more than a month removed from high school and Paul Pettit was on a diamond with big-leaguers. It was not all bubbly and enthusiastic, however. His new teammates were wary. Some were curious, others held animosity, and a few were angry. The Pirates were a veteran club. Most of the players were in their thirties with families and hadn't made $100,000 in their entire career. Indicative of their feelings was a comment that a player who didn't want his name used made to *The Sporting News*. "If we cut that bonus up 25 ways," he said, "everybody on the club would get a $4,000 raise."

Whatever optimism some Pirates fans may have held that Pettit would be their team's savior was misguided. He was not going to pitch for the Pirates beyond a week or two of spring training. The team's Class AA farm club, the New Orleans Pelicans, was the prospect's destination for the 1950 season. Still, when exhibition games began, Billy Meyer couldn't help but whet the appetite of the Pittsburgh faithful. The Pirates' manager sent Pettit to the mound in an early game and was awed when the 18-year-old unleashed crackling fastballs to strike out the side. "You did that on 14 pitches," Meyer gushed. "That's great! Keep it up!"

A few days later Meyer called on Pettit to pitch in an exhibition game against the mighty New York Yankees. The young left-hander was nervous but retired the side in order. "Great, just great!" Meyer praised. A week later, however, Pettit was on his way to the minor leagues as was planned. When the young phenom joined the New Orleans Pelicans, he arrived with a humble nature and a determined work ethic that evoked the friendship of his teammates rather than envy or scorn over the record-signing bonus. Realizing that enormous expectations enveloped him, the rookie was determined to outwork his teammates. "If they are asked to run ten wind sprints, I'll run 20," he told his father before leaving California.

New Orleans was a city that loved its baseball. Fan excitement at the bonus baby's arrival had been stoked by three competing newspapers vying daily for the most insightful story about the prospect. "The Finest the Pelicans Have Had in Years!" read one headline when the pitcher got to town. "His Fast One Can Take Care of Itself!" read another.

The Southern Association was not a good place to send Paul. New Orleans was in a tough league, a hitter's league. Almost every club had former major-league ballplayers. Atlanta's player-manager was Dixie Walker, the National League batting champion with Brooklyn. Some of the parks were band boxes. In Nashville it was 262 [feet] to the right-field fence. It was 302 to the right-field fence in Memphis. This was the sort of league that would challenge the confidence of any veteran pitcher. It was not the league for a boy right out of high school, no matter how good he was as an amateur.

New Orleanians relished their baseball. The annual attendance at Pelicans Stadium was among the highest in the Southern Association, fueled in part by a gambling culture that was rampant in the stands. A veteran player called the city "a great place to play when you were going good. When you weren't, the fans could get nasty."

The Pelicans traversed Louisiana for a series of exhibition games leading up to their season opener. It was the last of the preseason games that got the attention of the men in Pittsburgh. Luby planned to use both Bob Purkey and Pettit in a game against the defending Southern Association champions, the Nashville Vols. Purkey would start, pitch the first four innings, then give way to Pettit.

Roy Hamey and one of the Pirates' owners, Tom Johnson, flew to town to take advantage of the chance to see two of the Pirates' prized pitching prospects in regular season form on the same night. The men were not disappointed.

Purkey mowed down the Vols without allowing a hit. Pettit took over and barely skipped a beat. In the ninth inning almost everyone in the ballpark was riveted to the fact that something special was taking place. Everyone, that is, except Paul Pettit. When the final out was recorded, the pitcher couldn't understand why his teammates were dashing from the dugout in his direction. It was only when they mobbed the newcomer that Pettit was told that he had just teamed with Purkey to pitch a no-hitter. Hamey was astonished. When asked if he would consider selling Pettit if offered double the record signing bonus, Hamey shot back, "It was worthwhile to gamble $100,000 on him, it's worthwhile keeping him." Ben Tincup, the Pirates' minor-league pitching consultant, told an inquiring reporter after the game that Pettit "can't help but become a major-league pitching star!"

Hal Luby read the comments and waded through the euphoria with trepidation. The Pelicans' manager had his own ideas about pitching, and they did not mesh with what he saw from Paul Pettit. Never mind that Hal Luby had never pitched. As the season got under way, the former New York Giants infielder instructed Pettit to change the way he threw and adopt a "windmill" delivery. Luby did not like the brief mid-delivery hesitation Pettit employed. The windmill had become a trend in the game. It involved an exaggerated windup in which the pitcher would swing his arms back while taking one step back before thrusting the arms forward and upward to a point where the pitching hand and glove came together above and even slightly behind the player's head. The ensuing dropping of the arms would initiate a slight upper-body rotation, followed by a leg kick, and then the drive forward into the delivery of the pitch.

Proponents pointed to physics and said the windmill gave a pitcher better body control, enhanced his rhythm, and put the pitcher into a proper release position. Some crowed that the momentum it generated would improve fastball velocity. Opponents argued that the more movement in a pitcher's delivery, the less accurate his pitches would be. In Paul Pettit's case, that is exactly what happened.

High expectations shadowed the Pelicans on their season-opening road trip to Mobile. Those expectations sprouted from hype over Pettit, Purkey, and another prized Pirates pitching prospect, Vernon Law. Luby's plans for Pettit during the season-opening series, however, only involved pitching batting practice, the better to repeat his altered pitching mechanics into habit. The manager's plan for Pettit was tested when the Pelicans lost three of their first four games and then needed ten innings to win the final game of the series.

Before the series concluded, Luby responded to a sportswriter's question with a hint that he was thinking of pitching Pettit for the first time when the team returned home to New Orleans the following week. It was like throwing a lit match to gasoline. The city's three newspapers pounced on the story. Each ran bold headlines to trumpet Pettit's potential debut. Joe Tracy stoked the fires. The Pelicans' business manager was concerned that a slow start on the road might be met with less-than-usual enthusiasm when the ballclub came home. Once Luby let him know that Pettit would make his professional debut in the Sunday afternoon game against Chattanooga on April 23, Tracy was on the phone to the press, and more headlines and broadcasts with the news ensued.

3. Painted by the Numbers

Throughout the week publicity was incessant. Pettit's debut gained added box-office appeal when the opposing manager, Fred Walters, announced he would pitch Bobo Newsom, a four-time All-Star who had twice won 20 games in the major leagues. When Sunday afternoon arrived, long lines snaked about the ballpark as ticket sellers furiously worked to accommodate the rush, and turnstiles spun almost nonstop. On the field Pettit and Newsom were brought together by photographers. "You know, most of this crowd has turned out to see me," the affable former big-leaguer cracked. "I sincerely hope the kid wins 'em all," Newsom said to the newspapermen, "except when he's pitching against us."

When the top of the hour came, radios in homes around New Orleans, in taxi cabs at the airport and in downtown, in tight cubby holes that passed for offices, and in French Quarter restaurants were spun to 940 on the AM dial for the call of the game by local icon Ted Andrews on WTPS.

Five minutes later, loud cheers greeted the 18-year-old pitcher as he walked to the pitcher's mound for the start of the game. The buzz from the stands drowned out the crack of Pettit's warmup pitches smacking his catcher's mitt as over 11,000 people—the most ever to see a Pelicans game—had pressed into a ballpark built to hold 9,000.

Under a bright, sunny sky with a breeze blowing from first base toward left field and in front of a noisy crowd, Paul Pettit's much-anticipated professional career began. The young sensation was nervous, more nervous than he had ever been before. He unleashed a cracking fastball to strike out the first batter. After walking the next hitter, Pettit coaxed a fly ball to medium left field. What should have been an easy out swung open the doors to disaster when the Pelicans left fielder lost the ball in the sun, and it fell untouched to the turf. Before the game Luby told people he worried that Pettit would "overdo himself trying to win," and suddenly his worst fear manifest. Intent to keep the two baserunners from scoring, Pettit pursed his lips and went into a delivery that reeked of heightened intensity. The pitcher coaxed a pop up to shortstop that was misplayed, landed in the grass, and loaded the bases. Tension, both in the stands and the Pelicans dugout, was heightened by another crack of the bat and a single that sent two runners dashing home to score. After notching the second out of the inning, a Pettit curveball was driven to deep right field. Frank Thomas had to navigate the standing-room fans who had been herded onto the warning track by the ballpark's lack of seating. The tall right fielder reached as high as he could and successfully snagged the fly ball to end the inning.

The second inning offered more of the same. Bobo Newsom opened the second inning with an infield hit. Pettit pressed. His new mechanics betrayed him. The once impeccable control that had left scouts in awe only a year earlier was now a memory. He struggled to put the ball in the strike zone and walked the next two batters. When the rookie tried to guide a fastball into the strike zone on Dick Guyton, the veteran expected as much and hammered the pitch over the left-field fence for a grand slam.

From the third inning on, however, Pettit was a different pitcher. He recorded outs, relaxed, and fell into a smooth rhythm that made throwing strikes a thing of ease. Over the fourth, fifth, and sixth innings, the phenom was overpowering. "Better than any 18-year-old boy I ever saw," said Tincup. Five of the nine outs in those innings came by strikeout. In the sixth inning, Pettit struck out the side.

In the eighth inning Pettit got two quick outs on groundballs then began to tire. He walked two hitters then gave up a single to score a run. After a third walk, Luby strode to the mound and removed his rookie sensation from the game. "You did better than I thought you would," Luby praised while waiting for the relief pitcher to arrive. "You showed you have the guts to overcome bad breaks, and you really looked fine after the second inning."

The press box was instantly a den of clatter as sportswriters pressed and pecked their typewriter keys to produce stories before their deadlines. A *Times-Picayune* columnist noted that Pettit "did not work with the ease and smoothness" of his exhibition game no-hitter. The scribbles and symbols in scorebooks tallied 11 walks and seven runs allowed by the debutant. Luby offered assurances that "with a game under his belt, he'll be alright." Still, this was not the same pitcher who had made scouts marvel and impressed the Pittsburgh Pirates' manager with his work in intrasquad and exhibition games.

Pettit's first game, however, failed to dampen the fervor that had hiked him to celebrity status in New Orleans. Almost every day the city's three newspapers carried stories with large photos of the heralded pitcher. Their write-ups ranged from the inane to the insightful. They covered everything from dissections of his pitching skills to life in Pettit's Canal Street apartment with his roommates, Bob Purkey and Dixie Upright, which noted that Upright did the cooking while Pettit cleaned and dried the dishes.

The new professional's forays about the city were met with treatment reserved for motion picture or other entertainment celebrities. After dining at the famed Antoine's restaurant, Pettit was asked by the owner for an autograph. It was hung proudly on the establishment's wall. That Pettit dined on Oysters Rockefeller, filet de sole Colbert, filet de boeuf béarnaise, crêpes Suzette, and a glass of milk somehow managed to get written up in the gossip columns.

Most of Pettit's time was spent at the ballpark, where he continued his breakneck work habits. He jogged to improve his conditioning. Pettit threw every day, though he had been instructed to throw only every other day. Through it all, Pettit concealed something troubling. The adjustments to his pitching mechanics were putting stress on his left shoulder, which made the effects of his high school shoulder injury return. There were occasional tinges of pain when he threw, especially when he tried to snap off a curveball. Pettit tinkered and tried to alter his arm angle in hopes it would get rid of the discomfort. Sometimes the discomfort grew so bad that he abandoned his normal over-the-top angle and dropped down to throw sidearm. Complaining was the last thing Paul Pettit was about to do, not with his every throw shrouded in such high expectations. He felt every ounce of the enormous pressure he was under to live up to the massive signing bonus he had received.

It was another week of pitching batting practice and running for conditioning before Pettit got into his second game. He was given the start in the second game of a doubleheader in Little Rock, Arkansas, where wildness was once again a nemesis. His teammates had staked Pettit to an early five-run lead when trouble with his control flared in the bottom of the third inning. By the time he was taken out of the game, Pettit had walked five batters, given up two hits, and Little Rock had scored six runs. So amiss was the phenom's control that he had gone to three ball counts on 11 of the 14 batters that he faced.

The Pelicans' manager tried to remain positive. "All we want him to do is forget about the bonus price," Luby told reporters. Unfortunately, it was too late for that. The heralded pitcher was being crushed by the weight of expectation. The money and the immense press coverage had served to paint a picture of brilliance in the minds of opponents and fans. When Pettit wasn't brilliant, patience was tested, frustrations grew, and ire sparked. With every pitch that missed the strike zone, heckling spewed from opposing dugouts. Every time a batter belted Pettit's fastball to or over the wall instead of swinging and missing, jeers abounded from the stands. In the city that had initially offered adoration, derision flared. "Pettit, you stink!" a man shouted at the pitcher as he sipped a cup of chickaree coffee in the French Quarter one morning. While looking over a friend's flashy new sports car, Pettit was recognized by a man who hollered, "Pettit, you'll never make it!"

Few if any 18-year-olds anywhere in America carried such a heavy weight of expectation as Paul Pettit did. Every pitch was supposed to be a $100,000 pitch—travel with awe-evoking speed, cross the plate with precise accuracy, and make every batter swing and miss. When it wasn't and the phenom missed the strike zone or surrendered a hit, Pettit grit his teeth, tensed his muscles, and fired his next one with added zeal in hopes that it would produce the sort of result that would prove to people he was worth every penny of his record-signing bonus.

Following the fiasco in Little Rock, Luby gave Pettit two weeks off. It was the middle of May before he would pitch again. Once the Pelicans' manager made it official that Pettit would pitch the May 13 game against Birmingham, all of the New Orleans papers trumpeted the news. Despite his failings, Paul Pettit was still a phenomenon in the Crescent City. That was proved by the near-capacity crowd that came out on a Monday night to see him pitch despite the Pelicans sitting in the bottom four of the Southern Association standings.

It didn't take long for the buzz of excitement to fade. Amidst a chorus of groans, Pettit walked the first three batters that he faced. Words of encouragement were rewarded when the pitcher struck out the next two batters. It was quick thinking that got Pettit out of further trouble in the inning. When the pitcher went into his windmill windup, the Birmingham runner at third base thought he could successfully steal home. Shouts alerted Pettit to the theft attempt, and he managed to hurry the ball to his catcher just in time to cut down the runner for the third out.

An inning later problems surfaced that turned into disaster. Pettit fell behind in the count to the first batter of the inning. He was in danger of walking the man when it happened. Pettit wound up to throw a curveball, but as he began to flex his wrist to snap off the pitch, a sharp unmistakable pain shot from his left elbow. Concern that bordered on panic filled the pitcher's thoughts. He shook off his catcher's call to throw another curveball. Instead, he fired one fastball then another. Each missed the strike zone and Pettit walked the batter. Red Mathis, a veteran and a good hitter, was up next. Mathis noticed Pettit shake his left arm and sensed something was wrong. Experience told him the rookie might ease up and try to guide a ball into the strike zone. That's exactly what happened, and Mathis drilled the pitch off the wall for a double that scored Birmingham's first run.

Pettit battled through the pain and retired the next three hitters. Once back on the dugout bench between innings, however, worry weighed on his mind. When the third inning began, the pain persisted. Finally, Pettit summoned his manager to the mound. He explained what had happened. "Throw a couple more," Luby said. Pettit flung a curveball, turned to his manager and said, "It hurts more."

In an instant a chain reaction of events ricocheted into action. Phone calls to Pittsburgh with news and updates, appointments with doctors, and amidst it all, the press was clamoring for answers. Luby told the writers that Pettit had pulled a muscle in his arm. He estimated the injury would keep the pitcher out four or five days. Fans were just as anxious as the press. Mail poured from sacks at the local newspapers. "How long is Pettit out?" and "How do you think this will hurt his career?" the letter writers asked.

When the Pelicans' team doctor reported that he could find nothing wrong, Pettit tossed his suitcase on the bus and accompanied his teammates on their road trip to Atlanta and Mobile. Escaping New Orleans didn't mean escaping questions from the press. In Atlanta, Luby told a local radio host that "Pettit will recover and win a lot of games this season. I plan to pitch him every fifth day once his arm gets well." A perceptive New Orleans *Times Picayune* sportswriter, William Keefe, wasn't buying it. "A hurt elbow on the pitching arm is a serious matter. Not many get over it," Keefe wrote.

Before a game in Mobile ten days after the injury, Pettit played catch with a teammate and still felt pain. Luby sent him back to New Orleans with orders not to throw. In Pittsburgh, anxiousness was growing. Roy Hamey made arrangements to have Pettit fly to Baltimore and be examined by the top pitching expert in the medical profession, Dr. George Bennett at Johns Hopkins University in Baltimore. "My arm doesn't hurt me very much, though it does pain me just above the elbow when I throw a curve," Pettit told the doctor. After a two-hour examination that involved twisting, bending, and squeezing the elbow, Bennett phoned Hamey with the news that there was "nothing permanently wrong with Pettit's pitching arm. He said the pitcher was free to resume throwing but warned against throwing any curveballs "until the arm gets better."

Three weeks after he suffered the injury, Pettit threw batting practice to his teammates. When he reported to Luby that there was no pain, the manager announced that he would start Pettit one week later against Memphis. His return start did not go well or last long. The second batter Pettit faced hit a home run. In the second inning, the left-hander walked two batters and hit two others. After giving up a three-run double, Pettit was removed from the game after retiring just four batters.

By the end of June, the problems coming out of New Orleans had reached a high level of concern in Pittsburgh. Pettit's injury and continuing struggles were so alarming that on July 1 Roy Hamey and the Pirates' farm director, Fred Herring, took action. They changed managers. Hal Luby was replaced by Bill Burwell, a pitching guru who was renowned for his work with young hurlers.

Pettit found the 55-year-old to be grandfatherly and a calming influence, but Burwell offered little advice and no teaching. He used Pettit in relief for a few weeks to build back his confidence. In the first start he made under Burwell, Pettit pitched eight innings, seven of which were impressive. One bad inning, though, did him in—a fourth inning in which he walked three, hit two batters, and gave up three runs. "There are plenty of pitchers in the big leagues who would love to have his stuff," said Little Rock's left fielder, Red McQuillers, after the 4–1 defeat. "It's the best pitching he's done this season," said his catcher Bobby Ganss. Burwell offered reporters a sly grin, nodded and said, "He's sneaky, ain't he?" Still, the "stuff" that had impressed on that night in Little Rock didn't compare to what people had seen back in Lomita.

I had been assigned to Chattanooga by Washington. When we played New Orleans I faced Paul. He wasn't the same pitcher I had seen when he was in high school. He didn't have the kind of velocity that I had remembered. He had good control in high school. Now he was wild. I was pretty certain that Paul was hurt.

"Erratic" replaced "sensational" in newspaper descriptions of Pettit. Walks far exceeded strikeouts. Wildness opened the door to runs, all of which added up to defeats. As his struggles mounted Pettit grew envious that his teammates Bob Purkey and Vernon Law had been able to break into pro ball in the low minors. Both had started in Class D ball, where they pitched with less pressure, began their careers without fanfare, and didn't have to face lineups that were stacked with former major leaguers.

Burwell offered encouragement and gave the prospect regular turns on the mound. On August 10 Pettit earned his first professional win, defeating Birmingham 3–2. "The plate looked bigger than it has all season," he told the sportswriters before dashing off to send a telegram with the big news to his parents. Bill Keefe wrote in the *Times Picayune*, "No pitcher who ever won a game at the local stadium ever got a more enthusiastic round of applause."

Over the final four weeks of the season, there were more promising performances. Pettit beat the Memphis Chicks, 3–2, on a four-hitter. He engaged in a ten-inning pitchers' duel on a sweltering night against Atlanta that was spoiled when the Crackers' 19-year-old prospect, Eddie Matthews, clouted a home run over the 50-foot Coca Cola sign in right field. Ugly results flared as well, such as the game against Memphis, where Pettit not only walked four batters in an inning but beaned an umpire. The arbiter had jumped up from behind the catcher to call a balk just as Pettit released his pitch. After Pettit lost the season finale in Nashville, his first year in professional baseball concluded with a two-win, seven-loss record, an earned run average of 5.17, and 76 walks allowed in 94 innings pitched.

Upon returning home to Lomita after the season, Pettit met up with Gar Myers. The buddies swapped tales about their first season in pro ball. Myers was particularly anxious to hear about Pettit's summer in New Orleans. When Pettit told Myers how Luby had changed his pitching mechanics and the problems it had caused, the catcher couldn't believe it. "Paul is a mess," Myers told a friend.

The failure of such a heralded and highly-paid prospect reverberated in the Pirates offices at Forbes Field in Pittsburgh. The Pirates' president, John W. Galbreath, pushed Roy Hamey out of the general manager's chair. Branch Rickey, the man who had built World Series winners at Brooklyn and in St. Louis, was brought in to take over the day-to-day running of the ballclub.

In addition to the changes taking place in his professional life, Pettit's first professional baseball offseason brought change to his personal life. In January Pettit married his high school sweetheart, Shirley Jennings. Three weeks after the wedding, Pettit was right back at work. He joined the Pirates for spring training in San Bernardino, only this would not be a mere flirtation like the year before. Branch Rickey had promised Pittsburgh a youth movement to give young prospects a shot at turning the dismal Pirates around. Paul Pettit received every opportunity to make the Pittsburgh Pirates pitching staff.

Pettit made a strong showing in the very first intrasquad game. He pitched three innings, faced only nine batters, and didn't walk a single one. Babe Herman, who had scouted Pettit in high school, said it was the best he had seen the pitcher throw. "Just about the best stuff I ever had," Pettit seconded to a sportswriter.

As the days in spring training dwindled, Rickey ended the questions about whether the bonus baby would begin the 1951 season in the major or minor leagues. "Pettit will remain with us," he declared. "He needs his self-confidence built up. He's a better pitcher than he thinks." No sooner had Pettit received Rickey's assurance than his performances took a downward turn. He was tagged for four hits and three runs and blew a lead in the ninth inning of a 3–2 loss to the Chicago Cubs. The St. Louis Browns got to him for four hits and two runs in the final two innings of another exhibition game in San Bernardino. During another outing in which Pettit struggled with his control, Clyde McCullough, the Pirates' catcher, grew angry and marched to the mound to chew out his pitcher. "Every time I throw, my arm hurts," Pettit revealed.

Still, despite Pettit's poor outings he made the ballclub. It was three weeks, however, before he saw action in a game. His major-league debut came on a Friday night, May 4, in the Polo Grounds in New York. The Pirates were losing, 5–1, to the Giants. Meyer sent Pettit in to pitch the ninth inning. Rickey moved from his customary seat behind first base to one behind the plate to get a better look at the pitcher. He watched as Pettit induced Bobby Thomson to ground out to shortstop, Hank Thompson to ground out to second base, and Ray Noble to fly out to left field. While the sportswriters noted that Pettit was the only Pirates hurler to escape the game unscathed, Branch Rickey groused, "Doesn't throw hard enough to suit me."

In a column in the *Pittsburgh Post-Gazette*, sports editor Al Abrams related a story from a ride on the Pirates' team bus. Pettit had been seated next to another rookie, Bill Koskie. A veteran player seated a few rows back turned to a sportswriter and with a nod toward the rookies said, "There's a $100,000 pitcher sitting next to a boy who cost this club practically a bag of peanuts. I'll bet you the boy who's worth a bag of peanuts will outlast the $100,000 bonus pitcher. He has shown me more stuff."

Baseball rules allowed each team to begin the season with three additional players on their roster. One month into the season, three would have to go. On May 14 Paul Pettit was one of three players that Branch Rickey dispatched to the minor leagues. A sportswriter typed about the demotion, "Somewhere along the way he lost his fastball."

Pettit was first sent to the Pirates' top farm club, Indianapolis. After just four games he was shuttled back to New Orleans. He only pitched in one game for the Pelicans then was demoted to the Pirates' Class A farm club in Charleston, South Carolina. There he was no longer a failed bonus player but was once again heralded. His first game drew the team's largest crowd of the year, but the excitement was drowned in the sixth inning, when Pettit was hammered for a triple and three singles, walked two men, threw a wild pitch, and gave up four runs.

Pettit failed to win any of the first ten games he pitched for his new club. Pummeling's brought tired phrases disguised as pep talks: "Get tough. Bow your neck," or "Buckle down and throw strikes." With three weeks left in the season, Pettit finally gained reason to celebrate. On August 16 he earned his first win of the season. Two days later Shirley gave birth to the Pettit's first child, a son.

In the final days of the season, Pettit suffered a knee injury that sent him into the offseason earlier than his teammates. His second season of pro ball concluded with a less-than-sterling 2–2 won-loss record. Pettit's struggles with control and high hit totals in a majority of his starts fueled derisive rumors. The most inflammatory commentary appeared in a September issue of *The Sporting News*, in which columnist Oscar Ruhle suggested that the Pittsburgh Pirates had given up on 19-year-old Paul Pettit.

If Branch Rickey had given up on Paul Pettit, Fred Haney hadn't. The Hollywood Stars' manager jumped at the chance to add Pettit to his ballclub for the 1952 season. The first meeting between the pitcher and his new manager during spring training energized the once-prized prospect. "Paul, have you ever been fined by any club you've played for?" Haney asked. When the lefty said no, the manager barked, "Well, you'll be fined $100 on this club anytime I catch you listening to anyone who is telling you how to pitch!" The Stars' skipper had seen Pettit pitch in high school. "You can pitch winning baseball anywhere if you pitch like that again!"

The Hollywood Stars were run by men who were promotional wizards and never missed a trick to try to hike ticket sales. Having the onetime local high school sensation on their ballclub was right up their alley. Pettit's first home start was promoted like a Hollywood premier. Klieg lights were rented to bounce beckoning search beams off the clouds prior to game time in hopes that fans would follow. What wasn't counted on, however, was an unseasonable cold snap that few fans were willing to brave. Barely more than 2,000 persons came to Gilmore Field for the game. Pettit's debut was, however, heavily watched—on television. An estimated 500,000 Southern California television sets were tuned to the live telecast of Pettit's 5–3 win over Seattle.

By the end of May, the one-time sensation had won five of six starts. But it wasn't just Pettit's pitching that was gaining notice. During a game in Portland, Pettit had four hits and batted in four runs. Against San Francisco he had a single, double, and triple. His batting average was .457. Despite the pitching and hitting success, negativity continued to follow Pettit. In late June he was held up to public scorn, the focal point of a heavily promoted *Saturday Evening Post* article about bonus-baby flops. By now it was rare for any newspaper or magazine to print Paul Pettit's name and not accompany it with "$100,000 bonus player." When the title lead into reports of his struggles, it inferred failure or worse; it glaringly blared bust.

What was not receiving the notice it was due was that Paul Pettit was pitching his way back into the role of a big-league prospect. Heading into July, his record was 9–2. Pettit's ninth win ranked as one of the most memorable of his career. An overflow crowd of 12,682 packed Gilmore Field to see the onetime wunderkind. In the top of the first inning, Pettit was shaky.

He surrendered three singles that led to a run for the rival Los Angeles Angels. Following the third hit in the inning, Pettit took advice from Haney and adjusted his position on the pitching rubber. The suggestion paid off. Pettit pitched no-hit ball over the next eight innings. Hollywood won, 6–1, and Pettit looked to Haney and others like the pitcher they had been awed by in high school.

After a win over San Francisco in mid–August boosted Pettit's record to 13–5, Fred Haney declared to the press that his pitcher was ready for the major leagues. On September 15 Pettit beat Portland to earn his 15th win of the year and sew up the Pacific Coast League pennant for Hollywood. While his velocity was not that of his high school years, and hits and wildness pocked many of his performances, Pettit generated interest from the Pittsburgh Pirates. He was returned to the team's 40-man roster and invited to spring training.

It was Fred Haney who greeted Pettit on the first day of the Pirates spring training camp. He had been hired by Branch Rickey to manage the Pirates and vowed to give Pettit every opportunity to make the ballclub. In the early exhibition games, observers said that they had never seen the left-hander throw harder. One was the veteran umpire, Augie Donatelli, who told sportswriters, "He surprised me with his speed and his control." When the club broke camp and headed for Pittsburgh to start the season, Pettit had pitched his way back to the big leagues.

By the first of May, the once-hapless Pirates were playing good baseball. Three straight wins had generated an enthusiasm that peaked on May 1, when Pettit was announced as the starting pitcher against Cincinnati. A crowd of 7,500 was expected, but the box office was caught off guard when twice that many people showed up. The game had been under way for almost 15 minutes before half of the 14,826 ticket buyers finally settled into their seats. By then they had missed Pettit breeze through the top of the first inning and strike out Ted Kluszewski to end the frame.

Through five innings, Pettit throttled Cincinnati with ease. The majority of the outs recorded were mild groundballs. He had allowed just two hits and only walked two men. With one out in the seventh inning, Pettit gestured for his manager to come to the mound. Fans drew quiet, fearful perhaps, of another bout of arm trouble. Haney was somewhat relieved to find that wasn't the case. The pitcher had developed a painful blister on his left heel and had no choice but to come out of the game. Pittsburgh held on to defeat the Reds, and Pettit was credited with his first major-league win.

It was eight days before Pettit recovered and was able to pitch again. This time the result was much different. Against the Giants in the Polo

3. Painted by the Numbers 69

Grounds, Pettit failed to record a single out. He was yanked by Haney after giving up a walk and three consecutive singles. The performance was the beginning of a downward spiral for the onetime pitching prodigy. One week later, at Wrigley Field in Chicago, Pettit breezed through the first three innings without allowing a baserunner against the Cubs. In the fourth inning, however, three successive Cubs hitters singled, scoring two runs, and Pettit was pulled from the mound.

By the end of May, Branch Rickey's patience in Pettit had worn thin. He had never believed Pettit's complaints about arm trouble and told others he felt the problem was in the pitcher's head. Rickey's tolerance reached its breaking point following a May 27 doubleheader with Philadelphia. Over two innings Pettit gave up seven hits and seven runs. Six days later, Rickey sent him to the minor leagues with a record of 16 runs and 22 hits in 16 innings pitched.

At New Orleans, Rickey watched him toss seven shutout innings against Nashville. Not long after, Pettit developed a dead arm and was demoted to Charleston. There his arm recovered and his performances sparked Rickey's interest, but it had nothing to do with pitching. Against Montgomery, Pettit singled twice and clobbered a grand slam. During his six weeks with the club, Pettit had eight hits in 21 at-bats for a .381 average.

Following the season in Charleston, Pettit was summoned back to Pittsburgh to finish the season with the Pirates. Rickey and Haney wanted to evaluate young prospects in preparation for the 1954 season. Being back in the big leagues was only part of the exuberance that Pettit felt in September of 1953. Days after he rejoined the Pirates, Shirley gave birth to their second child in California. Only hours after receiving the news, Pettit went to the mound to pitch against the Chicago Cubs. He retired eight of the first nine hitters he faced. In the fourth inning Pettit gave up a walk and four straight hits before Haney sent him to the showers. Four nights later Pettit pitched again. He was staked to a four-run lead over Cincinnati but failed to hold it. It would be the last time the 21-year-old would ever appear in a major-league game.

Paul Pettit's fifth season in professional baseball brought dramatic change. Branch Rickey sold Pettit's contract to Hollywood. The press had a field day. "Colossal Flop" screamed one headline. Articles called the 21-year-old a "100-G lemon" and an "abysmal failure." Harry Keck wrote in the *Pittsburgh Sun-Telegram*, "The case of Paul Pettit is tragic," adding "He may never return to the majors."

During Hollywood's opening series of the season, Pettit was called upon to quell a rally against Portland. Instead, he allowed two runs on a hit and two walks then was removed without ever recording an out. A former high school opponent who witnessed the game said, "He isn't throwing anything like the way he did when I saw him in high school. He could really fire in those days." Four weeks into the season, the Stars were boarding a bus to the airport for a road trip to Portland when Pettit was pulled aside. "We want you to go to Salinas," he was told. "We want you to try and play every day."

I was managing our farm club at Hutchinson, Kansas, when Mr. Rickey called me. He said he was sending me to take over the club at Salinas, California. Mr. Rickey said he had a project he wanted me to handle. He wanted me to try and salvage Paul Pettit. Mr. Rickey wanted to try and make him an everyday player. When I got to Salinas, Paul and I talked. I told him he would pitch every fourth day, but the other days he was either going to play in right field or first base. He went on a tear!

Filled with confidence by his new manager, Pettit thrived. He was the hitting star of the Salinas Packers. Even though he played in only three-quarters of the season in Salinas, Pettit finished in the top ten in the Class C California League in home runs, doubles, runs batted in, and batting average. He hit .324, belted 20 home runs, and drove in 103 runs in the 108 games that he played. Were it not for a pair of *faux pas*, Pettit's totals might have been even higher. Playing in a dimly-lit ballpark in Visalia, Pettit came up with the bases loaded and slugged a ball that cleared the fence for a home run. However, only Pettit seemed to know that it had cleared the fence. The Visalia right fielder had leaped and pretended as if he had caught the ball. It fooled the runner on first base, who turned and raced back to first base. Pettit had just jogged around first base and was unable to stop before his teammate passed him, which was an automatic out. Later in the season a ball Pettit hit in Stockton caromed off the top of the wall and into the right fielder's chest. The player cradled it then held the ball aloft as if he had made the catch. The performance confused the umpire, and Pettit was called out.

Mr. Rickey assigned me to manage Mexico City in 1955. We badly underestimated the level of talent in the Mexico League and got off to a slow start. Our club was in last place, and the locals wanted me fired. Branch Jr. gave me a list of players the Pirates were thinking of releasing from the Hollywood club. When I saw Pettit's name on the list, I said "I want HIM!"

Pettit initially balked at the assignment. He didn't know what to expect of conditions and was wary of taking his wife and small children to Mexico.

Once Pettit arrived, however, he went on a hitting tear that awakened the last-place Tigers. Over his first four games Pettit hammered out nine hits and launched the team on a win streak. In Monterrey he smashed a home run over the center-field fence that locals called the longest ever hit out of Parque Cuauthemoc. When the win streak reached six, it was Paul Pettit's grand slam that was a highlight. Two nights after that, Pettit's three singles, double, and home run helped the Tigers extend the streak to eight. The tally grew to double digits after a game in which Pettit hammered out two singles, a double, and drove in five runs. "You're a house afire," his teammate Gail Henley exclaimed. By the time the streak had been snapped, the Tigers had won 14 games in a row to climb out of last place and contend for the pennant.

Newspapers throughout Mexico regularly ran stories about him. His face appeared often on the cover of *El Hit*, the Mexican baseball magazine.

I talked to Mr. Rickey and his son, Branch, quite regularly. Every time we talked I told them the switch was going to work. Paul was really hitting the ball. I said I felt he should get a look with Pittsburgh. He would be the ideal 25th man. He can play the outfield, he can play first base, he can even pitch in an emergency.

For three months Pettit flirted with a .400 average and dueled his teammates Henley and Leo Rodriguez for the Mexican League batting title. On the final day of the season, Rodriguez won the crown with a .385 mark to Henley's .3836 and Pettit's final average of .3830. Pettit's 80 runs batted in and ten home runs helped his team win an improbable Mexican League pennant.

Pettit told sportswriters he hoped that his play in Mexico would earn another opportunity with the Pirates. It didn't. There were new sensations in the farm system. A 20-year-old by the name of Roberto Clemente had his name affixed to right field. Bob Skinner was fast tracked for left field, and many in the organization saw Dick Stuart as the Pirates' future first baseman. In time Pettit saw the writing on the wall. When a strong 1957 season for Hollywood, in which he hit 20 home runs, drove in 102 runs, and batted .284, failed to generate so much as an invitation to spring training with the Pirates, the once-heralded talent realized his days in baseball were likely numbered. That realization was delivered bluntly on May 2, 1959. The Pirates had cut their final check of the ten-year bonus payout agreement. The obligation fulfilled, they traded the one-time wonder to Seattle of the Pacific Coast League. Paul Pettit's ten-year struggle to fulfill expectations and reward the largest investment ever made in an amateur player was over.

Pettit played well for Seattle, but reality shifted his emphasis. He skipped the 1961 season to concentrate on school. Pettit attended classes in the evening and did his student teaching by day. He often worked nights in a bakery, then dashed home to catch what little shut-eye he could. Pettit graduated with a degree in secondary education and was hired for a teaching job to begin in September of 1962.

In the interim he decided to give baseball one last shot, but the Seattle Rainiers had become a Boston Red Sox farm club. They had to play the prospects supplied by their new parent club. There was little playing time for Pettit. Things had changed off the field for Pettit as well. His children were busy with school and activities. Shirley stayed in Southern California with them. The pain in his throwing arm flared up from time to time. The factors added up to one decision. Paul Pettit followed it and retired from the game.

Paul became a teacher and did a lot of coaching. He helped me out as one of my associate scouts. He was never bitter about the way his career turned out, and he really had a great love for baseball, even after he retired. Paul did some coaching, and he helped a couple of young players who went on to play pro ball. One of them, Gary Allenson, reached the big leagues then became a manager. I really felt Paul should have made it back up as a hitter. Why the Pirates didn't, I'll never understand. But, boy, back when he was in high school, he was really something.

For decades Pettit and the members of the 1949 Narbonne High School baseball team have gathered sometimes twice a year for dinner. Their evenings are filled with storytelling and laughs made special by the bonds of remarkable friendship. When talk evolves from families and jobs, grandkids and hobbies to baseball, it is inevitable that stories from Paul Pettit's career become a topic. Asked one evening about pitchers that he had caught during his six seasons in the Dodgers' farm system, Gar Myers rattled off the names of Larry Sherry, Johnny Podres, Roger Craig, "and a few old timers—Rex Barney, Joe Black and Don Newcome." Without hesitation, Myers slid into comparisons to his former high school battery mate. He gushed that there was only one pitcher he ever saw that came close to the Paul Pettit he caught at the height of his talent. That one pitcher threw from almost the same over-the-top arm angle, had a fastball that was comparable to Pettit's, and a curveball with a bit more break. The pitcher Myers felt most closely compared to the 18-year-old Paul Pettit amassed a career in which he won three Cy Young Awards, a Most Valuable Player Award, and was in the Hall of Fame—Sandy Koufax.

4

LESSONS FROM THE COLLEGE OF BASEBALL

Conversation of the latest pitching sensation was in the air. Talk wove from the many predictions and expectations to the largess of the signing bonus baseball's nouveau phenom was expected to receive. It was a topic that took Ed Cereghino back some 65 years. A chuckle came through the phone and then a recitation of Mark Twain: "History doesn't repeat itself, but it does rhyme."

I faced Ed Cereghino in 1951 in the Pacific Coast League. He was the youngest player in the league by almost three years. The boy was just 17, right out of high school, and he was competing in the strongest of all the minor leagues. The Coast League was filled with future and former major leaguers. Ed had a real good fastball, and he was quite a competitor. Everybody was predicting a big future for him.

The photographer waved his right arm in an exasperated plea for the men yakking and laughing to move into position. A half dozen or so took direction and moved to the left of the primary subject. Another group stepped to the right of the lad in the middle. The men wore trench coats over their suits and ties to ward off the chill of a San Francisco summer night. Fedoras perched atop the scalp of almost every one of the men. The photographer peered into his view finder. Some of the men offered stern looks while others forced a grin or gave a wry smile. In the middle of the mass stood a 17-year-old boy. A Jefferson High School letterman jacket covered a baseball jersey that was dotted with sweat.

The men in the trench coats were baseball scouts. Each had come to watch the most coveted professional prospect in the country, Ed Cereghino. Over the previous two and a half hours, Cereghino had complied with the scout's request that he pitch one more time before they made their contract offers. The teen had agreed to pitch in a semipro game at Funston Park in the city's Marina District, and with the scouts scribbling evaluations into their notebooks and squinting in the dim light to judge the break on the right-handed hurler's curveball, Cereghino struck out 22 batters in the game. Now as the savvy photographer recognized the opportunity for a historic photograph, several of the scouts waited for the burst of the flashbulb. Some were flush with an anxious unease that their ballclub's offer might be rejected by the coveted pitcher.

Baseball had been Ed Cereghino's passion since the age of seven. His father, Ed Sr., had been a semipro player. As the son's talents grew, coaches with amateur and semipro teams recruited the younger Cereghino to pitch in games and tournaments up and down the Peninsula.

The wins as a junior pitching for the Jefferson High School varsity and a string of no-hitters over teams like Joost Coffee and Five Mile House in the Golden Gate Park summer league drew the attention of professional baseball scouts. Charlie Walgren of the Boston Red Sox was the first to come around. Soon after, Bill Brenzel of the Dodgers, "Sloppy" Thurston of the White Sox, and Eddie Montague of the Giants became regular followers. During four years at Jefferson High School and in the Golden Gate Park League, Cereghino threw seven no-hitters, 39 shutouts, and won 120 games.

The pursuit of Cereghino's talents by professional baseball's evaluators took on a new dynamic when one scout made the teen his target. Joe Devine was a legitimate super scout. His work had funneled Joe DiMaggio, Charlie Silvera, Jerry Coleman, Billy Martin, Gil McDougal, Bobby Brown, and Andy Carey to the New York Yankees. Devine was a personable Irishman, quick to laugh and with a keen ability to listen. He was a round man with a receding hairline covered by a few strands that he combed over. Devine had a knack for forging relationships with the parents of the players he wanted. In the spring of 1951, Joe Devine's master skills at charm were unleashed in full force on Ed Cereghino's parents, Ed and Nora.

Whenever the Yankees' scout turned up to watch the younger Cereghino pitch, he would squeeze between the pitcher's parents, toss a blanket over their legs, and engage in nine innings of conversation, primarily aimed at the teenager's Irish mother. This sent Walgren, Thurston, and Bob Fontaine of the Pittsburgh Pirates into a tizzy. After games the pursuing scouts scurried after the younger Cereghino, keen to learn what his mother and Devine had talked about in the stands. It was an inquisition that was almost always met with an ignorant shrug.

4. Lessons from the College of Baseball 75

The flock of scouts following Cereghino became a show in itself. "Scouts have clogged the stands for all-important games," wrote Darrell Wilson in the *San Francisco Chronicle*. "When Cereghino blows his nose, scouts watch his hand action from hip to face," the writer chided.

In May, Cereghino struck out 11 and scattered just three paltry hits as Jefferson High beat San Mateo, 5–1, to claim their league title. Gary Wilshire, writing in the *San Francisco Chronicle*, praised Cereghino as "the greatest pitcher in Peninsula Athletic League history."

With graduation nearing, scouts began to press for information into what sort of signing bonus it would take to land the coveted pitcher. Across the bay one year earlier, J.W. Porter from McClymonds High School in Oakland had received a $67,500 bonus from the Chicago White Sox. The figure was a record signing bonus for a prospect from Northern California.

Around this time Cereghino's father made a pronouncement to answer the scout's persistent questions—that to land his son would take $100,000. The large figure hiked pressure on the scouts. Suddenly, their evaluations received greater scrutiny from upper management. The men were grilled by their scouting directors, general managers, and in some cases, team owners, who were faced with the prospect of making a substantial financial outlay for a 17-year-old prospect.

Opportunities to evaluate the hard-throwing pitcher dwindled to one final game. On June 8 the best high school seniors from the San Francisco and Oakland areas would assemble in Seals Stadium for the region's annual East-West all-star game. Cereghino would pitch. His selection fanned greater interest in the game than usual. A throng of 7,208 fans streamed into the Pacific Coast League ballpark to see the young phenom pitch. Cereghino was dazzling. He held the Oakland standouts at bay with a sizzling fastball. In the seventh inning Cereghino came to bat and drove a pitch over the left-field wall for a three-run home run to give his team a commanding lead. By the game's end he had tallied 15 strikeouts, and his home run had been the big blow in his team's 5–1 win. It was hardly any surprise when he was announced as the game's Most Valuable Player. The only real surprise came from Cereghino himself when he learned that the prize brought with it a trip to the World Series.

After the game, several scouts gathered in the Seals Stadium lounge, and once a few drinks had been tossed back, a baseball version of liar's poker broke out. Diminishing the value of Ed Cereghino was the objective.

"He has no changeup."

"His curve isn't sharp. You can see it coming. He doesn't fool anybody."

"You've got to realize he's bigger than most boys his age. In a pro league he'd be cut down to size."

One by one the scouts spewed criticism of the teen's pitching skills, each one attempting to make the other scouts reconsider their level of interest in the boy. Four hours later those same scouts slammed their glasses on the table, grabbed their coats, made a dash for their cars, then beat a path to 412 Willets Street in Daly City, where they tried to muscle past one another and into the front door of the Cereghino home to gain an audience with and lavish praise on the coveted ballplayer and his parents.

Pressed by their front office, several scouts asked Cereghino if he would agree to pitch one more time. The White Sox' general manager, Frank Lane, wanted to travel to San Francisco to see the pitcher for himself. Harry Jenkins of the Braves insisted on flying out from Boston for a first-hand look. In Pittsburgh, Branch Rickey wanted opinions from not just his two California scouts, Bob Fontaine and Bob Clements, but also his son, Branch Jr.

A semipro game was assembled for Funston Park, just blocks from the waters of San Francisco Bay. Cereghino would pitch for Panama Tile in their Golden Gate Park League game against Johnnie's Billiards. Fourteen men representing nine big-league clubs trickled to the diamond to watch Cereghino pitch. Nods and a few handshakes recognized rivals. The night was chilly. In stark contrast to the weather, Cereghino's fastball was blazing. One scout muttered to his colleague that the teen's pitch resembled Bob Feller's legendary blazer.

Throughout the game the 17-year-old amassed a staggering number of strikeouts. Heading into the ninth inning he had yet to give up a hit. In the final frame an outfielder muffed a fly ball. The official scorer ruled the play a hit. Many in the stands scoffed that it was clearly an error. The decision robbed Cereghino of a no-hitter. Once tallied, the prospect had struck out 22. There were few, if any, scouts that were not greatly impressed.

After the game, a reporter quizzed some of the scouts about Cereghino's performance. Joe Devine said he could find no flaws. Branch Rickey, Jr., said, "I think 50,000 is more like the right figure for him," then added that the Pirates' offer would depend upon whether Cereghino wanted his money in one lump payment or was willing to have it spread over several years.

Before leaving, four of the scouts made offers. The Boston Braves were the first to talk money. The Pittsburgh Pirates made the highest offer, close to $75,000. Jack Fournier of the Chicago Cubs made an appointment to meet privately with the family to extend his club's offer. Ed Cereghino,

Sr., had promised Joe Devine the chance to beat whatever offer turned out to be the highest.

As the scouts stomped through the grass toward their cars, Ed Cereghino, Sr., turned to his son with a bit of mischief in mind. "Wadda ya say we make 'em sweat. Let's go to Yosemite for a week." The next day the Cereghinos packed suitcases and drove to Yosemite National Park, where they spent the next week camping.

Once the family returned, more proposals waited. The Boston Red Sox monetary offer was well short of that of the Pirates. They attempted, however, to sweeten the value of their deal by including a full scholarship to Stanford University. The Cereghinos summoned Devine and were taken aback when the scout showed up at their door missing several teeth. He apologized and explained that he had come from the dentist where he was being fitted for dentures and was suffering the effects of a Novocain injection.

The scout complimented the pitcher. "One of the big reasons I like you," Devine said, "you have a great value system. Your parents did it right." The Cereghinos thanked the scout. After small talk, Ed Cereghino, Sr., shared that his son had received an offer that was close to $75,000. "Give me an hour," Devine requested. He then left to phone his boss, George Weiss. After conferring with the Yankees' general manager, Devine returned. The New York Yankees offered $74,000. The figure topped the record $60,000 bonus the team had given to Bobby Brown in 1946. Heads nodded around the table as the deal was agreed to. As Devine expanded on the offer, enthusiasm between scout and pitcher rose.

"Listen, we got an opening with the Seals."

"The *San Francisco* Seals?"

"We could start you at C ball."

"No, I'd like to go with the Seals!"

Ed Cereghino and his father were Seals fans. They regularly trekked to watch the Pacific Coast League club play, sitting in box seats just behind third base and the Seals dugout. "Gosh, now I'm going to be *in* that dugout!"

Ed was very fortunate. Six months before he signed, baseball did away with the bonus rule. To try and stop teams from paying big bonuses, baseball created a bonus rule back in 1947. It said that any player who got a bonus of more than $6,000 had to spend a year in the big leagues. This hurt a lot of guys. They weren't ready to play in the big leagues, so they sat around, didn't play, and their skills suffered. At the Winter Meetings in December 1950, the rule was rescinded.

It was a day later when Devine dropped by the Cereghino's home with the contract. Sportswriters, photographers, and newsreel cameramen were summoned. Devine, looking especially dapper in a black double-breasted blazer, flashed his broad smile as his prize bent at the waist, leaned forward to bring a pen to the document, and signed the contract on his parents' dining room table. Alongside the scout, Cereghino's mother and father smiled at the happy occasion.

The cameramen asked father and son to grab mitts, step outside, and engage in a friendly game of catch on the sidewalk. Flashbulbs popped and the whirr of the film camera filled the air as father and son chuckled while tossing a weather-beaten baseball back and forth.

Once the media had packed their things and left, Devine offered sage advice. He instructed the teen to never reveal the amount of his signing bonus. With a wink, Devine suggested that if Cereghino were backed into a corner and made to answer, he should "throw out a figure $10,000 higher than what you got. That'll make the organization look good."

While joviality enveloped the occasion, Devine's visit concluded with somberness. The Yankees' scout had recently received a serious medical diagnosis. He had cancer and the disease was at an advanced stage. "Kid, DiMaggio was my first and you're going to be my last," he said. Three months later while in Los Angeles preparing for a game with the Hollywood Stars, Ed Cereghino would receive a phone call with the sad news that Joe Devine had passed away.

Cereghino's deal with the Yankees reverberated throughout baseball. Publications from *The Sporting News*, *The New York Times*, *St. Louis Post-Dispatch*, and *The Brooklyn Daily Eagle* ran headlines that trumpeted the Yankees' feat. Not all penned the news in glowing fashion. In his column in the *San Mateo Times*, Art Knight wrote, "Are the New York Yankees that stupid?" Knight castigated the Yankees for launching the prized prospect's career in such a lofty level of minor-league ball. The columnist accused the Seals of "caring more about padding their gate than they do about Cereghino's future in baseball." There was a basis for Knight's supposition. The San Francisco Seals were not only floundering near last place in the Pacific Coast League standings, they were swimming in red ink. The team's poor play had affected attendance, and Paul Fagan, who owned the ballclub, was staring at the prospect of losing a quarter of a million dollars for the season. In June, before Fagan left to spend the summer at his vacation home in Hawaii, the multi-millionaire demanded that his manager, Lefty O'Doul, and Joe Orengo, the Seals' business manager, get the club into the first division. "This is an order! Understand?"

4. Lessons from the College of Baseball 79

On June 27 Cereghino stepped into the clubhouse at Seals Stadium to join his new team. As he shook hands with his new teammates, he was in awe. Here was a kid who had cheered these very players on from the stands and was now their teammate and anxious to begin his career.

Except for talent-depleted times during World War II, the recent high school graduate was the youngest player to suit up for a Pacific Coast League club since a 17-year-old Ted Williams played for San Diego in 1936. After the introductions Cereghino received two gifts. He was wide-eyed when the equipment manager handed him a pinstriped flannel jersey with the word SEALS in block letters over the left breast and the number 17 on the back. The second gift was a new baseball mentor—his manager, Frank "Lefty" O'Doul.

Lefty O'Doul was a larger-than-life figure in San Francisco, more well-known during the summer of 1951 than even Ed Cereghino. He was charismatic, hugely popular, and sported a baseball pedigree that was beyond reproach. During an 11-year, big-league career, O'Doul won two batting titles, was an All-Star, and finished second in the MVP voting in 1929, when he batted .398. During the winter of 1934, Fagan, the owner of the Seals, coaxed O'Doul to leave the New York Giants and come home to manage his ballclub. By 1951 Lefty O'Doul had managed the Seals to the Pacific Coast League title five times.

O'Doul's mentoring covered both facets of the game of baseball: playing and professionalism. He put Cereghino through workouts and schooled the young hurler on pitching strategy. In fact, Cereghino heard his manager urge, "Change speeds. Pitch corner-to-corner," so much that the refrain echoed in the young pitcher's sleep.

Schooling extended beyond the walls of Seals Stadium. One afternoon, O'Doul nodded in the direction of a taxi then barked to his new pitcher, "Come on, kid, hop in!" The Seals manager slid into the front seat alongside the cabbie, and the trio sped off. Whenever the taxi came upon a congested intersection, O'Doul would give a wave and holler to the cop who stood in the median. "Hey, Lefty! How ya doin'?" the officer would shout back. Immediately the taxi would be allowed to drive through. Sitting in the back seat, Cereghino was enthralled with the show. In almost every case his new manager knew the police officer by name. O'Doul was the unofficial mayor of the city.

After traversing several city blocks, the taxi screeched to halt on Geary Street near Powell, where the Seals' manager led his new pitcher into McIntosh, a tailor, and directed the purchase of three new $150 suits for the rookie.

The jump from high school to the Pacific Coast League was almost unheard of. People called the league the third major league. In fact, the owner of the San Francisco Seals was one of the men working hard to get it declared a third major league. Ballclubs in the league were filled with former big-leaguers as well as guys who were knocking at the door to go up to the major leagues. The coast league had the most talent and was the most competitive of all the minor leagues.

Throughout the week, O'Doul had Cereghino pitch batting practice to his teammates. The manager had his doubts about a 17-year-old's ability to compete successfully at the highest level of the minor leagues and in a league dotted with former major-league players. O'Doul initially thought he would use Cereghino only in selected relief situations. The more he watched Cereghino throw, however, the more impressed O'Doul became. Tidbits began to appear in various newspaper columns about O'Doul's plans for his new pitcher. The first said that Cereghino would be used only in relief, another said he would work from the bullpen for his first two weeks in pro ball. They were followed by a note that Cereghino might start the game against Seattle on July 8. His manager remained tight-lipped about plans for the teen until a midweek session with the local press. The Seals' skipper responded to a sportswriter's question by saying that the Yankees' record bonus signing would make his professional debut at the end of the week on Sunday, July 1. Cereghino would start the second game of the Seals' doubleheader against the San Diego Padres.

For a solid week the teenager was inundated with interview requests. Sportswriters from the *San Francisco Chronicle*, *News*, and *Examiner*, radio reporters from several San Francisco area stations, and sportscasters from area television channels thrust microphones in his face, focused bright lights in his eyes, and showered the young pitcher with questions.

On Sunday, July 1, the usual sounds of pregame batting practice and the echo of batted balls reverberating from empty grandstands was replaced by the buzz of hundreds of fans pouring into the ballpark. Outside, on 16th and Bryant, anxious fans searched for parking spots. The lot behind center field and another in back of the third-base stands filled quickly. As game time neared, almost 75 percent of the 16,000 seats in the park were filled.

That San Francisco beat San Diego, 5–4, in the opener was of little consequence to the throng. It was the second game that held their interest. When Ed Cereghino emerged from the Seals dugout, a loud murmur rippled through the stands. Almost every fan turned to watch his walk to the warm-up mound in the left field corner. The pitcher's parents sat in box seats behind the third-base dugout. Ed Senior chewed on a cigar, dapper in a three-piece suit and fedora. Nora warded off the chill with a dark overcoat, her hands nervously clinging to the purse that rested on her lap.

Photographers and cameramen built a semicircle around the 17-year-old as he began his warm-up tosses. After four or five pitches Cereghino paused. He scanned the crowd. His gaze flicked to the field, the pitcher's mound, home plate, and the backstop. *"No different than the all-star game,"* he thought. *"I can do this."*

The smack of Cereghino's fastballs hitting the palm of his catcher's mitt were partnered by the pop of flashbulbs and the buzz of Bell and Howell film cameras. Each time he told his catcher that he was done, another one of the camera wielders hollered for Cereghino to throw a couple more. Their demands forced the young pitcher to warm up much longer than he wanted, and he paid a price for it in the first inning.

A loud cheer filled the air when Ed Cereghino took the mound to begin his professional baseball career. Seals stadium boasted its biggest crowd of the season, more than 12,000 fans. Among the curious and ardent was Bing Crosby. Festive pregame cheers were quickly replaced by groans once the game began as Cereghino struggled to control his fastball. It lacked the zip and movement that had so impressed covetous scouts two months before. San Diego's veteran hitters capitalized. Loud thwacks echoed through the ballpark as the Padres rapped out four hits that sent three runners across home plate.

Despite falling three runs behind in the top of the first inning, Lefty O'Doul never moved a muscle in the dugout. He saw the situation as a learning opportunity and let Cereghino work his way out of trouble. With his fastball lacking, Cereghino relied on his curveball. When he did use the fastball, he nibbled the corners with it rather than trying to overpower the hitters. The manager's faith was rewarded when his prospect got out of the jam and for the next four innings blanked the Padres.

San Francisco fought back and tied the game, 3–3. In the bottom of the sixth inning, Cereghino came to bat with the bases loaded. In the press box, sportswriters questioned O'Doul's decision to let the young pitcher bat rather than use a pinch-hitter. With a two-ball, two-strike count, Cereghino swung and sent a fly ball toward right field. Once it was caught, Bill McCawley tagged up from third base and slid under the catcher's tag to give the Seals a 4–3 lead.

Fans rose to their feet when Cereghino marched to the mound to pitch the seventh and final inning. All 12,285 stayed on their feet when Whitey Wietelmann flied out to left field. They continued to stand and roar when Ed Sauer caught Jack Graham's fly ball up against the right-field wall to put Cereghino one out away from winning his professional debut. But two pitches later, Seals Stadium fell silent, muted by the loud crack of Clarence Maddern's bat. The San Diego batter sent a drive over the left-field wall for a home run that tied the game.

An inning later fatigue caught up with Cereghino. Two walks and two weakly-hit balls produced a pair of San Diego runs. The Padres spoiled the heralded prospect's debut with a 6–4 victory. Cereghino had thrown 135 pitches, and only 50 were strikes.

After the game, a throng of reporters pressed into the Seals locker room to seek out the 17-year-old. They found the pitcher exhausted, sitting on a stool in front of his locker, head down, and awash in disappointment. "One pitch did it," Cereghino muttered. "I gave Maddern a fastball and waist high. That was my big mistake."

Not everyone was dour and glum after the loss. Joe Devine, the scout who had signed Cereghino, flashed a big smile to reporters. "I'm proud as heck of him," Devine beamed. Thirty miles south of the Seals Stadium clamor, Ty Cobb had quietly listened to the game on the radio at his home. When a reporter from the *San Francisco Examiner* phoned to ask the legendary Hall of Fame outfielder for his thoughts, Cobb said Cereghino had done "a remarkable job."

Only weeks after the largest of Cereghino's signing bonus had sparked curiosity among San Francisco's baseball fans, the dynamics changed. An almost daily diet of newspaper articles, reports on radio stations, and even television news programs grew fan intrigue into legitimate interest. The platitudes contained in the reports and coming from such lofty experts as Ty Cobb helped to fuel newly-whetted appetite into full-blown fervor.

So great was the fans' zeal that an even bigger crowd stamped into Seals Stadium one week later for Cereghino's second professional start. This one would again be in the second game of a doubleheader but against a far more daunting foe than his first—the Seattle Rainiers.

The standings in the morning paper told Cereghino he was facing the first-place team in the Pacific Coast League. Lefty O'Doul offered a run-down on the Rainiers batting order. They were the best-hitting team in the league. Five of their eight position starters were veterans of the major leagues. Two more were being aggressively pursued by big-league clubs, including "Jungle Jim" Rivera, the leading hitter in the league. O'Doul didn't stop there. He warned his fledgling that the Seattle manager was to be reckoned with, too. Rogers Hornsby was a legendary heckler, notorious for getting under the skin of and rattling even the most seasoned veteran. "Don't listen to him. Don't pay him any attention," O'Doul ordered.

Once they had won the first game of the July 8 doubleheader, the Rainiers were riding a nine-game win streak. By the time Cereghino reached the pitcher's mound to begin the game, Seals Stadium was buzzing with anticipation. Curley Grieve, the *San Francisco Examiner* sports editor, described the atmosphere being "as tense and dramatic as that which surrounds a World Series." Ticket takers reported the crowd count at 14,525—of which 2,000 turned up just for the second game to see Cereghino pitch.

No sooner had the young sensation taken a couple of his pregame warmup tosses when sportswriters in the press box noticed something different. When not doing interviews with the media during the previous week, Cereghino had spent extensive time with Joe Sprinz, the Seals' pitching coach, to iron out some flaws. The biggest change Sprinz had made was to have Cereghino throw with a stiffer right leg rather than bend the leg almost to the point of kneeling. Results from the modification were dramatic. "Better hop on the fastball and the changed delivery gave me better control," the pitcher told his father.

It didn't take long for the Seattle Rainiers to find out how dramatic those results were. Firing a much quicker fastball, Cereghino retired the first five Rainiers batters in order. With two outs in the top of the second inning, the dominance was punctured. Cereghino's attempt to catch the inside corner with a curveball went awry. The pitch didn't break as he wanted. It hung out over the plate and was hammered over the fence for a home run.

Between every pitch, Hornsby hollered insults from the visitors' dugout. Cereghino maintained his concentration and kept the Rainiers in check in the third inning. With one out in the fourth, his catcher called for a slow changeup, and the Rainiers' batter sent it into the right-field pavilion for another home run. It would be the last run Seattle would tack on the scoreboard that afternoon.

Cereghino set down the Rainiers with relative ease in the fifth, sixth, and seventh innings. In only 98 minutes the 17-year-old had pitched San Francisco to a 3–2 win over the best team in the league. Jubilation surged through Seals Stadium. No sooner had the final out been recorded when 2,000 exuberant fans hurdled the railing and rushed toward the pitcher's mound to congratulate their new hero. Worried for his son's safety, Ed Cereghino, Sr., vaulted the railing and pushed his way through the mob. "Let him through," O'Doul hollered. Fans complied as Cereghino's father ushered his son toward the clubhouse.

Once in the sanctity of the Seals clubhouse, O'Doul gushed to the reporters. "Sensational! I can't believe he's only 17. His fastball was hopping.

See him crowd those left-handers like Rivera? And that curve. It fooled those right-handers plenty. What a kid!"

Across the hall in the visitors' clubhouse, Hornsby groused to the San Francisco press. "He beat the league's leading club. What the hell more can you ask?" Cereghino, who completed the game on just 73 pitches, heaped praise on his pitching coach, Sprinz. "That suggestion was the answer!"

The *San Francisco Chronicle* trumpeted "Cereghino Wins" in a banner headline on page one. The paper's baseball writer, Bob Stevens, called the performance "The miracle of Sixteenth Street," and anointed the teen pitcher "this newly-arrived sensation to the conqueror's throne."

O'Doul ditched his plan to use Cereghino only as a relief pitcher. He added the young sensation to the starting rotation. Despite his age difference, Cereghino fit in well with his older teammates. Lew Burdette, Al Lien, Joe Page, and Manny Perez took the newcomer under their wings. The veteran players offered advice that was often mixed in with a fair heaping of good-natured razzing.

On the heels of Cereghino's success came a disagreement which drew the young player into controversy. Teams around the league were not happy that the Seattle Rainiers declined to join into an agreement with everyone else in the PCL to share 40 percent of box office receipts with the visiting club. Cereghino's third start was expected to come in Seattle, and the Rainiers had been promoting that fact in the papers and on radio to try to draw a big crowd. O'Doul, who also wasn't particularly fond of Hornsby, the Seattle manager, pulled Cereghino aside the day before his scheduled start. "I'm going to hit him where it hurts," he said, then announced that his young sensation would not pitch while the Seals were in Seattle. The Rainiers were furious and complained loudly, but O'Doul stuck to his plan and held Cereghino back until the Seals reached Portland later in the road trip.

The road trip saw a trend begin that would fester for much of the remainder of the season. Cereghino would pitch brilliantly for five or six innings then run out of steam and falter. It first occurred in Portland, where he pitched six strong innings then waned in the seventh. Against the pennant-chasing Hollywood Stars, Cereghino was outstanding through the first four innings, only to grow weary in the fifth then exit the game. Five days later the young sensation again stymied Hollywood for six innings before he weakened and was clobbered, 8–1.

When we went up there to play the Seals, you could see that Cereghino was a quick learner. San Francisco could have its advantages for a power

pitcher. At night it got cold and the fog would come in. A good power pitcher could use that to his advantage, and he did. Cereghino threw a heavy ball. He could make it run in on a right-handed hitter. If you caught it on the wrong part of the bat, it would really sting your hands. You'd feel like they were full of bees. He could make aggressive hitters a bit tentative.

Against Oakland, Cereghino held the Oaks to just three hits over the first five innings. In the sixth, in the words of the *Chronicle's* Bob Stevens, "He again grew weary and ran out of gas." San Francisco lost to its crossbay rival, 11–8. More than 8,000 fans turned up on August 13 to see the prized prospect take on the Los Angeles Angels in Seals Stadium. As Stevens wrote in the *Chronicle's* account, Cereghino "pitched brilliantly through the first five innings." In the sixth inning, the Angels exploded for five runs and beat San Francisco, 8–1.

On August 26 in Sacramento, almost 6,000 fans endured a scorching-hot night to see the young phenom pitch. The 17-year-old's fastball was as searing as the weather. Cereghino carried a no-hitter into the fifth inning then ran out of steam in the sixth and exited the game.

On the next to the last day of the season, the Seals were playing Sacramento in a battle to avoid finishing in last place. In a tie game, Joe Page, a onetime Yankees standout whose better days in the game were behind him, pitched his way into a jam in the final inning. O'Doul summoned Cereghino to relieve Page. With the potential go-ahead run at second base and former American League Most Valuable Player, Joe Gordon, stepping to bat, O'Doul ordered Cereghino to pitch out and intentionally walk the hitter. After throwing his first two pitches intentionally wide of home plate, Cereghino's third offering came closer to the strike zone than he wanted. Gordon reached out and drove the ball to right field. The runner who was on second base broke into a dead sprint in a desperate attempt at heroics to score the winning run. When the throw home went awry, the Seals were consigned to not just defeat but a last-place finish, and the slow, dejected walk the young pitcher made up the tunnel to the clubhouse was in stark contrast to the way his season with the Seals had begun.

Finish aside, Ed Cereghino's inaugural three months of professional baseball stirred a great deal of zeal within the New York Yankees' hierarchy. The 17-year-old made 12 starts in the most competitive minor league in baseball and had finished five of them. He won four games and lost six. His earned run average was 5.64, bloated by a couple of short and lopsided outings.

Once the season had concluded, Cereghino couldn't wait to cash in his high school all-star game prize and travel to the World Series. It featured his new ballclub, the Yankees, who would face the New York Giants. On arriving at Yankee Stadium, Cereghino was ushered into the clubhouse to meet the men he hoped would soon be his teammates. "Hey, gimme a loan!" Yogi Berra grinned. Cereghino was welcomed with back slaps and handshakes by Vic Rashi, Allie Reynolds, and Art Shallock. It was when he was introduced to Joe DiMaggio that the mood chilled. The Yankees' superstar was curt and unfriendly toward his fellow San Franciscan. "He's jealous," Cereghino was told. "He's read in the papers how much the Yankees paid to sign you. They only paid 50,000 to get him."

As Cereghino walked down a hallway beneath the stadium, he heard a familiar voice holler. It was his manager, Lefty O'Doul.

"Hey, Kid!"

"Lefty!"

"Go get your shots. I'm taking you to Japan."

"Why? What for?"

"I'm going to teach you to how to pitch out!"

O'Doul had selected Cereghino for a team of all-stars that he was taking on a tour of Japan. The team was made up of major leaguers and several former major leaguers who were with Pacific Coast League clubs. They would play 15 games against Japanese teams and all-stars.

The Americans received a greeting fit for icons when they arrived in Tokyo. Almost one million people jammed Tokyo's Ginza District to see the team parade through the streets in open-topped automobiles. Flowers were tossed at Joe DiMaggio. Paper rained from office buildings.

Two days after arriving, the U.S. All-Stars walloped the Yomiuri Giants, 7–0, before an overflow crowd of 50,000. The opening win set a tone of big crowds watching one-sided American wins.

For Cereghino, every day was eye-opening. The people and the culture were beyond anything he had previously experienced. American politicians, bureaucrats, and military leaders became exuberant fans, anxious to greet, host, and spend time with the ballplayers. Cereghino snapped up gifts and souvenirs in almost every city the team visited. By the latter weeks of the tour, silks and Noritaki China filled his trunk.

Few stops on the tour carried the astonishment of the visit to Sendai. Six years after World War II, rubble was still everywhere. Even more stunning was watching more than 30,000 fans stream into the ballpark for that evening's game. The Americans wondered where the fans had come from.

O'Doul worked Cereghino into occasional relief stints. He pitched an almost flawless ninth inning of a 6–1 win over the Yomiuri Giants. When the rookie wasn't pitching, he peppered the veteran big-league pitchers,

4. Lessons from the College of Baseball

Bobby Shantz, Mel Parnell, and Ed Lopat with questions. It was the 14th game of the tour when O'Doul selected Cereghino to be the starting pitcher. The Americans were to face an all-star team made up of players from Japan's Pacific League.

Dating back to the very first tour of Japan made by big-leaguers in 1913, Americans had never lost a game to their island counterparts. With just two games to the conclusion of the 1951 tour, the latest all-star team was closing in on their latest sweep.

After completing his warmup tosses, Cereghino was nervous. The 25,000 fans in Okayama's stadium were loud. With encouragement from his catcher and other teammates, the 17-year-old got through the first inning with ease. In the second inning, however, the Japanese scored twice on a walk, triple, and single. An inning later they added one more run. Cereghino kept the Japanese from scoring any more than the three runs before he gave way to Bobby Shantz after four innings. Even though Shantz held the Japanese scoreless over the final five innings, the Americans struggled to erase their deficit. When the final out was registered, the Japanese fans celebrated wildly. Their players had defeated a team of American pros for the first time, 3–1.

Despite the setback, O'Doul heaped praise on his young pitcher. "Cereghino had good stuff. He walked only one man," the manager told American writers. "He was good." O'Doul pointed out that his rookie happened to pitch on a day when the Americans didn't manage much offense. "He could have won any other game over here if we had started him."

It was on Thanksgiving Day when Cereghino and the all-stars arrived home in the United States. The team returned to San Francisco, where Ed and Nora Cereghino greeted their 17-year-old son with broad smiles and hugs. They made up for a disrupted family Thanksgiving 48 hours later with an 18th birthday party for the new pro ballplayer.

High spirits enveloped the teen's initial foray into professional baseball. If anything proved distracting, it was the barrage of solicitations from the schemers, salesmen, and out-and-out shysters who sought to bamboozle the recent high school graduate out of a slice of his celebrated signing bonus. The Cereghinos, however, had an ironclad defense against the nuisance makers. Because the pitcher was underage, his bonus funds went into a court-administered trust. Ed Cereghino, Sr., was its trustee. The pitcher's father was an astute businessman who guarded his son's money well. The younger Cereghino was hardly naïve to the world of finance. He had become interested in accounting and voraciously studied investing strategies.

Prior to the start of spring training, Casey Stengel invited Cereghino and a dozen other Yankees prospects to his "How to be a Yankee" camp. The man who had managed the Yankees to three successive World Series titles opened the camp by proclaiming, "It is a privilege to be a Yankee." Stengel and several coaches schooled the prospects on not just the drills and schedules they would experience in a few weeks' time in spring training but also the deportment and comportment that came with being a member of the New York Yankees.

Sportswriters turned up with notepads and were accompanied by photographers. Stengel dismissed the notion among the scribes that the prospects weren't candidates to make the 1952 Yankees. He pointed out to the writers that Mickey Mantle and Tom Morgan had successfully made the jump to the big leagues the previous season at both a young age and with very little minor-league seasoning. "Cereghino has a lot of stuff. Perhaps Cereghino will induce me to keep him," Stengel told the writers.

In mid–February the rookie pitcher's quest to make the Yankees began. Eight months removed from high school, Cereghino changed at a locker while surrounded by many of the biggest names in baseball: Berra, Mantle, Rizzuto. He felt no awe. Intimidation never entered his mind. The Seals experience was one reason why. The trip to Japan, another. Perhaps the biggest reason, though, was something Cereghino explained to his father in a phone call one evening. "This place is a dump," he exclaimed of Miller Huggins Field. "Jefferson High School was better!"

Cereghino took his turn with the veterans—Allie Reynolds, Vic Rashi, Eddie Lopat, and Johnny Sain—in the daily fielding drills, throwing sessions, and the batting practice rotation. Each was more than willing to answer the 18-year-old's questions and offer advice. Cereghino worked to develop a slider while Jim Turner, the Yankees' pitching coach, tutored the young prospect on the nuances of the craft. "Stare down those hitters," the Tennessean said with a drawl. "You don't look away. You make that hitter look away."

Five days into March, Cereghino was among the pitchers used during the Yankees' first intrasquad game. Four days later the gates to Al Lang Field swung open to the general public, and 7,000 fans took seats to see the Yankees' first exhibition game. They met their St. Petersburg spring-training neighbors, the St. Louis Cardinals. In the bottom of the sixth inning, with the score tied, 4–4, Casey Stengel summoned Cereghino from the bullpen.

Resorting primarily to his fastball, the prized Yankees' prospect struck out the first batter he faced. The Cardinals then sent their All-Star second baseman, Red Schoendienst, to pinch-hit. He tagged a Cereghino fastball to the outfield fence for a double. A minor leaguer who was getting a look in camp, Earl Weaver, singled and sent Schoendienst to third base. Solly Hemus then singled to give the Cardinals a 5–4 lead. Cereghino remained calm. He struck out the next hitter and got out of the jam with no further damage. In the next half inning, Cereghino's teammates erupted for seven runs. The 11–5 margin wound up being the final score, and in his first game wearing a major-league uniform, Ed Cereghino was the winning pitcher.

Five days later he entered a tie game with the Philadelphia Phillies in the seventh inning. Cereghino blanked the Phillies in the seventh, eighth, and again in the ninth innings. The 2–2 game went to extra innings to settle. After the Yankees failed to score in the top of the tenth inning, Cereghino went to the mound for his fourth inning of work, trying to give his teammates another chance to win the game in the 11th. It would never happen. Smokey Burgess tagged a Cereghino fastball over the left-field fence to give Philadelphia a 3–2 victory.

Euphoria at his successful stint was short-lived. Two days after the game Cereghino was dispatched 85 miles east to the minor-league camp in Lake Wales. His dream of breaking camp with the Yankees was over. The pitcher would, instead, open the season with the Yankees' top farm club, the Kansas City Blues.

Cereghino's addition to the club only increased the expectations that Kansas City writers trumpeted about the team. Those expectations helped squeeze more than 15,000 fans into Municipal Stadium for Opening Day.

The season began in a suspect way for Cereghino. After a string of stellar exhibition outings in Florida, the young pitcher struggled with his control in Kansas City. Cereghino failed to win any of his first three starts. Walks were a problem. George Selkirk, the Blues' manager, was mulling whether to remove the prized prospect from the starting rotation.

In what was a make-or-break start in Columbus, Cereghino was stellar in beating the Cardinals' farmhands. His curveball was breaking better than in his first three games. He got ahead in counts, kept the Red Birds off balance with an effective changeup, and most importantly, he cut down on the walks. Cereghino took a two-hitter into the ninth inning before he tired and saw Columbus string together three hits to ruin his shutout.

Cereghino whipped through the month of May undefeated. When he shut out Toledo on June 1, the youngest player in the American Association led all of the league's pitchers with a 5–0 record. Five thousand fans cheered every swing and miss served up by the 18-year-old in his next start, when he beat Louisville on a four-hitter.

By the time Cereghino's win streak reached eight, Yankees scouts Joe McDermott and Tom Greenwade were regular attendees at Kansas City games. Both were sent by George Weiss, the Yankees' general manager, who routinely asked if they felt the 18-year-old was ready for the major leagues.

In early July Cereghino's record was a perfect 10–0. His pitching had helped to push Kansas City to the top of the American Association standings. By the middle of July, however, the prized Yankees' pitching prospect would endure a monumental collapse. On July 18 a crowd of more than 16,000 fans filled Municipal Stadium for Cereghino's start against the Louisville Colonels. In the second inning it had become obvious that something was not right. The standout's curveball was not breaking. Cereghino's fastball lacked its usual snap. The Colonels kept Cereghino on the ropes all night before winning to end his streak.

Soon Cereghino was in the throes of a different streak—a losing streak. With each defeat the young pitcher's mind went into a dissecting overdrive. Worried that his curveball had flattened and his fastball lacked his usual zip, he picked apart his pitching mechanics. Modifications made things worse. The real root of Cereghino's troubles had nothing to do with his mechanics. It was the heat. Not the heat from expectation but literally the weather. The oppressive Midwest combination of searing heat and high humidity was nothing like San Francisco's temperate climate. One opponent called Kansas City "the hottest place on Earth in the summer time." In start after start, the 18-year-old would literally wilt in the latter innings of his games, drained of both energy and strength.

Teammates offered both empathy and advice. They explained that it sometimes took anywhere from two to five years to adjust to the Midwest weather. Eddie Erautt, who was from Oregon, said he had struggled with the stifling weather for five years before he finally acclimated and enjoyed a breakout season, winning 21 games.

When the regular season ended, Cereghino had lost eight games in a row. The Blues entered the playoffs. Selkirk removed Cereghino from the pitching rotation and used him just once in relief. The appearance came in Milwaukee on a cool night, and Cereghino finally felt the life return to his fastball and the healthy break to his curve. He struck out two of the four batters he faced. Selkirk, however, chose not to pitch Cereghino in the Junior World Series, which Kansas City lost in seven games to Rochester.

The Yankees assigned Cereghino to Kansas City again for the 1953 season, and his struggles continued. He lost his first three starts. Control was an issue. Cereghino had a 2–4 record when the decision was made in mid–June to demote the once-prized prospect down to Class A.

On Cereghino's first start for the Binghamton Triplets, he failed to escape the second inning and was mauled by the Scranton Miners, the worst team in the league. Cereghino had yet to notch a win after three starts when his fortunes took a dramatic turn on July 2. He notched his first victory and in the process initiated a win streak. By the time Cereghino completed a four-hit shutout of Scranton in late July, he had rediscovered his missing fastball velocity, and the bite in his curve was back. In Schenectady, Cereghino spoiled Baseball Appreciation Night and sent 4,000 fans home disappointed. In the seventh inning he slammed a home run to tie the game, 3–3. A pitchers' duel waged for 13 innings when Cereghino blasted another home run to win the game, 4–3. The triumph was Cereghino's ninth in a row.

The young pitcher's performances helped send Binghamton into the playoffs. In the semifinal game against Albany, Cereghino pitched no-hit ball for eight innings. He finished with ten strikeouts and a 5–2 victory that was his 11th of the season.

Cereghino finished the season with an 11–3 won-loss record and an impressive 2.59 earned run average. The statistic that got the attention of the Yankees' brass was his walks total—just 37 allowed in 139 innings pitched, an indication that perhaps their once-prized prospect had cured his control issues. They were statistics that impressed the Yankees enough to assign Cereghino back to their top farm club, Kansas City, for 1954.

The Ed Cereghino who arrived in Florida for spring training in February 1954 brought with him a different set of priorities than he carried the year before. Now 20, he was married and a father. The scales of career interest had shifted. While in high school, two of Cereghino's teachers, Frank Kane and Marge Riondo, had sparked his interest in education. Riondo's bookkeeping class and an economics book that Kane had lent to the student over the summer sparked an interest in one day becoming a teacher. The once-heralded Yankees' prospect found his ambition drift toward attending college and the pursuit of a different career path.

Once games began, however, there was no doubting that Cereghino's focus was on baseball. He pitched eight innings of one-hit baseball in his final spring training tune-up then opened the regular season in impressive fashion.

Cereghino won his first two starts for Kansas City. When he finished May by throwing a one-hit shutout, *The Sporting News* wrote that he "appeared finally to have made the grade." By the end of June, Cereghino had five wins. When he didn't win, it was in low-run games where he came out on the short end of a pitchers' duel.

At the season's halfway point Cereghino had eight wins. Just like the year before, however, he plunged into a downward spiral from the middle of July on. Coinciding with an increase in the temperature came another losing streak. By August he had been removed from the starting rotation after winning just once in six decisions. Cereghino finished the season with 11 wins and 13 losses.

During a summer morning, the Californian was shopping in a grocery store when he looked to his right and was struck by the sight of a very public figure. It was the former President of the United States, Harry Truman. Cereghino introduced himself and broke into a broad grin when he learned that the former President was a baseball fan and followed the local ballclub. Cereghino offered to leave Mr. Truman free tickets any time he wished to see a game, an offer the former President enthusiastically accepted. "Mr. President, I will have the tickets delivered to you," Cereghino suggested. Truman refused the offer, and said he was happy to wait in the pass line like everybody else. Several times during the summer, Truman contacted he pitcher for tickets. Each time Cereghino cringed at the thought of the former President of the United States sweating in 95-degree heat and high humidity while he waited with other fans to pick up his game tickets.

Despite Cereghino's second half of the season struggles, the Yankees added him to their 40-man, major-league roster for 1955. The timing was fortunate. "I have to reorganize the pitching staff," Casey Stengel proclaimed to a group of New York sportswriters. "I have to get up a new relief department." Vic Rashi had been sold to the St. Louis Cardinals. Allie Reynolds, the mainstay of the Yankees' staff, had retired. A blockbuster trade was made with Baltimore for Bob Turley and Don Larsen, but both were unproven at the major-league level. For the first time in several seasons, spring training brought real competition for jobs on the Yankees' pitching staff, and Ed Cereghino found himself in the thick of it.

With two weeks left in spring training, Cereghino and Tom Sturdivant were in a battle for the final spot on the Yankees' pitching staff. The pair were roommates and had been teammates the previous summer. Every pitch and every inning worked in the exhibition games formulated evaluations that would encompass the final decision. As the deadline date for the end of camp neared, the Yankees traveled to Bradenton for an exhibition game against the Milwaukee Braves. Cereghino received the start. His hopes of departing Florida for Yankee Stadium took a beating that after-

4. Lessons from the College of Baseball

noon. During Cereghino's three-inning stint, the Braves scored seven times. Their powerful lineup hammered out six hits while the pitcher surrendered three walks.

In the outfield the next day at Miller Huggins Field, a throng caught Cereghino's attention. He turned to his roommate and said, "Sturdy, I think I see the press coming to talk to you. Could be that Casey's told them he's sending me out, and you're going to stick with the club." Days later, the Yankees were being hammered by the Philadelphia Phillies. A fifth-inning rally by the Phillies forced Casey Stengel to make a pitching change. He brought Sturdivant from the bullpen. Over the game's final four innings, Sturdivant didn't allow a baserunner. Watching from the bullpen Cereghino dropped his head and muttered to himself, "Oh, that's it." The next day he was summoned to Stengel's office, where the manager said matter-of-factly, "Kid, we're sending you out."

Cereghino was to report to the team's new top farm club, the Denver Bears. He, instead, made a special request. "My wife is expecting. She's out in California and she's due in June. Is there any way I can play on the west coast?" The Yankees did not have a farm club on the west coast, but Lee McPhail, the farm director, worked the phones and found the Sacramento Solons in the Pacific Coast League willing to take Cereghino.

By mid–May, Casey Stengel was up in arms. His starting pitching was in crisis. Don Larsen was a huge disappointment. Bob Turley was struggling with his control. He pleaded with George Weiss for a starting pitcher. Weiss polled the Yankees' minor-league managers for a solution. In Sacramento Ed Cereghino was struggling. He was being bounced between relief and starting roles, and his control had again gone awry. After Weiss received a negative evaluation, he felt there was no other way to solve the problem but to make a trade for a pitcher outside the organization. It was a move that effectively erased the title of prospect from Ed Cereghino's status in the organization at the age of 21.

The once-promising ascent became an odyssey. The Yankees shipped Cereghino from Sacramento to Toronto to replace an injured pitcher. Once Cereghino arrived he found that the injured pitcher had recovered. Without ever getting into a game for the Maple Leafs, he was sent to the Denver Bears. By this time words like "failure," "bust," and "flop" began to accompany Cereghino's name in articles. His thoughts wandered to life after baseball more than ever before, and he began to examine the steps to take to become a teacher.

When the Yankees assigned Cereghino to their new Class AAA farm club, the Richmond Virginians, for the 1956 season, a new wave of prospects were drawing the attentions of the front office. Ralph Terry, Jim Coats, Jack McMahon, Johnny James, and Marshall Renfroe were putting up impressive numbers. Still, Eddie Lopat, the Richmond manager, pledged to salvage Cereghino's career. The task, however, became mired in frustration. Cereghino went the first three months of the season without a win and ended it with a dismal 3–9 record.

Responsibility and visions of life after baseball tugged at Cereghino. He and Janet had three children, and being away for the eight-month baseball season weighed on him. The pitcher enrolled at San Francisco State, where he found classroom experiences stimulating.

When spring arrived, he returned to the Yankees and was again assigned to the Richmond club. After just four appearances Cereghino confided to Lopat that intense pain in his right elbow accompanied every pitch he threw. McPhail ordered Cereghino to report to New Orleans. He reasoned that the warm weather would heal the injury. Cereghino refused and was suspended. Frustrated, Cereghino packed his belongings, told his manager that he quit and headed for home.

During the offseason McPhail phoned to urge Cereghino to come back. The pitcher pondered the matter and somewhat reluctantly agreed. The Yankees assigned the one time phenom to pitch for the New Orleans Pelicans, where he found the conditions horrendous.

The Pelicans' longtime home, Pelicans Park, had been torn down to make way for a hotel. The team had moved into a high school football stadium. The left-field wall was a mere 257 feet from home plate with a 40-foot-high screen erected above the wall to cut down on home runs, but it didn't.

The Mayor of New Orleans, deLesseps Morrison, owned the ballclub along with the parish coroner and two city council members. To say the ownership group meddled was an understatement. Morrison frequently pitched batting practice. The coroner was at the park almost every night. Whenever the Pelicans lost at home, one of the owners was guaranteed to enter the clubhouse, verbally berate the players, and vow that they would not be paid for that game.

Throughout the summer there were flashes of the once-prized prospect—a shutout in Mobile, a four-hitter in Birmingham, and a well-pitched game that ended in frustrating defeat in Memphis. Pitching at home in the Pelicans' makeshift ballpark, however, produced altogether different results. Cereghino and his teammates learned early that every pitch they threw would have to be put in the lower part of the strike zone. Get a pitch up and hitters could loft the ball in the air, where it might easily sail over the screen for a home run.

No pitcher was affected more adversely by the tiny dimensions of the makeshift New Orleans ballpark than Ed Cereghino. Throughout the summer he gave up 30 home runs, twice what he had ever allowed in a season before and far and away the most in the Southern Association. Trying to spot his pitches to avoid fly balls resulted in 109 walks, more than he had ever before allowed in a season. Cereghino's earned run average of five runs per every nine innings pitched was his highest season mark since he broke in with the San Francisco Seals.

He lost 16 games, the most he'd ever lost in a season, and with each defeat, every home run, every "ball four" called, and each night spent in a hotel away from his wife and children, Ed Cereghino's frustration and disenchantment with baseball grew.

By the final weekend of the season, Cereghino had had enough— enough of the second-rate ballpark and its effect on his pitching, enough of the team's meddling owners and their penny-pinching antics, enough of being away from his family, and enough of baseball. Anxious to exit New Orleans as quickly as possible and convinced that the Pelicans' owners likely had one last act of deceit up their sleeve, Cereghino hatched a plan. The night before the team's final game, he packed his belongings. Before going to the ballpark the next day, he took his suitcases to the airport and stuffed them into a locker. As soon as the final out of the game was made, Cereghino bolted for the locker room. He hurriedly changed clothes without showering then dove into a waiting taxi and dashed for the airport and his flight to San Francisco.

Days later Cereghino learned that his suspicions had been true. While his teammates changed to shower, the owners of the ballclub had entered the locker room, announced that nobody could leave, and that the players would not receive their transportation money or a final paycheck until they were compensated for every sweat-stained, tattered or torn cap, uniform, or piece of equipment.

For Ed Cereghino there was no looking back, not at New Orleans or at professional baseball. He notified the Yankees that he was done and filed for voluntary retirement. Jerry Coleman, a friend and the Yankees' second baseman, phoned to urge Cereghino not to quit. McPhail made the same appeal. He even offered incentives.

"We'd like you to go with Fred Hutchinson to Seattle."

"No. I'm going back to school."

"Listen, we're putting a farm club in Modesto. It's not too far from your home. What would you say to being the player-manager? You'd only have to pitch one day per week."

"I'm going to do what I'm going to do. I'm going to concentrate on my studies."

When the Yankees' persistence was repeatedly rebuffed, McPhail retaliated and placed Cereghino on the permanently suspended list.

None of the Yankees' threats fazed their once-prized prospect. Ed Cereghino had reached a point in life where he was more likely to respond to McPhail by quoting Hamlet—"Methinks he doth protest too much"—rather than with anger. There was no wavering, not a flinch of second guessing, or sliver of doubt. By February when the Yankees' pitchers strode onto the field at Miller Huggins Field in Florida, Ed Cereghino was well on his way to earning degrees in Business, Social Science, and English Literature and embarking on a career as a high school teacher. Baseball was the furthest thing from his mind.

If you were in the Pacific Coast League in 1951, you were as good as in the major leagues. For some guys the pay was better. There were guys who refused to go to the big leagues because it meant taking a pay cut. You traveled by plane and the big-leaguers were still going by train. There were 16 teams in the big leagues then and eight AAA clubs in the Pacific Coast League. Today there are 30 teams in the big leagues. What Ed Cereghino did in the Coast League that summer was tremendous. Remember, he was only 17 years old!

In the years following his playing days, a keen interest in economics led Ed Cereghino to make wise investments of his bonus money and enjoy a comfortable life. While interest in education had eclipsed the once-burning desire to succeed in professional baseball, there was still reverence for the nine-inning game. "I learned how to be a better human being," the former pitching standout reflected, "thanks to college—the college of baseball."

5

GREATNESS SHACKLED

A bright summer sun bathed the small ballpark in Batavia, New York. Bill Dougherty, the historian for the local ballclub, walked his guest on a tour. Dougherty pointed out changes that had been made to the ballpark throughout the decades. He explained that during World War II, in an act of patriotism, the ballpark was named for General Douglas MacArthur. Dougherty chuckled and recalled the team's Miss Batavia Clipper Pageant during his 18th summer in 1952. The two men then stopped in front of a wall adorned with pictures of Chase Utley, Ryan Howard, Ned Yost, and several others—big-leaguers who had once played for the Batavia club. The guest nodded and noted perhaps the most talented player to ever play for a Batavia club and the tragedy that kept his from being one of the pictures on the celebrated wall of fame.

1952 was my first season with the Pirates. During spring training Branch Rickey called me into his office and said, "George, you've slowed down a step. You're not going to go back to the big leagues. I think you've got a good career ahead of you, though. I'd like to make you a manager." Mr. Rickey offered me the job managing the Pirates' Class D club at Batavia, New York. When we put the club together in spring training, I had some talent—one boy in particular—Howie Jennings.

The popping sound from balls zipping through the heavy air and smacking palms of leather baseball mitts filled the warm Florida air. Smiles abounded. The players were a collection of rookies who were in their first days in professional baseball. A mixture of exuberance and anxiousness stirred within both the players and their manager.

Like the players, the manager was in a new environment, too. These were his first days on the job. A week earlier in New Orleans, his career path had been diverted from trying to play in the major leagues to becoming a minor-league player-manager. The orchestration was conducted by the man who ran the Pittsburgh Pirates, Branch Rickey.

The manager was handed the reigns to a club on the lowest rung of the Pirates' minor-league ladder—the Batavia Clippers, a Class D club whose roster for the 1952 season would be primarily filled with players just out of high school and a smattering of college products. As he worked out his players, humidity partnered with the Florida heat to bead sweat on the manager's brow. The anxiousness at the new responsibilities was suddenly amplified by the vision of a man walking toward him. This wasn't just any man. It was the Pittsburgh Pirates' director of scouting and a baseball legend—the holder of the single-season record for hits and a member of the Baseball Hall of Fame. George Sisler himself was keen to have a conversation with the newest manager in the Pirates' farm system, George Genovese.

George Sisler came to me and said, "George, I've signed a boy that I'd like you to take a look at. He's had a rough life, but I think he can be a ballplayer." He said that he had just signed a prospect out of a reform school in Cleveland. George told me the boy had been a Golden Gloves boxing champion and was very athletic. "George, I think you can help him. Would you take him with you?" I agreed, and by the end of that day Howie Jennings had joined my ballclub.

Only a few weeks earlier, long before he was to depart for spring training, Sisler had received a phone call from a man who was the business manager of a Pirates farm club. The man had attended a Golden Gloves boxing tournament in Columbus, Ohio, and ran into an old friend. The friend was coaching several fighters, one of whom was a 19-year-old by the name of Howie Jennings. The man couldn't stop praising Jennings' talents. He had been a standout football player, a champion sprinter in track and field, and a boxing champion. But the coach cautioned that Jennings had a dark side. He had just completed an 11-month sentence for armed robbery. It was his second brush with the law. At the age of 13 he had been convicted of assault and battery. Jennings had spent the last two years in a reformatory, the Boy's Industrial School in Cleveland. The information about Jennings, both his problems and skills, was conveyed to Sisler. He was intrigued. Sisler made arrangements to work the young man out. What he saw impressed him enough to sign Jennings to a contract.

Branch Rickey had instructed all of his scouts to leave no stone unturned in the search for talent. Our club showed the results. We had a Native American who had been born and raised on a reservation in Northern

California, Sonny Pivar. My first baseman was going to be R.C. Stevens, who came to spring training looking for a tryout after Mr. Rickey sent his scouts looking for talent in the black schools in the South. And there was Jennings. Mr. Rickey didn't mind giving a second chance to a boy with talent if he thought it could pay off.

When the Clippers arrived in Batavia from spring training, they were greeted by a headline in the local paper that screamed "It's A New Deal Fans!" A genuine enthusiasm for baseball rippled through the small northwestern New York town. Only six months earlier, there had been despair among Batavia's baseball fans. Financial losses from the 1951 season were exorbitant, and a nine-year relationship with the Cleveland Indians had ended. The team's future was in serious doubt. Enter a savior: Branch Rickey. In early November the legendary executive was hired to run the Pittsburgh Pirates. One of his plans was to add more clubs to the Pittsburgh farm system. The Clippers' management pounced on Rickey's proclamation. The two sides struck a deal that made the Clippers a Pirates farm club. "This is the promise of better days ahead for local baseball," Paul Bostwick wrote in the *Batavia Daily News*. Once the agreement was struck, "Duke" Labruzzo, the Clippers' business manager, rolled up his sleeves and worked feverishly to try to boost community interest and attendance. He announced that ticket prices would be "the lowest in the league." A knothole gang was formed so children could attend games for a special nominal price. Once the team had arrived in town from spring training, the community was invited to McArthur Stadium to watch the Clippers take batting practice. The Batavia High School marching band was recruited to play at the event.

Before Howie Jennings could receive his Silver Bat award, he was behind bars and his career was over. (Courtesy Ohio History Connection)

The Pirates did their part to drum up excitement. The day before the season opener, a welcome luncheon was held at the local Elks Lodge. Among the speakers was Branch Rickey's right-hand man, Harold Roettger, who proclaimed that many of the Clippers "are part of an accelerated youth movement. It is possible some of these men will be in a Pittsburgh uniform this year!" When Genovese was asked who his starting pitcher would be in the opener, he didn't hesitate in providing the honor to Howie Jennings.

On a cold and windy May 4, the Clippers launched the 1952 season against the Olean Yankees. In the cramped Clippers' offices, Labruzzo, Roettger, and Ed McCarrick, the Pirates' east coast scouting director, looked at their watches, and at three o'clock set out to squeeze through a throng of more than 1,700 fans and make their way to their seats. Five minutes later the nine Clippers starters trotted onto the field from the team's third-base dugout. They were greeted by loud cheers from an overflow crowd and weather conditions that were far different from the sunshine and warmth of their spring training base in Deland, Florida. Wind swept against Howie Jennings' cheeks as he threw his warmup pitches. Teammates blew into their fists to ward off the effects of the chill.

It didn't take many pitches after the home-plate umpire waved his right arm, then bellowed "play ball" for McCarrick and Roettger to recognize that an immense yet raw talent stood on the pitcher's mound. Jennings displayed a live arm. His fastball streaked past the opposing hitters with an extremely high velocity. On the downside, however, it was clear to all that Jennings was inexperienced and his pitching talent, to put it mildly, was raw. By the eighth inning Jennings had struck out eight batters, but he had walked ten.

At this stage in the game, however, it was no longer Jennings' arm that was gaining attention; it was his legs. In the stands, McCarrick and Roettger had become overwhelmed by what they had witnessed. Already, his own manager was reevaluating Jennings' role on the ballclub. In his previous at-bats, the young Ohioan had displayed remarkable running speed. It was game-changing speed.

In the bottom of the eighth inning, Batavia trailed, 5–4. With two outs, Genovese shot a fly ball toward the right-field corner. As the Olean right fielder raced in hot pursuit, the ball bounced over the fence for a ground-rule double that put the Batavia player-manager on second base.

Bunny Mick, the Olean manager, walked to the mound and gestured to the umpire that he wanted a new pitcher. Jack Katchik trotted from the Yankees bullpen. He would face the Batavia pitcher. While in most instances this would overwhelmingly bear the look of an easy, inning-ending out, the pitcher in this case was Howie Jennings. Already in the game, Jennings' speed had turned two sure infield outs into singles.

Katchik's first pitch skipped in the dirt in front of home plate and right past the Yankees' catcher to the backstop. As the crowd cheered, Genovese ran to third base. Mick whistled to get his pitcher's attention then gestured for him to issue Jennings an intentional walk, which he did.

Fans hollered encouragement as Sonny Pivar dug into the batter's box. As Genovese took a walking lead off of third base, it was Jennings who commanded Katchik's attention. The fleet Batavia baserunner danced about, feigning a break for second base. Genovese eyed the situation, and when the Olean pitcher dipped his left shoulder and turned his body 90 degrees to throw to first base, the Batavia player-manager broke for home. Shouts flew from the Olean dugout to alert their first baseman to the daring dash for the plate. Throughout the small ballpark fans rose with anticipation as the throw streaked toward the plate. Genovese kicked up a small cloud of dust with his slide, and the fans roared with delight as the umpire threw his arms out to the side to signify the player-manager was safe and the game was now tied, 5–5.

The Yankees' attention to the excitement at home plate allowed Jennings to sprint to second base, and two pitches later, Pivar stroked a single to left field that enabled Jennings to speed home with what would prove to be the game-winning run.

An excited crowd of 1,732 fans pressed through the exits for home with the promise of a new day realized. The next day the *Batavia Daily News* fawned over Jennings in its account of the season-opening Clippers win. "Fans were amazed by the speed of Jennings, who twice turned ordinary infield outs into hits," the paper enthusiastically reported.

During the final days of spring training, players had queried teammates about sharing apartments. In the case of Stevens, Charles Berry, and Jennings, they were forced by the color of their skin to share accommodations. When they arrived in Batavia, they learned that the town of 18,000 had just three African American families, and one had agreed to board ballplayers.

After the game the trio took a short walk to the downtown area. They happened upon an Italian restaurant, Mancuso's, and decided they would stop in for a meal. When the three were ushered into a separate room in the back, Stevens was quick to realize what was happening. The back room was for people of color, something he did not expect to find this far north of the Mason-Dixon Line.

As the three young ballplayers got to know one another, Stevens and Berry were taken aback at revelations Jennings shared. Not that his father was a mechanic or that the man had moved his wife, three sons, and one daughter north from Piedmont, Alabama, for a better life. It was not the track and field, football, and boxing heroics. It was the tales of arrests, criminal activity, and jail time that shocked Berry and Stevens. "One tough character," Stevens said when a teammate asked what Jennings was like. "He was always in jail."

While Jennings, like his teammates, got settled into summer living quarters, his playing situation was becoming unsettled. Genovese pondered how best to utilize him: *The kid could be a tough out.* Ed McCarrick conveyed similar questions to Branch Rickey and his son, Branch Jr., who ran the Pirates' farm system.

To keep Jennings on the mound would be to waste his greatest asset. There weren't many players in the game that could run like Jennings could. Mr. Rickey always impressed upon his scouts and managers that there were three things that couldn't be taught: power, speed, and a strong throwing arm. What I saw Jennings do on opening night left me thinking—*Maybe we should make him an outfielder.*

Five days later the local paper reported, "The mercurial-footed speed king is being moved to left field … to take advantage of his speed. He's been on base almost every time he's batted." The switch had the effect of a spark plug and gasoline. It produced combustion, igniting an unrealized talent. Against Wellsville in his first start in the outfield, Jennings hammered out two hits. The next night he slammed four more. By the end of his first week as an everyday regular, Jennings was batting .800.

In late May the Clippers were throttled by six rainouts over a nine-day stretch. It was the sort of inactivity that would cool any hot streak by disrupting the rhythm of any player who was going good. Once the storm clouds cleared and games resumed, Jennings picked right up where he left off, however. He had three hits and a stolen base against Jamestown. Near the end of May, the league issued its weekly statistical release. Howie Jennings was the runaway batting leader with a .647 average.

A buzz rippled through the Clippers' tiny clubhouse. Branch Rickey had dispatched Harold Roettger for a firsthand look at the team's red-hot left fielder. Unfortunately for Roettger, the rain returned and he had to sit idly for three nights before he could watch Jennings play. Once he did, the Pirates' executive was impressed by a three-hit game against Jamestown, and the next night he witnessed the left fielder make what the *Batavia*

5. Greatness Shackled

Daily News labeled, "the fielding gem of the year." Tony Lupien, a former big-leaguer and Jamestown's player-manager, shot a drive to left center field. Jennings took off running at the crack of the bat. He reached out and stabbed Lupien's drive then juggled the ball several times before clutching it. Jennings then spun and fired the ball toward first base. When the throw reached R.C. Stevens' mitt before the runner, fans cheered the rookie's remarkable catch and double play.

By the end of May, it was clear that one player in the PONY League possessed the sort of raw, God-given talent that had the major-league luring power of a neodymium magnet—Howie Jennings. "This fellow is one of the fastest men I have ever seen," praised Hal Contini, the Hamilton Cardinals' manager. "We hold him down by playing a bag ahead of him." Genovese tried to utilize Jennings' success to energize the rest of his batting order.

I moved Jennings to the leadoff spot. With Jennings on base, Pivar and Stevens would get more fastballs to hit. It worked out well. One of the first nights we did that, Stevens hit two home runs against Hamilton. A few nights later, Mitch Francis came up with Jennings on base and hit two home runs against Olean.

The move up in the batting order helped Jennings, too. In his first game batting leadoff, Jennings rapped out three hits to help Batavia defeat Corning. The next night Jennings flied out to center field to lead off the game, then singed in each of his next four turns at bat to highlight a 10–4 win over the Athletics.

When the Dodgers' farm club in the league came to Batavia, speed stole the show. The Clippers battled Hornell for 11 innings before falling 9–8. Jennings came to bat seven times and reached base in five of those at-bats. It was another player whose dynamic speed won the game, however—Hornell's Maury Wills. The 19-year-old shortstop was a terror on the base paths, particularly in the top of the 11th inning, when he led off with a walk. Genovese then summoned Al Galindo from the bullpen to pitch. Wills promptly stole second base off the hard-throwing left-hander. When Wills strayed too far off of second base, Galindo thought he had a chance to pick the pesky Dodger off. The young pitcher's throw, however, sailed way wide of the bag and into center field, and Wills was able to easily scamper safely to third base. Wills danced off third trying to distract Galindo. The trick ultimately worked. With the pitcher's concentration split between the speedster on third base and the Dodgers' batter, Galindo let loose with a pitch that zipped past his catcher all the way to the backstop. Wills sprinted home to give the Dodgers the lead. They won, 9–8.

Whenever we played Hornell we couldn't get Wills out. He'd get on base and steal second then steal third. We tried everything, pitch outs, you name it, but we couldn't slow him down. Sometimes I'd slap a hard tag on him and try to leave his leg sore so he wouldn't think of stealing third. That didn't work. I'd talk to him, try to intimidate him, but he had the guts of a burglar.

The next night Jennings rapped out three hits and scored twice to highlight Batavia's revenge, a 10–4 win over the Dodgers' farmhands. Watching his fleet left fielder gave Genovese an idea.

During the game when Maury reached second base, I said, "I've got an idea." I pointed toward Jennings. "How would you like to race my left fielder? I don't think you can beat him." Wills didn't bat an eye. "Okay." After another pitch, he turned to me and said, "Mr. Genovese, can I have some time? Can we do it the next time we come to town?" I nodded and said, "Sure. That's not a problem."

The Clippers' manager shared the news with Duke Labruzzo, and the team's business manager set the wheels in motion to try to draw a big crowd when the Dodgers returned the following month. In the meantime, Jennings continued his torrid hitting pace. His skills were improving. He added a knack for dropping short fly balls into the no-man's-land area between the retreating infielders and the onrushing outfielders to his skill of outracing infield chops. Jennings' speed built an impressive tally of extra base hits. Line drives into the gaps were easily turned into doubles. Shots into the outfield corners were legged into triples.

By June 6 Jennings sported a .461 batting average with 36 hits in 78 turns at bat. He led the second-place hitter in the batting race, Charlie Lau, by 64 points. Late June brought the Clippers to Hornell. It was not an easy road trip for the ballclub. Their aging team bus lacked the power to climb through the Allegheny Mountains. Genovese had to phone ahead, and after explaining the problem, he was relieved that the Dodgers dispatched their own bus to fetch the stranded Clippers.

Once the series began, the on-field speed sparked more fury and frustration. Maury Wills wreaked havoc on the Clippers. Between delays for rain and lightning, Wills' base running and some questionable calls by the umpires ignited the ire of Genovese. He argued a call so vehemently that he was thrown out of the game. When he refused to stop arguing, the umpires summoned police, who led the Batavia skipper off the field so play could resume. The night ended with Batavia losing its fourth in a row.

5. Greatness Shackled

As June turned into July, Jennings was on a tear. Three hits helped the Clippers stop their losing streak at eight games with a 6–5 win over Bradford. He had two more hits to highlight a 3–1 win that concluded the series. When the season reached the halfway mark, another three-hit game pushed Jennings' league-leading batting average to .462 and helped Batavia begin a series against the Olean Yankees with a win. After each game, Genovese would dictate reports back to Pittsburgh. His evaluations would be read by Branch Rickey, Jr. Some of the reports made their way to Rickey Senior himself. George Sisler made a point to sift through the minor-league reports and stay abreast of Jennings' progress. Pleased by his signee's performance, the Hall of Fame hitter penned a letter to the protégé. "You have the necessary physical qualifications to be a good baseball player, and I want you to get up fast. I will certainly help you from time to time when I have the chance, and I am going to watch you very closely." Genovese too offered motivation to the rookie.

I told Jennings that *The Sporting News* magazine offered the Silver Bat Award to the best rookie hitter in the minor leagues. "You're hitting .462! You've got a good chance," I told him.

In mid-July Jennings fell into a brief slump that saw his average fall 21 points to .447, but the rookie did not succumb to self-doubt or see his confidence wane. He snapped out of the slump with three consecutive three-hit games and finished the month of July with 12 hits over a six-game span.

The weather that had left the Clippers with so much idle time in May exacted its revenge in August. The 11 May rainouts were rescheduled as doubleheaders during the high heat and humidity of the warmest month of the year. In some weeks, the Clippers were forced to makeup games with doubleheaders over four consecutive days. To no one's surprise, fatigue set in. Bat and leg speeds slowed. Howie Jennings saw his batting average begin to fall.

Fatigue and frustration ebbed into a fracas during an August 10 game with the Olean Yankees. Bunny Mick, the Olean manager, had been particularly abusive toward Batavia's African American players. Jim Coates, one of the Olean pitchers, seemed to take particular delight in knocking Jennings and Stevens down.

I told Jennings and Stevens to try and ignore them. "Don't pay attention to what those people are saying," I said. "If you do your job well, you will be rewarded!"

In the second inning, the Olean bench hurled verbal abuse at Genovese. It became bad enough that the home-plate umpire called time and warned the Yankees to stop. Things remained calm for another four innings until Pivar was knocked down and injured by a hard slide into second base. Angry, the Clippers' second baseman retaliated with his fists and was ejected from the game.

When Howie Jennings came to bat in the bottom of the sixth inning, Coates threw a fastball that buzzed under his chin. The Clippers' hitting star stepped out of the batter's box. He pointed his bat toward Coates and warned the pitcher not to do it again. Coates did. Jennings immediately dropped his bat and charged the mound. Before he could reach the Yankees' pitcher, Frank Rico, the Olean catcher had grabbed Jennings. He threw a punch in the direction of Jennings' head but missed. The former Golden Gloves champion spun around and retaliated. His punch landed squarely on Rico's jaw and knocked the catcher out cold.

Mayhem erupted. Players raced from both dugouts to join the fray. Coates fled with Jennings in hot pursuit. Fans spilled onto the field. Coates ran past them. He dashed out of the ballpark to take refuge in the team bus, locking the door behind him while the umpires fought to bring matters under control.

Anticipation about the Hornell Dodgers' return to Batavia had grown through the first two weeks of August. The planned match race between Jennings and Maury Wills had been the subject of debate among fans and the Clippers' players. Before the final game of the series, the two players strode toward home plate and shook hands. Genovese pointed out that they would race a 60-yard dash from home plate up the first baseline. The speedsters took their positions. Jennings bent at the waist while Wills lowered into a crouch. On cue the two became whirring engines of propulsion. Legs churned. Arms pumped. Fans and teammates alike shouted encouragement as the two players sped to be the first to the finish line. Gasps came from the home fans, and looks of shock covered the faces of Clippers players when it was Wills who crossed the finish line not more than a hair's width ahead of their teammate.

Maury came to me later and said, "Mr. Genovese, do you know why I asked for extra time before we had that race? Because your man was three inches taller than me. He had longer legs. I figured the race would be won or lost at the start, so I wanted to practice my starts."

As much excitement as the match race had stirred, nobody could have predicted that one night later an even bigger event would take place. The

5. Greatness Shackled

Bradford Phillies followed Hornell into Batavia for a series with the Clippers. Only 423 fans turned up to see the game. The lack of local interest was proof that there was nothing to suggest the sort of unique history-making game that would unfold or the way Howie Jennings would be part of it.

Batavia's starting pitcher, Jim Mitchell, retired the first 13 batters he faced. Bradford's starting pitcher wasn't nearly as sharp. Frank Etchberger struggled with his control, but the lanky hurler kept the Batavia hitters off balance and recorded a string of ground-ball outs. After six innings neither man had allowed a hit. A hit batter was the only way Bradford had managed to get a runner on base against Mitchell.

We weren't hitting the ball, but their guy was walking a few. When we got runners on base, I tried to take advantage. Twice R.C. Stevens walked, and each time I had him try and steal second right away. Both times he got thrown out. We got Jennings on with a walk with two outs, but before we could try anything, the next hitter flied out to end the inning.

In the top of the seventh inning, Jennings was involved in a play that would wind up being debated for decades. Bradford's Tom Keane sent a drive in the air to left field. Jennings initially started in then realized he had misjudged the fly ball. He made a 180-degree turn and broke into a full-out sprint. As he saw the ball descending, Jennings extended his right arm. The ball came down on the top of the webbing of Jennings' glove, caromed away, and fell to the ground as Keane ran to second base. The official scorer, taking in the play from the press box, ruled it a double. After giving it more thought, after perhaps remembering an unwritten baseball rule that the first hit of a no-hitter should be a clean hit, the scorer changed his mind. Jennings was charged with a two-base error.

When the game reached the ninth inning, it was clear that Mitchell was tiring. He walked the leadoff hitter, the first batter he had walked all night. A sacrifice bunt moved the runner to second base but only briefly. Mitchell uncorked a wild pitch that would send the Bradford runner to third base with only one out in the inning.

I hollered to our infielders and motioned for everyone to move in. We wanted to be able to get the runner at home if the ball was hit on the ground in the infield. Sure enough, it was hit to me at shortstop. I knew I had to get rid of the ball in a hurry if I was going to get the runner at home, but trying to grab it and throw it, I bobbled it. By the time I was able to grab the ball and make my throw home, the runner had that split second that he needed. He scored.

Mitchell got out of the inning without giving up a hit, and his teammates came up determined to try to pull out a win for his no-hit efforts. Genovese led off and grounded out to shortstop. Next up was Dave Brennan, and he too grounded out to shortstop. Sonny Piver represented the Clippers' last hope. He swung at a breaking pitch and hit a slow-rolling ball that dribbled over the infield grass. The Bradford shortstop charged, scooped up the ball, and fired it toward first base in one motion. Two thuds were heard a fraction of a second apart. Pivar was convinced that the thud of his foot hitting the bag came first. The umpire felt otherwise, thrust his fist, and bellowed an "out" cry that ended the game. "I was safe!" Pivar shouted to no avail. The umpire's call made official the first time in professional baseball history that both pitchers in a game had thrown no-hitters.

Going hitless in four at-bats during the no-hit game capped a six-week slump that dropped Jennings' batting average below .400 for the first time all season. Still, his .394 mark was 47 points higher than his closest pursuer in the race for the league batting title.

On Thursday night of the season's final week, 1,664 fans squeezed into McArthur Stadium for Booster Night. Between the prize drawings and giving of gifts, the Clippers beat Hornell, 5–3, and with two hits, Howie Jennings secured the batting crown.

Two days later the Clippers played their final home game. In a steady drizzle, Batavia clobbered Hamilton, 21–7. After the game fans held a party and gave food and gifts to the ballplayers. Teammates congratulated one another, especially Jennings on a scintillating first season in professional baseball. He had finished with one hit in the finale to make his final batting average .373. Two veteran player-managers in the league finished second and third in the batting race. Thirty-five-year-old Tony Lupien, who had played five seasons in the big leagues, hit .352, while Hornell's player-manager Andy Alexson finished with a .348 batting average.

Some in Batavia were surprised when the league announced its postseason awards. Despite running away with the batting title, finishing second to Maury Wills in hits and third in triples, Howie Jennings received nothing. The league's managers voted Hamilton's third baseman, Hal Miller, as the Rookie of the Year. Robert Umfleet, who won 23 games and lost just four for Hamilton with a 1.60 earned run average, was pegged by the managers as the most likely to go far.

Before all my ballplayers went home for the offseason, I sat Jennings down for a talk. "You have the chance to be a major leaguer," I told him. "I think you can be a pretty good ballplayer. But you have to stay out of

trouble." Jennings said he would. "Don't worry, Mr. Genovese, I will. You can count on me, Mr. Genovese." I pointed a finger at Howie and added, "You have to stay away from the people who get you into trouble, too." He promised me he would.

While Jennings returned home to Cleveland, Genovese traveled to Pittsburgh. He had been summoned to the team's Forbes Field office by Branch Rickey.

He asked me if I would help Pie Traynor and George Sisler with a tryout camp at Forbes Field. My wife and I were put up at a nice hotel near the ballpark, and Mr. Rickey and his wife had us out to their home for dinner while we were there. We talked about my season, and I made a point to give Mr. Rickey and Branch a favorable report about Jennings.

The Pirates were sold on the young prospect, but the planned rate of his future progress sparked debate. Sisler felt the speedster could and should move through the organization quickly. The Rickeys, on the other hand, wanted Jennings to progress prudently. Branch Rickey, Jr., made the decision to send Jennings a contract to play for the Pirates' Class C club in St. Jean, Quebec, for the 1953 season. Genovese would manage the club.

On the first day that the St. Jean Canadians assembled for spring training, two men had their enthusiasm for a new season of baseball shattered.

I was headed to the field when Harold Roettger, Mr. Rickey's assistant, stopped me. He broke the news that my father had just died. Harold said he had made arrangements for me to fly home. "Go get dressed. I'll take you to the airport," he said. After I had showered and changed, Harold and I were walking to his car in the parking lot when two men in suits passed us. My mind was elsewhere, and I didn't give it much thought. As we prepared to drive off it struck me that the men in suits might be detectives. I looked back toward the field. The two men were leading a ballplayer off the field. I was sure it was Howie Jennings. When I got back a few days later, Jennings was gone and nobody knew what had happened to him.

On June 11, while the St. Jean Canadians' players were preparing to head to the ballpark for that night's game, prisoner number 51860 was being processed to begin his incarceration at the Ohio State Reformatory. The prisoner was Howie Jennings. Days earlier, Jennings stood before Common Pleas Judge Joseph H. Silbert in a Cleveland courtroom. He pleaded guilty to his crimes. The police report about those crimes was stark.

On March 22, just days before Jennings had planned to leave for spring training, the ballplayer joined four friends for a night of criminal exploit. Jennings' friends broke into the Quality Poultry Company and made off with $200 worth of fish and poultry. Their heist also included the company's safe. Jennings drove the getaway car.

When the five men managed to forcibly open the safe, they found just $10.60 inside. Their action, however, was enough to get safecracking added to the charges, which heightened the potential punishment. After he entered his plea, Howie Jennings stood silently as the judge handed down a prison sentence of one to 20 years.

That spring a guy from *The Sporting News* called me in St. Jean. He was very excited and said that Howie Jennings had won the Silver Bat Award for being the best rookie hitter in the minor leagues in 1952. They wanted to arrange a presentation for him. I said, "I don't know where he is." The guy wouldn't believe me. "What do you mean you don't know where he is?" I told him nobody in the organization had any idea what happened to him or where he was.

In 1959 the *Batavia Daily News* selected its all-decade team to honor the best Batavia Clippers players of the 1950s. In a footnote the writer noted that Howie Jennings would have been recognized but was intentionally omitted "due to the unfortunate incident that happened later in his life."

6

ONE GLORIOUS NIGHT

Polite applause welcomed the special guest onto the diamond prior to the Pittsburgh Pirates' March exhibition game. A shock of hair that had grown white and a mid-section that had expanded slightly since the end of his playing career belied the athleticism that had riveted Pittsburgh Pirates' executives, managers, and scouts on similar walks to the pitcher's mound 60 years before. While the name Ron Necciai was not recognized by most of the fans in the Bradenton, Florida, ballpark, a proclamation from the local mayor and the public-address announcer's introduction told of his crowning achievement—the greatest single-game pitching performance in baseball history, which had taken place 64 years earlier.

Mr. Rickey was very excited about Necciai. He had taken over the Pirates in 1951 with a mandate to produce a winner. One of the first things he set out to do was evaluate the prospects in the Pirates' farm system, and when he saw Necciai for the first time, he saw a real live arm and a guy with a very good curveball. When I saw Necciai that spring, I could see why Mr. Rickey was so excited.

A hard rain pelted the metallic roof of the bus. Inside, a driver, 22 ballplayers, their manager, and trainer fidgeted. Restless chatter echoed, and an idling engine hummed as the bus sat parked outside of a ballpark in Bristol, Virginia. The men, most no more than 19 years of age, had been sitting in uncomfortable seats since leaving their spring training camp in Florida 11 hours earlier. Now, an intense storm prevented manager and players with the Batavia Clippers from gaining the relief that usually accompanied one's arrival at their destination.

The Clippers' wait had exceeded more than half an hour before clarity emerged in the form of a man cloaked by a large black raincoat and protected by a large umbrella. The man stepped into the bus, leaned toward the manager and said, "There's no game tonight. We won't be able to play." George Genovese turned to the driver and said loud enough for his ballplayers to hear as well, "We're rained out. Let's go get something to eat and head for Batavia."

We had finished spring training and were going to head for Batavia, New York, to begin the season. Along the way, we were supposed to stop in a town and play an exhibition game against another Pirates' farm club, our Class D Appalachian League club, the Bristol Twins. I love baseball and I never wanted to lose a ballgame. But that was one day when I was glad we got rained out because we were going to have to face Ron Necciai.

Prior to the 1952 season, intimidating was the last definition anyone would give to Ron Necciai. Nor would they have expected to hear the legendary baseball executive Branch Rickey say, "There have been only two young pitchers I was certain were destined for greatness. One of those was Dizzy Dean. The other is Ron Necciai."

Spindly, at 6 feet 2 inches, and closer to 150 pounds than a sturdy 200, Ron Necciai was hardly the picture of athleticism. He had been raised by a mother who was widowed before her son's fifth birthday. The woman spent the ensuing years instilling integrity and a work ethic in her five children while never letting on that the family was poor. Like many boys in Monongahela his age, toiling in sports brought fun and an injection of self-confidence before it became time to follow in the footsteps of fathers and uncles to carry a helmet and lunch pail into the coal mines or steel mills.

Baseball was Necciai's teenaged nirvana. He initially became engrossed in the game at the behest of his best friend, Alex DeRosa. The two boys were inseparable. DeRosa was the athlete, star of Monongahela High School's football and baseball teams. Come the spring, DeRosa's talent lured droves of professional baseball scouts. Necciai had once been a pitcher, but an errant fastball had broken a batter's ribs. He'd been scolded over it by his coach and from then on concentrated on playing first base.

By the end of spring in 1950, the Tigers, New York Giants, and Pittsburgh Pirates were in covetous pursuit of DeRosa. Worried that his club was about to lose DeRosa to the Detroit Tigers, Pittsburgh Pirates scout Tony Rikino made a suggestion that would change the tide of Ron Necciai's future.

The Pirates planned to hold a tryout camp in their ballpark, Forbes Field. Rikino hoped that if Necciai were invited and showed up, DeRosa would attend as well. Scouts tested the players' running speed and throwing skills and held batting practice. Necciai hit a couple of balls off the outfield wall. At the end of his audition, Necciai was surprised when a scout offered him a contract along with a bus ticket to join the Pirates' Class D farm club in the North Carolina State League.

While training with his new teammates on the Salisbury Pirates, Necciai agitated the team's shortstop. Throws that the newcomer made on the first-to-shortstop play were made with such ferocious velocity that they almost consistently knocked the shortstop back toward left field.

After one such incident, George Detore called Necciai over. "Son," the manager said, "from now on you're a pitcher." Necciai was taken aback. "You're crazy," the rookie shrieked. "I'm a first baseman!" No amount of argument or pleading could make Detore change his mind.

George Detore was a veteran baseball man who had seen great pitchers during his 17-year playing career. He had played with the All-Star Wes Farrell in Cleveland and had witnessed such pitching greats as Lefty Grove and Lefty Gomez while with the Indians. Detore felt Necciai had potential. His skills were raw but worth nurturing.

Once on the mound in a game for the first time, Necciai's lack of pitching skill was glaringly apparent. The 18-year-old had no idea where the ball was going once it flew from his right hand. The first five batters that Necciai faced all reached base, three via walks, and the other two were hit by pitches. Regardless of the pitch his catcher had called for, every ball that Necciai had thrown was a fastball. It was all he knew how to throw. Mercifully, Detore had seen enough. He trudged to the mound and removed Necciai from the game.

Necciai's next game was worse. By his third appearance in a North Carolina State League game, Necciai's wildness was showered with catcalls from fans and heckling by opposing players. "Even the fans are grabbing bats," he said to a teammate, "because I can't get anybody out." In just three games Necciai had pitched a total of three innings, walked eight batters, given up five hits, and allowed ten runs. Detore stopped using him in games.

Before a month of the season had expired, failure had eroded Necciai's confidence. One afternoon it reached a breaking point. The pitcher marched into his manager's office and announced, "I quit! I'm a first baseman. I don't even know how to throw a curveball!" With that, Ron Necciai packed a suitcase, boarded a bus for the eight-hour ride home to Monongahela, and left professional baseball behind. Within days the bat and mitt had been replaced by a sturdy black lunch pail and a silver hard hat. Ron Necciai was punching a time clock and working in a steel mill.

Several times during the winter of 1950, Charlie Muse, a Pittsburgh Pirates scout, dropped by the Necciai home to visit. "How are you doing,

Ron?" he would ask. Quietly, Muse hoped for a negative answer. He could sense that Necciai hated life in the mill, but pride wouldn't allow him to let on. Muse kept coming back, sometimes three, even four times a week. When one day Necciai angrily blurted, "Terrible. I'm working in a steel mill," Muse pounced. The scout let Necciai know that a second chance with the Pirates was waiting. Necciai eagerly accepted.

The Pirates assigned Necciai to the Salisbury Pirates again for the 1951 season, which reunited him with Detore. This time the manager found a more willing pupil, and he guided the young student into a crash course on pitching. Detore explained the nuances of the craft. He displayed patience as he worked with Necciai on his positioning on the rubber, leg kick, drive, planting, arm angle, finger grips, and follow-through.

In the games that he pitched, Necciai's results continued to be dismal, however. He struggled to find the strike zone. By the middle of May, Detore wondered if the Pirates' patience in the young pitcher was running out. It was during a workout that the manager's frustrations with the young pitcher spilled out. "Can't you throw any harder than that?" Detore barked. Necciai told of breaking a batter's ribs in high school and that his coach, "made me promise not to throw that hard again." Detore demanded that Necciai cut loose with a fastball. The pitch whistled so fast through the air that it flew right past the catcher's mitt and smacked the player's shin guard. Detore's eyes widened in amazement. Attentions then turned to throwing a curveball.

The manager had taught Necciai the grip, arm angle, and wrist action necessary to throw the pitch, but the results had been dismal. Now Detore ordered Necciai to throw a curveball with maximum velocity. The result was devastating—a pitch that rocketed toward home plate only to break wickedly downward late in its trajectory as if it had fallen off of a table. "You got it," Detore exclaimed.

In one afternoon Ron Necciai's career had taken a quantum leap forward. Hitters became impotent, swings grew weak, flailing in frustration. Still, despite the improvement, Necciai was miserable. He constantly fought nerves when he was on the mound. His stomach burned and was frequently upset, to the point of vomiting.

Minor-league living didn't agree with the Monongahelan either. Necciai and his roommate, Kenny Barbao, struggled to make ends meet. The ballplayers earned just $150 a month. Each day the two pitchers would walk to Red's Café, order a hamburger with a plate of fries, cut the burger in half, split the portion of fries, and make it their meal for the day.

Even for a Pennsylvanian who had grown up poor, these were unbearable conditions. After weeks of complaining to Barbao, the pitcher took

6. One Glorious Night

his gripe to Detore. "I'm going back to the mill," Necciai barked. Detore was stunned but thinking quickly asked, "Can you drive a bus? If you drive the bus, I'll pay you an extra $100 a month." Necciai agreed, and over the next few nights when he wasn't pitching, the young prospect was outside of the ballpark, in the parking lot, learning how to drive the team's 1937 GMC bus.

In early July Branch Rickey, Jr., visited Salisbury. The son of the Pirates' general manager oversaw the club's farm system. Before a game, Rickey Jr. parked himself next to Necciai in the dugout. He was complimentary then said, "If you figure out how to throw strikes, we'll put you where you can make some money."

Nearing the end of July, Necciai had won four of six games. He had cut down on the walks and begun piling up strikeouts. So much so that after a game one night, Detore beckoned Necciai to his office and told the pitcher he was being promoted. The Pirates were jumping Necciai four classifications and sending him to New Orleans.

On the eve of Necciai's first start, the *New Orleans Times-Picayune* introduced the newest member of the New Orleans Pelicans to fans as "Boyish, gangly Ron Necciai." The tall hard thrower made his debut against the Brooklyn Dodgers' Class AA farm club, the Mobile Bears.

In the first inning, Necciai fell behind, 1–0, when a walk and two singles put a run on the Pelican Park scoreboard. An inning later he hit a batter then gave up a single and a double, which gave Mobile a 2–0 lead. Once the early-inning jitters subsided, the Bears faced an entirely different Ron Necciai. For the rest of the game, he shut out the opposition, though New Orleans lost, 2–0. The next day Necciai was praised in the newspaper as having "turned in a pitching job that had the fans cheering for him."

If Detore was his guru, in New Orleans Necciai found the professors able to polish raw stone into a gem. The Pelicans were skippered by Rip Sewell, who had been the ace of the Pittsburgh Pirates' pitching staff through the mid–1940s. Bill Burwell was the organization's pitching specialist and together with Sewell, worked to hone the raw 19-year-old's skills. It was initially a frustrating endeavor dotted by wildness, walks, and hit batters. Trouble calming Necciai's nerves remained a challenge. In eight games, Necciai lost five times and earned just one win before he was sidelined by a twisted ankle. Through the difficulties, Sewell and Burwell could see promise. Both felt that Necciai was on the cusp of a pitching breakthrough.

The encouraging words of Sewell and Burwell reached the ears of Branch Rickey, and the Pirates' general manager invited Necciai to take part in an experiment he was to launch—a fall instructional camp in

DeLand, Florida. Rickey brought together 60 Pirates prospects and a half dozen newly-signed players for what he called a one-month "innovation school." The idea was to correct flaws, sharpen skills, and quicken the prospects' ascent to the major leagues. Mornings involved a Branch Rickey lecture followed by instruction out on the field. After lunch the players were divided into teams and spent the afternoon playing games. It was during one of these games that Ron Necciai found himself in Branch Rickey's crosshairs.

Necciai was pitching to a newly-signed catcher, Harry Dunlop, from California. With runners on second and third base, Dunlop switched to alternate signals in order to disguise the pitch call so the baserunner couldn't steal the signs. He called for a curveball, but Necciai didn't realize the change and instead threw a fastball that shot past Dunlop to the backstop and allowed the runner on third to dart home to score.

The next morning Rickey interrupted his lecture to demand an explanation. He recited the previous day's situation then asked, "Mr. Dunlop, what happened?" The newly-signed player became nervous. The last thing he wanted to do was point blame at a teammate. "I don't know, Mr. Rickey. I guess I just missed it," he answered. Rickey's voice rose in anger. "Young man, one thing you can *never* do is lie! Don't lie to me. I know you got crossed up!" Next, Rickey ordered Necciai to stand, then asked for his version of the event. Sheepishly, the pitcher diffused the situation by admitted that he, not Dunlop, had been to blame.

Rickey told the press he hoped ten players would make enough progress from the camp to warrant an invitation to join the Pirates in spring training. One did: Ron Necciai. After just one full season in professional baseball, Necciai was in spring training with the major-league team. He heartily worked to expand his education. The pitcher soaked up advice from the team's veteran catchers, Joe Garagiola and Clyde McCullough. He never missed the chance to sit with the Pirates' ace pitcher, Murray Dickson, and pepper the veteran with questions during meals, in the dugout, or in the bullpen. The neophyte clung to every shred of advice imaginable from "Perfection from repetition," to "You can't look at broads in the stands. Look at your catcher!"

The Pirates played intrasquad and exhibition games against the White Sox, Indians, and Giants. Each time he was called upon, Necciai pitched well. As spring training whittled down into a final few days, he was in a battle with Ron Kline, Jim Waugh, and Ed Wolfe for a spot on the Pirates' pitching staff. When he mowed down the Giants with five innings of shutout baseball, Ron Necciai had made the team.

Improved performances and the chance to reach the big leagues hadn't quelled Necciai's problems with nerves, though. His stomach was often unsettled, and the young prospect felt ill whenever he was on the mound. Teammates offered suggestions—buttermilk, cottage cheese, even Melba toast. Necciai tried them all, without relief.

During the first few days of April 1952, the Pirates traipsed from one Texas town to the next playing exhibition games: San Antonio one night, Corpus Christi the next, and Beaumont the following afternoon. While on a train chugging through south Texas, Necciai suddenly became violently ill. He was doubled over by intense pain, and when it worsened he vomited blood. An ambulance was called to Union Station in Houston, and when the train arrived, Necciai was rushed to a local hospital. There, doctors said Necciai's nervousness had manifested into a bleeding ulcer. They treated him with pills and prescribed a special diet. Once his symptoms subsided, Necciai was placed on an airplane and flown to Pittsburgh, where he was checked into Presbyterian Hospital for a ten-day stay.

Branch Rickey paid a visit to his young pitcher to assure him that he was a big part of the Pirates' plans. "You've got to prove you are ready to play," Rickey explained. "We will do all we can to get you ready." Rickey told Necciai that he would go to the minor leagues and pitch himself back into shape. "Where do you want to go?" the general manager asked. With little hesitation Necciai replied, "Where is George Detore?"

Necciai's pitching mentor was still managing the Pirates' Class D farm club, and though Necciai certainly warranted pitching at a higher level of the minor leagues, he wanted Detore's tutelage. "I have some kinks in my delivery. He can help me to get done what I need." During the winter, the Pirates had switched their Class D affiliation from Salisbury to Bristol Virginia, and Necciai joined up with the Appalachian League club during the final days of their spring training camp.

Every night during spring training Mr. Rickey had a meeting after dinner. It involved all of the managers in the farm system, Mr. Rickey, his son Branch Jr., who ran the farm system, and Harold Roettger, Mr. Rickey's assistant. We would spend hours reviewing every player in the farm system. What club should they be assigned to? Should we move them to a higher classification or drop them to a lower one? Or, were they just not cutting it, and should they be released? When Ron Necciai's name would come up, you could hear in his voice just how much Mr. Rickey thought of him. He threw real hard. He had a great curveball. A good kid. He was as consistent as an old shoe.

When Necciai joined the ballclub, he recognized a familiar face. He smiled when he realized his catcher with the Bristol Twins would be his buddy from the fall camp, Harry Dunlop. From his very first start, Necciai overwhelmed Appalachian League batters. He struck out 20 in his first outing, then came back to whiff 19 batters in his next game. Detore used Necciai in a relief stint, and he responded by striking out 11 batters in four innings.

As astounding as Necciai's first three performances were, his fourth would make history. On the night of May 13, 1952, Ron Necciai did what no pitcher in professional baseball had ever done before.

We had a few guys on our club at Batavia who had friends on that Bristol club, so the news reached us like a lightning bolt. By the time our players had shown up at the ballpark, our clubhouse was buzzing. "Did you hear about Necciai last night?" It was hard to believe that anyone, Necciai or any other pitcher, could do what he did—strike out 27 batters in a nine-inning no-hitter.

Ron Necciai had spun the most commanding performance baseball had ever witnessed at any level. The 7–0 win over the Welch Miners wasn't perfect. Necciai hit a batter, walked a batter, and a third man reached base on an error. With two outs in the ninth inning, the third strike bounced past Harry Dunlop. The Welch batter managed to outhustle Dunlop's throw to first base. Faced with having to earn a fourth out in the inning, Necciai simply reared back and finished the game by striking out the Welch batter for his 27th whiff. "Do you know what you just did?" Dunlop gushed when he reached the mound and his pitcher after the final out. The only out that wasn't recorded by strikeout came on a groundball to the Bristol first baseman in the fourth inning.

In the ensuing days, sportswriters from all around the country phoned for comments. The Ed Sullivan show asked Necciai to appear. "Of all the pitchers I've seen in the big leagues, Necciai more closely resembles [Dizzy] Dean," Detore told a sportswriter from New York. Photographers posed Necciai with Detore. They had him sit at his locker and hold sheets of paper that displayed the number 27. Then he was asked to hold the baseball used to record the final out.

Necciai was an instant phenomenon. Teams around the Appalachian League calculated the schedule and Bristol's pitching rotation in hopes the new sensation would pitch when Bristol next came to town. Optimistic clubs arranged for extra ticket sellers, ticket takers, and hot dog vendors to work when they felt Necciai would pitch. An opportunistic Bristol

6. One Glorious Night

photographer took out an ad in *The Sporting News* and offered eight-by-ten pictures of Necciai for one dollar apiece.

Before the hoopla could fully escalate, Pittsburgh phoned. Necciai was being promoted. He would make one more start for Bristol then join the Pirates' Class B farm club in Burlington, North Carolina, along with Harry Dunlop.

Seven days after his epic performance, a crowd of more than 5,000 squeezed into tiny Shaw Stadium to witness Necciai's final game with the Twins. A parade of merchants took part in pregame festivities, each presenting the pitcher a gift to commemorate his remarkable feat. In a near replication of his history-making effort, Necciai struck out 24 and pitched a two-hitter to defeat Kingsport, 7–1. The hard-throwing prospect left for Burlington with a staggering 109 strikeouts in 42 ⅔ innings.

Before joining his new club, Necciai was summoned to Pittsburgh by Branch Rickey, who wanted the young sensation to take a physical. The trip became problematic when bad weather rolled into the Pittsburgh area. A number of flights that would take the pitcher back to Carolina were cancelled, preventing Necciai from joining his new team for a couple of days. Once he finally arrived at the ballpark, Necciai was made red-faced when he opened his suitcase in front of his new teammates and found it filled with ladies' unmentionables. Equally embarrassed was the airline who determined that the ballplayer's suitcase had been switched accidentally with that of a woman headed to her class reunion in South Carolina.

The history-making pitcher proved big box office in the Carolina League. Fans filled stadiums whenever it was Necciai's turn to pitch. Between innings of a game in Winston-Salem, Necciai was startled to hear fans boo loudly after an announcement was made. "Why are they on me?" Necciai asked Harry Dunlop. "You just broke Vinegar Bend Mizell's strikeout record, and he's from here," the catcher replied.

Two weeks after Necciai had joined the Burlington ballclub, Branch Rickey showed up in Greensboro for a firsthand look at the heralded hurler. Necciai's performance was impressive. He struck out 11. After the game, Rickey evoked excitement in Pirates fans when he told a reporter, "We plan to move him up to Pittsburgh soon, but I'm not certain just when."

The pronouncement brought plenty of ribbing to both Necciai and Dunlop. Teammates needled the pitcher as "Rickey's fair-haired boy." They teased Dunlop, "If he goes up, do you go up, too?"

It was six weeks later when Branch Rickey summoned Pittsburgh sportswriters, sports editors, and radio sportscasters to a luncheon at the swanky Duquesne Club and announced that Ron Necciai was joining the

Pirates. "He could be the answer to our prayers," Joe Garagiola exclaimed to reporters. Rickey declared that Necciai would make his major-league debut in a Sunday doubleheader against the Chicago Cubs on August 10.

The 1952 Pittsburgh Pirates were abysmal, so deeply mired in last place, they were 26 games behind their closest competitor, the seventh-place Cincinnati Reds. Billy Meyer, the Pirates' manager, had been made physically ill by the losses and gulped buttermilk in a desperate attempt to quell his stomach during games. Meyer, renowned for developing young talent as a New York Yankees minor-league manager, had become so disillusioned with Rickey's emphasis on inexperienced prospects that he was thinking of quitting. On August 9 the *Pittsburgh Post-Gazette* posed a question of its readers. "Is Branch Rickey Doomed to Failure?" Of the 439 letter-writing respondents, 434 answered yes.

When Sunday, August 10, arrived, none of the ticket sellers in the Forbes Field box office or the ticket takers at the Bouquet Street entrance expected much activity. Apathy toward the Pirates was almost rampant in Pittsburgh. Only 4,000 people had shown up the day before to see a Saturday game with the Cubs. In 1950 the Pirates had drawn almost 1.2 million fans. At the rate they were going, the 1952 Pirates would be lucky to draw half that tally. Once the gates to Forbes Field were unlocked and swung open, however, workers were surprised to see that more than 17,000 fans had lined up to buy tickets and pushed their way through the turnstiles.

Already nervous to be in the big leagues, Necciai was made even more jittery by involvement in pregame festivities. H. R. Buchanan, owner of the Bristol Twins, had chartered a plane that ferried two dozen fans and a pair of sportswriters to Pittsburgh for their hero's big-league debut. On the field before the game, Buchanan and Gene Thompson of the *Bristol Courier* presented Necciai with an oil painting of himself. While grateful for the support, the pitcher was embarrassed by the fuss and made nervous by the attention. Absent from the festivities was Branch Rickey.

Mr. Rickey was a man of considerable faith. He once said to me, "George, I made a promise to my parents that I would never attend a baseball game on the Sabbath." Then he smiled and said, "But I never said anything about listening to one on the radio."

While the Pirates' general manager listened to the KDKA broadcast from his home, expectation evaporated almost as soon as the game began. "Play ball" had barely been cried when Cubs hitters teed off on the rookie debutant. The first three batters rapped hits off of Necciai. He failed to retire seven of the first eight men who came to the plate. The Cubs scored five times before Necciai was able to quell the onslaught with a strikeout, but the visitors came back with more in the second inning and again in the third to extend their lead to 7–0.

Meyer pulled his rookie after six innings. Necciai had surrendered 11 hits, walked 5, and given up seven runs. It was hardly the debut that suffering Pirates fans had hoped for. But 24 hours produced a much different opinion of the pitcher.

The very next night during a lopsided loss to Cincinnati, Billy Meyer surprised fans when he brought Necciai in to pitch. The seventh inning of a seven-run deficit without the fans and reporters from Bristol and no pregame presentations or newspaper hype meant a far less stressful stage for the 20-year-old. That night, the 9,000 fans in Forbes Field saw a far better Ron Necciai than the day before. Necciai began his stint by striking out Grady Hatton then Andy Seminick before Roy McMillan flied out to center field to end the seventh inning. Necciai set the Reds down in order again in the eighth inning while the lone blemish to his line score came when his catcher, Joe Garagiola, mishandled strike three to Ted Kluszewski in the ninth inning. Necciai had faced ten batters, struck out five of them, and didn't allow a hit or a walk. After the game Necciai said he had better stuff than in his 27-strikeout game. Cincinnati's pitching coach, Earl Brudker, was unabashed in his praise for the rookie, "He's got a good chance of becoming a great pitcher!"

A week later Meyer gave the young sensation another start. This one came against Philadelphia and the best pitcher in the league, Robin Roberts. The Phillies' ace was in pursuit of his 20th win of the year. Through the first five innings it was hard to tell which of the two was the best pitcher in the National League. Both men surrendered a run in the first inning—Necciai on a hit, walk, and an error; Roberts on three hits—before each mowed down the side in order in four successive innings.

In the sixth inning Necciai's luck ran out. The Phillies hammered five successive singles then a double before Willie Jones smashed a three-run home run. The six-run outburst brought Meyer from the dugout, sent Necciai to the showers, and dropped the Pirates to a 10–5 defeat, their seventh in 10 games.

Despite the young prospect's struggle, Billy Meyer stuck with him. Five days after the loss to the Phillies, Necciai faced the Boston Braves and rewarded his manager's confidence by showing the stuff that had drawn raves in the minor leagues. He took a two-hit shutout into the sixth inning before the Braves managed to get on the scoreboard. Meyer lifted Necciai after eight innings, and with help from the Pirates bullpen, the 19-year-old earned his first major-league victory with a 4–3 win over the Braves. After the game, a reporter asked home-plate umpire Dusty Boggess about Necciai. "I thought the boy looked very good. His fastball was moving all the time, and his slow curve had the Boston batters in trouble," he said.

What encouraged Meyer, Rickey, and others, however, was not that their gilded prospect had finally won his first game, nor that the frequently wild hurler had only surrendered two walks, or even that Necciai had induced the Braves into 11 meek ground-ball outs and three double plays. The men were impressed with how the oft-nervous 20-year-old handled an incident in the third inning.

At the beginning of the inning, Necciai attempted to throw a curveball, only to have it slip from his grip and sail at the hitter. Rather than jump back and out of the way of the errant pitch, the Boston batter, Jack Daniels, twisted his upper torso away from the oncoming ball. With a sickening thud, the hard-thrown ball smacked Daniels in the head and sent him limply to the ground, briefly unconscious. The Braves' trainer rushed to the fallen player, and Daniels was taken to Presbyterian Hospital, where he was kept overnight.

Where Necciai may have lost his composure in the past, now the lessons of Detore, Sewell, Burwell, Meyer, and the Pirates' pitching coach, Bill Posedel, kicked in and helped to maintain focus that guided the hurler through the next three Boston hitters, whom he retired handily.

The inconsistency that often accompanies major-league rookies shadowed Necciai through the final month of the 1952 season. After his strong outing against the Braves, he was pummeled by the Cardinals. A lone bright moment came after the game, when Stan Musial summoned Necciai. The Cardinals' slugger and Pirates' pitcher were from towns just six miles apart. Musial was the pitcher's idol. "You can be in this league a long time," Musial encouraged. "Just throw strikes."

Boston avenged the earlier loss with a 16–0 pounding. Necciai walked eight batters, allowed eight runs, and saw two of them score when Jack Daniels hit a ball over the Chesterfield sign behind the right-field bleachers at Braves Field.

Branch Rickey felt there was more to it than just rookie inconsistency. He felt he had detected a flaw in Necciai. "He seems to let up when things get a little tough. In trying to get the ball over the plate and not work batters, he is not bearing down."

On a humid September night in Cincinnati, that flaw was removed, and others suddenly saw the greatness that Branch Rickey foresaw in Ron Necciai. A paltry crowd in Crosley Field witnessed a stellar pitchers' duel as Necciai and the Reds' ace Ken Raffensberger made the scoreboard operator put nothing but zeroes on the big board for five innings. Clyde McCullough, the Pittsburgh catcher, repeatedly rose from his crouch to holler, "Take your time," and "bear down." The pitcher responded by firing fastballs and bending sharp curveballs past the stymied Cincinnati batters, which induced weak fly balls and meek dribblers to the infielders, resulting in outs inning after inning.

The deadlock was broken in the sixth inning. Cincinnati strung together four successive singles, none of them hard hit, to produce the night's first run. One hour and 49 minutes after the game had begun, the contest was over, and the sixth inning tally was the only run scored all night. "He was firing. The kid really had it," gushed Cincinnati manager, Rogers Hornsby, after the game. His mound opponent, Raffensberger, said to a reporter, "They told me Necciai was wild. He wasn't wild. A little more experience and he's going to be plenty tough out there." Jack Hernon wrote in the *Post-Gazette* that "the 20-year-old right-hander from Monongahela put on the best performance of his brief career in the majors."

As the Pirates arrived at the date for their final home game, a tarnish was beginning to attach to Branch Rickey's sterling reputation. The Pirates' general manager was being painted as more carnival barker than astute baseball executive for touting the young prospects he had hastily promoted to the major leagues. Sportswriters mocked the young Pirates as "the Rickey-dinks." Columnists claimed Rickey wasn't altruistic but a penny-pincher.

The press really got on him. It made Mr. Rickey angry. He would say to me, "They call me El Cheapo? If they knew what we spent on bonuses and the farm system, they wouldn't call me that."

Rickey was steadfast in his belief that the young players would mature quickly. He predicted the Pirates would be a first-division club in 1953 and that stardom awaited Dick Groat, Jim Waugh, Bob Friend, and especially Ron Necciai.

On a sunny, 70-degree Sunday afternoon, it was Necciai who walked to the pitcher's mound when the Pirates took the field to begin their final home game of the 1952 season. A loud cheer ushered the players onto the field. More than 22,000 fans—the largest for a game at Forbes Field since mid-April—filled over half the wooden seats in the old ballpark. The crowd was a surprise, considering the Pirates had lost 14 of their last 15 games and sat buried in last place, 53 games behind the league-leading Brooklyn Dodgers.

From center field, a young player just up from the minor leagues watched his former New Orleans teammate work to the Cincinnati Reds batting order. *He's finally figured things out,* Frank Thomas thought to himself as Necciai set down the first three hitters in order.

In the top of the second inning, Ted Kluszewski sent a shot whistling past the scoreboard in left field for a home run to give Cincinnati a 1–0 lead. After the game the Reds' slugger would say that Necciai had one of the best curveballs that he had ever seen. The home run failed to rattle the young pitcher, though, and he retired the next three batters with ease.

In the third, fourth, fifth, and sixth innings, promise was being realized, and Branch Rickey's forecast was on display for all to see. Of the 13 Reds batters during that four-inning stretch, just one reached base—Roy McMillan—on a weak single, and had been promptly picked off.

The reality of youthful inexperience, however, bit back in the seventh inning. Necciai tired and hung a curveball. Bobby Adams belted the pitch off the fence in left center field. From the dugout, Meyer ordered his pitcher to walk the mighty Kluszewski intentionally. Necciai's fastball was losing its steam, and Jim Greengrass arched one that landed in the left-field bullpen for a three-run home run to give Cincinnati a 4–0 advantage.

Despite a ninth-inning rally, the Pirates would fall, 4–3, to leave Necciai's first stint in the major leagues with a 1–6 won-loss record, an earned run average of 7.08, and 63 hits allowed in 55 innings pitched.

When the season ended, Necciai dropped by Forbes Field to discuss his 1953 contract with Branch Rickey. A long cigar in his mouth, the Pirates' general manager was in an especially good mood that morning. The two chatted about several subjects before Rickey asked, "Well, what do you think we ought to pay you?" The young pitcher humbly answered, "I'll play for whatever you think I'm worth." Rickey reached into a drawer, pulled out a contract, wrote a figure on it, then handed the paper to Necciai to sign. He was surprised to read that it called for a salary of $7,000, which was an increase of more than $2,000 over his rookie contract.

During the winter of 1952, the Pirates' preparations for a new season were made more difficult by the ongoing war in Korea. Combat failures had American generals urging for more personnel. Congress responded and lowered the draft age to 18 ½ and mandated 24 months of service by the young men who were drafted. Significantly affected were the Pittsburgh Pirates, who had more young players called to duty than any other team in baseball. Each day it seemed that Rickey received news that another one of his prized young prospects—Vernon Law, Bob Purkey, Frank Thomas—

had received their draft notices and would miss two seasons of baseball. In January of 1953 the list grew to include Ron Necciai.

Rickey was distressed. He didn't see how the military could take someone who had the health issues that plagued Necciai. The Pirates' general manager instructed three different doctors to send letters to the Selective Service System to explain the pitcher's problem with ulcers. Each one failed to change minds. The Pirates' team doctor instructed Necciai to take his X-rays to the draft board. "There's no way they'll take you." Dr. Feingold was wrong.

On January 15 Necciai shelved the idea of wearing a Pirates uniform for the next two years and reported as instructed to Fort Eustis, Virginia, where United States Army khakis became standard issue. Days after arriving Necciai became sick. The chow line food was contrary to the diet his doctor had ordered. The already slender young man lost weight, and with each day his condition grew worse. From the infirmary, the Pirates' prized pitching prospect was sent to a military hospital at Fort Knox in Kentucky. To no one's surprise, Army doctors diagnosed Necciai's problem as bleeding ulcers, and after just 60 days in the military, he was given a medical discharge.

Once back in Pittsburgh, Necciai's doctor had the ailing pitcher step on a scale and was surprised to see that he had lost 30 pounds. Strict orders were given to rest at home. Pills were prescribed to help combat the problem along with strict instructions to follow a special diet. Fried foods and dry cereals were again out. Vegetables were to be drained.

Branch Rickey sent word from Cuba, where the Pirates were conducting spring training, that Necciai's priorities were to be health first and baseball second. He ordered Necciai to not even think about picking up a baseball until he had regained the weight he had lost and felt strong again. Unfortunately, it was an order that the young pitcher didn't agree or comply with. The season was not far off, and Necciai wanted to rejoin the Pirates as soon as possible. He slipped into Forbes Field with a catcher, and in a hurried effort to get back in shape, he began training by throwing off the bullpen mound.

Necciai was still recovering. He was far from being back to full strength. His weight was building, but it was still below his playing weight of a slender 180 pounds on his 6-foot-5-inch frame. During each subsequent workout session, Necciai increased the intensity of his throwing until one day, one throw brought a sharp, stabbing pain to his right shoulder. "Ah, shit!" Necciai hollered as he clutched his shoulder. When his catcher trotted toward him to ask what was wrong, Necciai shook his head and said, "That'll go away." It didn't.

Necciai, Rickey and the Pirates' team doctor all believed it was nothing more than a case of preseason soreness, a common condition that pitchers endured during the early days of spring training. Throwing too much too soon strained muscles that had atrophied from winter inactivity. That's what Necciai wanted to believe. When the usual prescription of rest was ordered, the pitcher heartily complied.

While the Pirates and their minor-league clubs began the 1953 season, Ron Necciai sat at home resting and hoping the pain in his shoulder would go away. In Pittsburgh, Branch Rickey resumed beating the drum for his young talent. During a press conference in early May, the Pirates' general manager told a room full of sportswriters and radio men that, "Bob Friend and Ronnie Necciai should be two of the best pitchers in the league by August 1," then explained that Necciai would join the Pirates once his doctor had finished treating his ulcers.

After two months of inactivity, Necciai agreed to report to the Pirates' Carolina League farm club in Brunswick and test out his sore shoulder. On Memorial Day, he entered a game against Winston-Salem with two outs in the fourth inning. He promptly struck out the first batter he faced, but back in the dugout Necciai told the team's trainer that each pitch had brought "terrible pain." In the next inning Necciai fought to ignore the pain. He struck out two more batters but walked three and was removed from the game.

A week later he was assigned to start against Reidsville. With each throw the pain from the shoulder was excruciating. Between innings the team's trainer asked how his arm felt. Necciai called the pain "unbearable." Still he managed to strike out 13 batters and pitch his team to a 4–2 win. The news quickly reached Branch Rickey, who made arrangements for Necciai to be examined by a specialist at Duke University. Dr. Lenox Baker determined that Necciai had a nerve disorder in his neck that was the cause of his shoulder pain. He said that Necciai should not pitch for the remainder of the season; rest was the only cure. The pitcher packed his bags and headed home, and on July 11 the Pirates placed him on the inactive list. Branch Rickey was crestfallen. "The loss of Ron Necciai due to arm trouble was very upsetting, to say the least," he told *Pittsburgh Post-Gazette* sportswriter, Jack Hernan.

During the winter, Necciai kept in shape by playing in charity basketball games on a team organized by the Pirates' shortstop, Dick Groat. He remained on the major-league roster, and in February of 1954 Necciai reported to spring training. Like everyone else with the club, he was curious to find out how his arm would tolerate pitching again.

Necciai was chosen to start one of the first games. On a wintry cold day Necciai pitched four innings against the Detroit Tigers. He gave up five hits and one run in an effort many called encouraging. Necciai was given another opportunity three days later, but this time the results were alarming. After facing just two batters, Necciai summoned his manager and the trainer to the mound. The pain in his right shoulder was intense. He couldn't continue and came out of the game. In the aftermath of his discouraging game, Necciai approached Branch Rickey and asked to be placed on the voluntary retired list. The Pirates' general manager complied, and the pitcher went home to Pennsylvania.

For a full year Necciai rested his arm. He took up work in the sporting goods industry and saw possibilities for a new career. During the winter the Hollywood Stars coaxed Necciai into giving pitching another try. He traveled across the country to train with the club for the 1955 season, and in April he took the mound for an exhibition game against the Los Angeles Angels. He pitched four innings but struggled with his control. Necciai gave up four hits and walked three. The pain was still there.

Frustration grew. The inevitability of this being the end of the line for his baseball career could no longer be ignored. Anxious for a definitive answer about the source of his arm pain, Necciai agreed to meet with the leading expert on baseball pitchers and their arm ailments, Dr. George Bennett of John's Hopkins University. The renowned orthopedist put the pitcher's right shoulder through several tests, then without saying a word, left the examination room. Necciai sat awkwardly for several minutes, all the while hoping the doctor might deliver good news. When Bennett returned, he was blunt. Without looking up at Necciai he blurted, "Son, go home and buy a gas station. You're never going to pitch again." Necciai's injury was a torn rotator cuff in his right shoulder. There was no surgery, type of medication, or amount of rest that would heal such an injury. With Dr. Bennett's blunt pronouncement, the brilliant promise that was the brief pitching career of Ron Necciai was over.

Mr. Rickey always thought that Necciai was one of the best pitchers he ever saw. Bob Feller was the best I ever hit against, but Necciai might have been one of the best I've ever seen. A lot of pitchers back in those days saw their careers ended by injuries. For Necciai, it was a shame. He was special.

The anniversary of Ron Necciai's remarkable feat annually makes his phone ring with interview requests. He has been inducted into Pennsylvania's sports Hall of Fame. On the day Necciai was honored in spring training by the Pittsburgh Pirates, players marveled at the story of his accomplishment. Harry Dunlop, the former catcher summed up the uniqueness of the 27-strikeout game best, "It'll never be done again."

7

THE HOT DEBATE

Off the main highway that links Phoenix and Tucson rests an oasis, or what once was. Longtime San Francisco Giants fans occasionally arrive in Casa Grande on a pilgrimage. They come to see what once was a state-of-the-art complex where their team held spring training. They grin at the swimming pool shaped like a baseball bat and the parking lot constructed in the form of a mitt. The hotel, motel, and the building that once was the clubhouse remain. So too does the meeting room, where in the second year of the complex's existence raged a ferocious debate that ultimately cost the organization one of its most prized pitching prospects.

We had some great young pitchers in the farm system at that time [1963]. Gaylord Perry went on to have the greatest career of the bunch. Several of the boys had success in the big leagues. But that spring I don't think there were very many pitchers in our farm system that were thought of more highly by the managers and the scouts than Bob Bishop.

By the time Bob Bishop approached his 18th birthday, visits by covetous scouts brought an air of excitement into the family home. Baseball had long been an intoxicant to the tall, athletic teen. As an adolescent, 40-mile round-trips from his home in West Covina to Wrigley Field in south Los Angeles to watch the Pacific Coast League's Los Angeles Angels fed the fixation. Baseball was part of the daydreaming that passed the time while he and his older brother Harry sat in the back seat, instructed to do their homework, while their father, a U.S. Marshal Captain, drove around Southern California to serve papers. In sandlot games, Bishop would try to emulate the behind-the-back catches he had seen the Angels' center fielder, Bobby Usher, make. When he was on the pitcher's mound, however, Bob Bishop could do things with a baseball that Bubba Church, Turk Lown, Bob Zick or any of the other Angels pitchers couldn't. He could throw it by hitters with a humiliating wickedness that made scouts yearn.

I was managing in the Giants' farm system at that time. I liked to get out and see games, and I had seen Bob while he was in high school in Southern California. He was a very good ballplayer. He played all over. Bob was a pretty good catcher, but where he really stood out was when he was on the mound. He had a real live arm, and he could throw hard. It was no surprise to see a lot of scouts at his games.

Of all the scouts to visit the Bishop's home during the spring of 1961, it was a San Francisco Giants scout, Rex Carr, who raised the emotions to excitement. Bob Bishop was an unabashed Giants fan and needed no sales pitch to be convinced that he should sign with Carr's employer. To add to the enthusiasm, the Giants' scout also wanted to sign Bob's older brother Harry, who was pitching at Mt. San Antonio College.

Following Bob's graduation from high school, the Giants, Boston Red Sox, and the expansion Los Angeles Angels extended offers. A part-time scout for the expansion Houston Colt 45s who had been following the Bishop brothers brought his supervisor to the family's home. "If you can wait, I might be able to get $50,000 for the two of you to sign with us," the scout proposed. The money was intriguing. The Bishops waited, but days of waiting for the Houston scout to respond turned to weeks. When Bob and Harry sought his counsel, their father said, "A bird in the hand is worth 40,000 in the bush." On August 7, Bob's 18th birthday, the Bishop brothers accepted Carr's offer. Each inked a contract with the Giants that called for a signing bonus of $6,000. It was only later that they learned what had happened to the Houston scout and his supervisor. Both men had been fired.

Within days of their signing, Carr arranged for the Bishop brothers to pitch batting practice to the San Francisco Giants before a game with the Dodgers at the Los Angeles Coliseum. When they entered the Giants locker room, Bob and Harry gaped at the big-league environment. The brothers spied two muscular men seated on a bench. One Bishop turned to the other and said, "What are the Rams doing here?" It turned out the players were not pro football players but rather Willie Mays and Orlando Cepeda.

Once on the mound in the large stadium, Bob Bishop heard words of encouragement from his catcher, John Orsino, whose 6-foot-3-inch frame was the largest he had ever thrown to. The brothers took turns pitching to their heroes—Willie Mays, Willie McCovey, Orlando Cepeda, Felipe Alou and Jim Davenport. "What do you boys think?" Carr asked at the end of the session. "Fabulous," Bob Bishop gushed.

Only three weeks remained in the minor-league season once the Bishops signed. Their pro debuts would wait six months for the start of spring training. In the early days of spring training, it was Bob who got the attention of the Giants' minor-league managers. Both Bishops were assigned to the Giants' Class D club in the Florida State League, the Lakeland Giants, but after seeing Bob pitch, Sal Taormina had other ideas. The manager of the Giants' Class C Fresno farm club was impressed by Bob Bishop's live arm. He piped up in a player evaluation meeting that he wanted the 18-year-old rookie assigned to his club.

Jack Schwarz and Carl Hubbell, who ran the Giants' farm system, weren't convinced that such a raw, inexperienced player should launch his professional career in a hitter-friendly league. The men conferred and agreed to lend Bishop to Taormina's club for a few days to see what he could do. Bert Haas, manager of the Lakeland Giants, was nervous about the arrangement. The former Cincinnati Reds All-Star had quickly identified Bob Bishop as the most talented pitcher on his ballclub. To have any chance at a successful season, Haas needed Bishop to anchor his pitching staff.

Much to Haas' dismay, Bishop's first outing for Fresno was a successful one. He breezed through four scoreless innings so effortlessly that Schwarz and Hubbell agreed to let him pitch again for Taormina's club. The second outing had a much different result. It was far from effortless, and the pitcher's lack of success was exclaimed by a long home run off the bat of a power-hitting first baseman, Moose Stubing. Bishop was returned to Lakeland.

The conclusion of spring training unfolds a mixture of excitement and apprehension. It permeated the airplane that carried the young prospects to their summer home and also the front office of the Lakeland ballclub. Lakeland, Florida, had been without a ballclub in five of the previous six years. Its small population of 40,000 and searing summer heat were nemeses.

Summer days averaged in the mid–90s, and regular afternoon thunderstorms brought stifling humidity. Despite boasting the best record in the league in 1960, the paltry crowds and the large amount of money lost drove the club's owner to turn his franchise back to the league. In the fall of 1961, a Tampa businessman and baseball fan, Howard Roth, was granted a Florida State League franchise, which he placed in Lakeland. Keen to change the town's professional baseball fortunes, Roth hired an eager Lou

7. The Hot Debate

Gorman as the club's general manager and secured an affiliation agreement with the San Francisco Giants.

Gorman spent the winter arranging promotional activities. Pony Day, Bicycle Day, Paper Boy Day, Ladies Nights, and Father-Son Days were scheduled to help boost attendance. It only took Gorman a week to realize that a very unexpected attraction might become his biggest draw—Bob Bishop.

Bert Hass boasted to the *Lakeland Ledger* that pitching would be the key to his team's success. He tabbed Bob Bishop to start the season opener. Harry Bishop would pitch out of the bullpen. The Giants began the season in Tampa, where more than 2,000 fans responded to the considerable pre-season buildup for a Cincinnati Reds farm team that boasted a lineup of some of the organization's prized young hitting prospects. Flashing a lively fastball, Bob Bishop stymied the Tampa batting order and, specifically, the heralded duo in the middle of that lineup, Lee May and Jimmy Wynn. When Haas removed Bishop after eight innings, he had struck out seven and helped Lakeland to a season opening win.

Four nights later Lou Gorman surveyed the stands at Henley Field. The Giants were headed out on a road trip after the game. While the Giants held a 5–0 lead on St. Petersburg, the sight dismayed Gorman. Barely a third of the benches in the 1,000-seat ballpark were filled. By the end of the third inning, whatever disappointment Gorman may have felt at the paltry crowd was cast aside by Bob Bishop's pitching performance. In the second inning Bishop struck out the side. In the third his overpowering fastball blew away the three St. Petersburg hitters on strikeouts. The 18-year-old repeated the feat again in the fifth inning and once more in the seventh. Cheers from the stands grew louder with each swing and miss. In the press box the strikeout tally kept by the official scorer swelled as each inning ended. Jack Slayton, the *Ledger's* sports editor, began to realize he not only had a story angle but a report he could sell to *The Sporting News*.

Following the final out, his teammates mobbed Bishop. Bert Haas pumped his young prospect's hand. Harry Bishop beamed for his younger brother. The Lakeland Giants' hurler had amassed a league-record 20 strikeouts. It was almost midnight when Haas telephoned his report to Jack Schwarz's office at Candlestick Park in San Francisco. In the press box Slayton pecked his game story on a black manual typewriter. He drew parallels to the celebrated Cleveland Indians' pitching prospect, Sam McDowell, the star of the 1960 Lakeland ballclub. "Bishop was fast," Slayton typed, "as fast as when Sam McDowell was here in '60." Long after the last fans had left the ballpark, Gorman tallied box office receipts and inventoried the hot dogs and soft drinks at the concession stand. In the still of the late-night hours Haas, Slayton, and Gorman independently had a similar thought, that the Lakeland Giants just might have the best pitcher in the league: Bob Bishop.

A week after his record night, Bishop pitched a shutout to beat Palatka and struck out 12. Five nights later the rookie blanked Sarasota and struck out 11. In Bishop's last start in the month of May, a crowd of 1,921 squeezed into Henley Field. They cheered each of Bishop's 11 strikeouts, but only one fan, Wendell Yohn, left the ballpark happy. He won a pony. The Lakeland Giants, however, lost the game, 3–2, to Palatka.

Yet for all of Bob Bishop's praiseworthy accolades, there were frustrating flaws to his game. He was raw. Bishop had only pitched 31 innings in his senior season of high school baseball. His mechanics were disjointed. While the velocity of his fastball could be awe evoking, his wildness could astound. Against Ft. Lauderdale, an errant Bishop pitch hit the Yankees' shortstop, Ian Dixon, in the head. Fans gasped as the ball bounced 30 feet in the air. Bishop lacked the know-how to hold runners on base. Speedsters took advantage and stole on him. When he fell behind in counts and took something off the fastball to get it into the strike zone, his pitches became hittable and opponents feasted. As the season approached the end of June, Bishop could not have known that a brewing storm would have significant consequences on his baseball future.

During the final week of June, Bert Haas startled Howard Roth. The Giants' manager told his boss that he had received a job offer that he felt was too good to pass up. An opportunity in the wholesale liquor business offered a salary far beyond what Haas could make in baseball. Roth alerted Jack Schwarz to the possibility that his club may need a new manager, and when Haas did resign, Schwarz quickly assigned Max Lanier to take over the club.

During the 1940s Max Lanier had been one of the best pitchers in the National League. Twice he had been an All-Star and helped pitch the St. Louis Cardinals to the World Series four times in his career. When he arrived in Lakeland, Lanier chose to watch a few games before taking over the ballclub. He very quickly realized the talent and potential within Bob Bishop. Almost immediately, Lanier made Bishop his project. He tweaked Bishop's mechanics to try to improve his control. Lanier instituted a fine for throwing a pitch in the strike zone on a no-ball- two-strike count. The manager offered tips on how to better hold runners on base and cut down on steals.

7. The Hot Debate

In Bishop's first start with Lanier as the manager, he endured a terrible first inning. Facing the Miami Marlins, the young hurler struggled with his control. Two walks and a single loaded the bases. A sacrifice fly brought a run home. A walk, a wild pitch, and another single gave Tampa a 2–0 lead. Bishop pitched his way out of trouble then settled into a rhythm to hold the Marlins at bay over the final eight innings. He did not allow another run and just two hits as the Giants rallied back to win, 5–2.

In late July Carl Hubbell traveled to Lakeland to watch the Giants' farm club in person. He watched Bishop strike out 15 batters and pitch a shutout to beat Tampa. After the game, Hubbell and Lanier nodded with agreement that the most impressive part of Bishop's performance was that he didn't walk a batter for the first time in a game all season. After speaking with Hubbell, Jack Slayton penned a column about Bishop in the *Lakeland Ledger*. In it he wrote, "The youngster should advance to the majors for a trial in 1964 and probably win a pitching spot by 1965." Lanier was also full of praise for his pupil. "This boy cannot help but make it," he said. "He has desire, keeps in perfect condition, wants to learn, and wants to pitch."

On July 30, with his parents cheering wildly from the stands, Bob Bishop extended his consecutive scoreless innings streak to 24 with a three-hit shutout of St. Petersburg. Lanier's teaching bore fruit. Bishop struck out 13 and walked only 1.

Twenty-three hundred fans squeezed into Henley Field for Bishop's next start. The fans' hope of seeing the scoreless streak grow ended in the top of the first inning, when Ft. Lauderdale's Art Lopez slammed a Bishop fastball over the outfield fence for a home run. The hard thrower retained his composure and quelled the visitors before fatigue set in during the seventh inning, and Lanier removed him from the game.

Bishop celebrated his 19th birthday with a 3–2 win over St. Petersburg. He took a three-hit shutout into the ninth inning that night. Winning made his record under Lanier, 5–1. There was no denying that his was a star on the rise. Lakeland's fans voted the young Californian their team's Most Popular Player. The rookie finished the season with 12 wins. His 2.28 earned run average was third best in the league. Bishop completed 19 of the 25 games he started, the most complete games in the Florida State League. In 197 innings pitched, the hard thrower struck out 224 batters, the second-best total in the league. He walked 87. Impressed that Bishop had a bright future, the Giants took steps to avoid losing him in the minor-league draft. During the offseason he was placed on San Francisco's 40-man, major-league roster and received a contract with a pay raise and promotion to Class AA.

During spring training in March of 1963, debate was a constant in the meeting room at Casa Grande. Each night upon the completion of dinner, Jack Schwarz, the director of scouting and the farm system for the San Francisco Giants, and Carl Hubbell, the Giants' director of player development, would convene a meeting of the organization's scouts and minor-league managers. On one wall was a large chalkboard that displayed the names of almost 250 ballplayers who were vying to make one of the Giants' ten minor-league clubs. One by one, Schwarz would call out the name of a player. Chatter ensued. The player's manager gave a review of his performance then stated an opinion of his prospects before the scouts and fellow managers weighed in. At times during the night differing opinions would spark debate. Promotions, demotions, and advocacy for the outright release of a player could hike the decibel level. The closer it came to midnight, the more fatigue and frayed nerves entered the equation. At times the men became enveloped in contention. Voices echoed in anger. Fists pounded on the table. Schwarz and Hubbell let the men speak their piece but all the while kept the meeting under control.

One night in particular it was Dave Garcia and Charlie Fox who initiated the argument. It was about Bob Bishop. The two Giants scouts pointed out that Bishop didn't have sound pitching mechanics. "You should change Bob's delivery," Garcia piped up. "Nobody's touching him," snapped the normally soft-spoken Hubbell. Fox joined in. He insisted that when Bishop extended his arm in his pitching delivery, he could see the arm separate, dislocate at the elbow. "His arm snaps back at the elbow," Fox bellowed. "Everyone can see it!" Hubbell's face grew red. The Hall of Fame pitcher shouted back at Fox, "He throws hard. He throws strikes. Don't change him!"

As the close of spring training drew near, another argument about Bishop erupted, this one over which farm club he should play for. For 1963 the Giants would have two Class AA clubs: Springfield, Massachusetts, in the Eastern League and El Paso in the Texas League. Jack Schwarz and Carl Hubbell had made the decision to assign Bishop to Springfield. George Genovese strongly disagreed.

I said that I thought sending Bishop to Springfield was a mistake. The boy was a power pitcher. I pointed out that the weather was usually very cold in the Eastern League during the early part of the season. Cold weather was not good for a power pitcher. I told Jack and Carl that Bishop should be sent with my club and go to El Paso, where the weather was warmer. If he pitched in that bad weather, he might get hurt. We

7. The Hot Debate

talked about it several times before spring training ended, but they stuck to their guns and sent Bob to Springfield.

Players who had played in the Florida State League found spring weather in the Eastern League offered sobering contrast. Cold temperatures and wet air could chill to the bone. Nighttime dew made fields damp. Heavy jackets and thick gloves were common garb in dugouts. The obscurity of some of the ballparks' bullpens empowered players to build fires that brought both warmth and relief.

The disparity was especially stark during the first few days of a season. Players who had spent six weeks training in sunshine and warm weather in Florida or Arizona were suddenly smacked with frigid conditions in their team's home. Such was the case when Bishop and his teammates arrived in Springfield, Massachusetts. An enthusiasm for the new season greeted the new Springfield Giants. The ballclub and a service organization partnered to stage a downtown reception that introduced the players to their fans. Though the day was cold, a welcoming warmth filled the air. When he introduced his players, Giants manager Buddy Kerr heaped praise on Bob Bishop. Kerr concluded by announcing that Bishop would be his starting pitcher on opening night. As the event drew to a close, the pitcher was approached by a young boy. "I don't care how many batters you walk; just pitch a no-hitter," the young fan implored. Bishop smiled and promised he would do his best.

That night as Bishop took his warm-up tosses in the bullpen, a breeze swayed the tall trees behind the outfield fence. One by one the large light towers fired to life. Fans trickled into the riverside ballpark. Once the pregame festivities began, almost all of Pynchon Park's red chairback seats were filled by more than 2,100 fans.

The Reading Red Sox were seeing Bishop for the first time, and by the end of the first inning it was clear that the young pitcher's fastball was going to be tough to handle. By the fourth inning the strikeouts were mounting. From the Reading dugout, the bench jockeys were in full gear. The Red Sox heckled Bishop with each pitch. They tried to break his concentration by pelting him with a verbal onslaught—and not just any oral barrage, but one that violated the very tenants of baseball and brought to the pitcher's attention that he was throwing a no-hitter.

By the seventh inning the fans had become part of Bishop's quest for history. They roared with every swing and miss or the strike calls that were bellowed by the home-plate umpire. Loud applause accompanied Bishop's walk to the dugout after he had struck out the side in the seventh inning.

When Bishop took the mound in the top of the ninth inning, he was tired. He had struck out 14 batters and walked six. Tony Torchia led off and worked the count to three-and-two before going down on strikes. Rico Petrocelli came up next and smashed a hard-bouncing ball toward second base. Hal Lanier, Max's son, bobbled the ball momentarily then managed to grab it and make a hurried throw to first base that beat Petrocelli to the bag for the second out.

By now Bishop was beyond tired. He was exhausted. Bob Lawrence, a strong, left-handed hitting outfielder stood between the 19-year-old and the first Opening Day no-hitter in the Eastern League's 41-year history. Bishop struggled with his control. His fastball lacked the zip it had in the earlier innings. Lawrence was patient and worked the count to three balls and two strikes. He unleashed mighty swings that caught part of Bishop's next two offerings, and the foul balls extended the at-bat. On the eighth pitch of the at-bat, Bishop made a concerted effort to end the challenge once and for all. He gritted his teeth and released a mighty fastball. Lawrence swung. When the ball popped into the catcher's glove, a loud cheer rose up from the stands, and Bishop's teammates ran to the pitcher's mound in celebration.

Once he had made it beneath the stands and into the Giants' clubhouse, Bishop collapsed into a chair. A sportswriter asked his manager, Buddy Kerr, how many pitches the right-hander had thrown. "Nobody counted," Kerr admitted then added, "probably about 180."

The feat was heralded both in the local paper and nationally by *The Sporting News*. In San Francisco, Schwarz and Hubbell smiled at the news that reaffirmed their belief that the Giants had a sensational prospect in the making.

Five nights later in Elmira, New York, Bishop made his second start of the season. The night was bitterly cold. "I can't feel my feet," the pitcher admitted to his catcher. In the bottom of the first inning, Bishop struggled with his control. He walked four successive batters to force in a run. However, that run would turn out to be the only run of the game. The Californian escaped the predicament without any further damage then breezed through the second, third, and fourth innings without surrendering a hit.

In the fifth inning Bishop utilized a pitch that he had not enjoyed much success with, a palmball. Out of the hand, the pitch looks to the batter to be a fastball but actually travels at a much slower rate of speed. This palmball, however, was a good one. In the split-second it traveled to the plate, the pitcher was certain it would provoke a swing and miss. The crack of the bat connecting with the pitch, however, said otherwise. The

7. The Hot Debate

ball shot through the infield, and Bishop's hope for a second no-hitter was done.

It was not until the sixth inning that Bishop surrendered his second hit of the game, and with one out in the seventh, Kerr removed him. His pitching opponent, John Papa, shut out the Giants on just three hits, and Elmira won, 1–0.

On June 4 the Reading Red Sox returned to Springfield for the first time since the season-opening series. Bishop drew the starting assignment and would be opposed by Gary Modrell, who was on the losing end of the opening-night no-hitter. Bishop had won four of his five starts. With four complete games, two shutouts, and an earned-run average barely above one through the first month of the season, Bishop had established himself as perhaps the top pitcher in a league teeming with big-league prospects. And at just 19, he was the youngest pitcher in the league.

Before the game the two pitchers jogged in the outfield. As they passed each other Modrell cracked, "Don't you go throwing another no-hitter at us." Bishop smiled and replied, "Don't *you* throw a no-hitter at *us*!" The night was cold, but it wasn't long before a fierce pitchers' duel was heating up. Bishop and Modrell worked their way through the batting order without giving up a hit. By the sixth inning each had gone through the other team's batting order a second time and still not surrendered a hit. Fans were riveted to a historic event taking shape before them: a double no-hitter.

First Bishop in the top of the eighth then Modrell in the bottom half of the inning retired the opposing hitters, and still not a single hit had been recorded. Bishop recorded the first out of the ninth inning when Gene Giannini, Reading's second baseman, stepped into the batter's box. Bishop went into his windup, and as he whipped his right arm forward to deliver a fastball, he felt a sharp pain in his elbow. *Uh-oh*, he thought. While his focus was on the pain in his elbow, Bishop hardly noticed that Giannini had swung and managed to rap out the game's first hit. Tom Williams, the Reading third baseman, followed Giannini's single with a triple that scored Giannini with the first run of the game. Bishop got out of the inning without further damage. In the bottom of the ninth, Modrell retired the first two Springfield batters. One out away from dishing a no-hitter back at the Giants, Modrell delivered a pitch that Springfield's Dick Pawlow sent right back through the pitcher's legs and into center field to break up the no-hit bid.

The loss paled in comparison with the alarm that filled the trainer's room at Pynchon Park. The usual ice-bag wrap that covered a pitcher's shoulder following a game was accompanied by a second bag of ice, this one wrapped to Bishop's right elbow to reduce both pain and swelling. Concern rippled through the Giants front office on learning the news. An appointment was made almost immediately, and Bishop was hustled to the train station for a trip to New York and an examination by the Giants' team doctor. As the young pitcher sat quietly pondering his future, the train began to pull away from the platform. A conductor made his way down the aisle and asked Bishop for his ticket. "You're on the wrong train," the man said. He pointed out the window to another waiting train and bellowed, "That's your train!"

Bishop grabbed his suitcase and hurried for a door. By now the train had picked up speed and was nearing the end of the platform. He pushed the door open and hesitated momentarily. The train was moving much faster. Realizing he had little choice, Bishop leaped from the train.

He reached for a pole to break his fall, caught it, then was spun by his momentum around it several times, all the while his left arm was extended by a firm grip on a flailing suitcase.

Bishop's injury was diagnosed as bone chips. The Giants' team doctor cited a loose elbow joint as a problem and said surgery would have to be performed to address both. The procedure shaved bone and left a once-powerful right arm with both a five-inch scar and one and a half inches shorter than the left arm.

Recovery took months, but Bishop was able to join the Giants for spring training in Phoenix. But he was not, nor would ever be, the same pitcher. The gifts that had shot him up the farm-system ladder so quickly were gone. Fellow pitchers in the organization who had heard glowing stories of Bishop's remarkable exploits were surprised by what they saw. "He's got nothin'," one said to a teammate. The once overwhelming fastball was gone and so was the awe that accompanied Bishop's performances on the mound.

Bishop spent the bulk of the 1964 season in the Texas League with El Paso, where he struggled. In a hitter's ballpark, he was hammered. His confidence suffered, he became moody. "I don't think I've seen him smile all year," a teammate noted. Bishop was used primarily in relief, pitching an inning here and an inning there. He got into 18 games, pitched 46 innings, allowed 60 hits, and finished the season with a 1–6 won-loss record and an earned run average of 7.43.

Nobody ever worked with Bob. He kept trying to pitch as if he still had that overpowering fastball. He kept trying to strike everybody out. He couldn't do that anymore. What he should have been doing was trying to fool the hitters, mix up his pitches, and change locations. Relying on

the fastball is what a lot of kids do. They stick with the pitch they think made the scouts like them in the first place.

The next two seasons brought more of the same, but headed into the 1967 season Bishop pressed for a change. Bishop pleaded with the Giants to let him catch. It was a position he had played in high school. The Giants relented, and the move breathed new life into a dormant career. Dave Garcia was the manager at Class A Fresno club, and he agreed to let the once-prized pitching prospect play in the field.

Bishop shared the catching duties. Garcia also took advantage of his athleticism and played Bishop at third base and in both left and right field. The enthusiasm for baseball returned, so too did his magnetic smile. Whether playing in the field and making plays, sitting in the bullpen having laughs with pitchers who offered baseballs to urge kids to run down the block and bring back a bag of tacos, or being a part of pranks in the clubhouse, the game became fun again for Bob Bishop.

In a June game against Bakersfield, Bishop belted three home runs. He had five hits, scored four runs, and drove in five in the win. On July 4 Garcia had to miss a game. He tabbed Bishop to manage the club. The interim boss made one change to the starting lineup. He took himself out. The move proved astute. His replacement, Tim Young, had four hits and drove in five runs to help Fresno to a 12–2 win over Stockton. Bishop concluded his first season of playing in the field with 16 home runs. In 107 games, he drove in 59 runs and batted .254.

I saw Bob a few times that season. He did a good job. I thought he could become a major-league prospect as a hitter! The organization was a bit thin on catching, and I thought Bob had a chance to move up. But there were people in the organization who had different ideas. I couldn't understand it.

The Giants had other ideas. They insisted that Bishop return to the mound. "Your arm looks fine," he was told. "We want you to pitch." It was a decision that left the onetime hard thrower both confused and disappointed. For the next two seasons, he pitched primarily in a relief role for the Giants' Class AAA and Class AA farm clubs before the organization gave him his unconditional release.

Bob finished up as a player-coach in the Mets organization, then he became a scout. The thing about Bob is he never expressed any regret about his career. He's very humble. So many people who know him never knew how good he was. He was very good!

In the years that followed his playing days, Bob Bishop became a scout. He spent close to 40 years in the profession working for the New York Mets, Los Angeles Dodgers, and the Kansas City Royals. Among the many players that he is responsible for recommending and signing is Eric Karros. In 2006, Major League Baseball named Bob Bishop the West Coast Scout of the Year.

8

THE WHOLE PACKAGE

Cheers blared and images of jubilation filled the television screen. The sounds and the pictures of the Chicago Cubs celebrating their first World Series title in 108 years swept both enthusiasm and pride through Fred Nori. It had been eight years since the career high school and college coach had first seen and trained a determined 15-year-old who had dreams and aspirations of big-league success. Now, Kyle Schwarber danced about in celebration, having been an important part of the Cubs' success. "I told the guys at Indiana University back then, 'You are never going to see another player like this.'" It was a boldness of conviction that took Nori back to his days in minor-league baseball and the way he felt the first time he saw the number one pick in the 1966 draft, Steve Chilcott.

He was a very strong boy, a good catcher. Everybody came to watch him play. There has been a lot of talk in hindsight about him over the years, but he got a lot of attention from every ballclub back then. A number one pick? I think it came out after the draft that everyone was split between him and Reggie Jackson, but he was a very good ballplayer.

Necks craned and eyes gazed upward to the sound of a screaming jet engine. More than 60,000 feet above, a speck streaked across the sky. White contrails streamed from the aircraft in spectacular contrast to the deep blue California sky. It was another test flight by one of the jet jockeys from nearby Edwards Air Force Base who stretched speed records, soared to the edge of space, and defied death on an almost daily basis. The headlines made by the daring pilots brought visitors and attention from every corner of America to the Antelope Valley, a sparsely- populated area in the Mojave Desert, an hour and a half north of Los Angeles. During the spring of 1966, so too did an 18-year-old high school baseball player, Steve Chilcott.

The youngest of three boys in an athletic family, Steve Chilcott first turned heads with his play in little league. He was in a league for 11- and 12-year-olds in Fullerton. Chilcott was recognized as the league's all-star catcher, but a startling revelation got him banned from the playoffs. "They didn't know I was only ten," he later told the *Antelope Valley Press*.

By the time he was a sophomore at Antelope Valley High School, Chilcott was a gritty, strong-armed quarterback on the football team and a powerful left-handed-hitting third baseman on the Antelopes' varsity baseball team. Word of the 15-year-old's play on the baseball diamond began to draw the attention of pro scouts. By the time Steve Chilcott was a senior, he had been switched to catcher, and the trickle of baseball evaluators had grown to a steady stream.

This was the second year of the baseball draft. Scouts had to expand their area and look for talent where they hadn't before. The Antelope Valley was a growing area. A lot of families were moving out there. Pretty soon every scout in Southern California was heading out there on a regular basis to see this catcher. Talk began to spread that he could be the first pick in the draft.

Professional baseball scouts weren't the only men in covetous pursuit of the 18-year-old. Coaches from UCLA, USC, Stanford, The Air Force Academy, and Fresno State coaxed the catcher to attend and play for their school. Chilcott would pare his list of schools and finally decide on Fresno State—if, that is, he did not decide to play pro ball instead.

By April the throngs of scouts that turned out to watch Chilcott play had grown in size. When Antelope Valley High traveled 100 miles south to participate in the Pomona Elks Invitational during Easter vacation, more than a dozen scouts took in each game. Chilcott failed to disappoint. He slammed a home run in a win over Victor Valley High, then another to help defeat Rowland High, and was named the tournament's Most Valuable Player.

Antelope Valley High surged into league play with a 13–1 record. Chilcott's four home runs, 15 runs batted in and .384 batting average were a significant reason why. The catcher's growing reputation lured Houston's general manager, Paul Richards, former Pittsburgh Pirates manager, Danny Murtaugh, and 19 scouts to the league opener with rival Palmdale High, where Chilcott banged out three hits and scored twice in a 4–1 win.

Six days later, the covetous pursuit reached a crescendo. It was a Friday afternoon in Lancaster when the whispers grew to urgings. From student to classmate, teacher to spouse, school employee to friend and fan, the

8. The Whole Package

news spread throughout the community that a baseball legend was at Antelope Valley High School. Wearing a suit and tie, Casey Stengel sat perched in the bleachers at the high school ball field. The legendary former New York Yankees' manager, now retired and a consultant for the New York Mets, had come to watch Steve Chilcott. Twenty-three other evaluators had come to watch the Antelopes' game, too. But they weren't creating the buzz that the former manager generated.

As the start of the game with Kennedy High drew near, more and more fans arrived, pulled by news of Stengel's presence. A handful became a dozen, then more than a hundred, and still more flocked. Autographs were sought until requests got in the way of the evaluation effort, and Stengel left.

I was there that day. When people heard that Casey was there, they came from all over to see him. When Casey left, it was just me and Bob Zuk, Charlie Silvera, Dutch Zwilling, Art Lilly, Jackie Warner, Jerry Gardner, and Rosey Gilhousen. There might have been more scouts than fans by the time the game reached the third inning.

As he prepared for the game, Chilcott noticed the larger-than-usual crowd and a commotion in the stands. "I took a look in the stands, saw a big crowd gathered in one spot, and sure enough, there was Mr. Stengel right in the middle," Chilcott told a local reporter. If the throng was a distraction, it didn't show in the catcher's play. The Antelope Valley standout slammed four hits and led his team to an 11–3 win. As he left the park Stengel commented, "One look is enough for me. He's got all the tools to become a major-league hitter."

Many of the same scouts who tracked Chilcott spent several Tuesdays and Saturdays 400 miles east in Phoenix, Arizona. Arizona State University was brimming with prospects. Eight Arizona State players had been selected in the inaugural baseball draft in June of 1965, including the first player chosen, Rick Monday. Nine months later another half dozen Sun Devils were on the scouts' radar with curiosity ebbing over Monday's successor in center field, Reggie Jackson.

Jackson had come west from Philadelphia on a football scholarship, but after the 1965 football season he joined the Arizona State baseball team.

The first time I talked to Reggie, he told me that my brother Chick had been the first scout to give him a card back when he was in Pennsylvania. He said my brother had seen him when he was a teenager and urged him

to concentrate on baseball. The first time I saw Reggie, it was in a series against Michigan State. He must have struck out 15 times. I don't think he even foul-tipped a ball. When I went back though, I saw him hit some long home runs. He had power. He had talent.

Jackson hadn't played baseball in two years, and then it wasn't at the elite collegiate level. His skills were raw. One night he might go hitless and the next afternoon drop two fly balls. A week later he would impress fans and scouts with a 375-foot home run.

The evaluation of Reggie Jackson was a challenge for scouts. He was draft eligible, which meant his first season of college baseball would be the only opportunity scouts would have to evaluate his potential for future success in professional baseball. They would have to develop that conviction over just four months of development and not the usual three or four years for a college prospect.

While the young man was chasing Arizona State's single-season home run record, he was also on track to break the school's single-season record for strikeouts. Naysayers noted that while Jackson exhibited tremendous power, a lot of his home runs came against the lesser opponents on the Sun Devils' schedule such as Sul Ross State and San Diego University. Jackson exhibited tremendous foot speed. He was among the nation's leaders in stolen bases. In the field, he possessed a strong throwing arm, but the speed that also enabled him to cover a great deal of ground in center field came with a penchant for muffing fly balls. Still, with each step closer to the school's home-run or runs-batted-in record that Reggie Jackson took, his standing in the draft rose.

As June neared, the pressure increased on scouting directors and their stable of evaluators. Adoption of the draft concept in 1965 had completely changed scouting methods. Gone were the days of permitting scouts to use their judgment to sign high school or college players that they considered prospects. Now internal decisions had to be made from the reports that scouts sent in from all over the country. Players had to be ranked and a selection plan created.

Until 1965 you worked hard to find talent and then tried harder to persuade the boy and his parents that yours was the organization he should sign with. It was a challenge to be a scout, but it was also very rewarding. In 1964 things changed. The Angels had spent over $200,000 to sign a college outfielder, Rick Reichardt. That was $30,000 more than the previous record for a signing bonus. They also gave a high school player, Tom Egan, a $100,000 bonus. Several clubs were upset about these large

bonuses. At the Winter Meetings, they proposed the idea of a draft. The Cardinals, Yankees, Mets, and Dodgers fought it. But in the end, it passed by a vote of 19–1. Under the plan, the team that finished with the worst record would choose first, while the team that won the World Series had the last selection. With no bidding for players, signing bonuses would go down.

It was the "worst choose first" criterion that gave the New York Mets the initial pick in the June 1966 amateur draft based upon their 1965 won-loss record. The Kansas City Athletics would select second.

Evaluators had reached an opinion that the draft-eligible talent available in 1966 was the best in years. "Last year I was wondering if we could pick up as many as three players," noted Paul Richards. "This year, give me the 20 of the first round, and in three years, I guarantee you that team would make trouble for anybody. And I mean anybody." At the head of that crop were two players, Steve Chilcott and Reggie Jackson. By the Memorial Day holiday Chilcott was batting a jaw-dropping .647 in league games, which hiked his overall batting average for the season to .500. The powerful catcher was clubbing an average of one home run a game through league play. Reggie Jackson had broken both the home-run and strikeout records at Arizona State. It became the consensus among scouts and executives of the 20 teams in major-league baseball that either Chilcott or Jackson would be the first player selected in the draft on June 7.

In the final two weeks before the draft, debate and decision-making grew intense within the New York Mets front office. Bing Devine, the Mets' assistant general manager, oversaw the team's preparations for the draft. Devine was a veteran baseball man who had laid the foundation for the St. Louis Cardinals' run of success as its general manager. He had made it his policy to respect the information from his scouts and pondered the reports about Chilcott from his men in Southern California: Nelson Burbrink, Charlie Frey, and Dutch Zwilling. Perhaps the biggest advocate for Chilcott, however, was Casey Stengel, who reminded Devine that the Mets' farm system lacked a legitimate catching prospect.

Days before the draft, Chilcott reaped a bevy of awards. He was named Antelope Valley High School's Senior Athlete of the Year and the Most Valuable Player on the baseball team. The Helms Foundation named the catcher its Southern California Player of the Year. Coaches voted Chilcott the MVP of the Golden League.

By Tuesday, June 7, 1966, evaluations had been completed. The debates were finished. Among the scouting directors of the 20 major-league clubs, tensions and expectations had reached their peak. Representatives of each club strode into a meeting room at the grand Roosevelt Hotel in midtown Manhattan in New York, baseball's second-ever amateur draft. A phalanx of phone lines resembling spilled spaghetti covered the floor. Rows of tables and chairs were set up for the clubs to operate from. The first order of business was to punch an index finger into the dialer and call the office to make sure communication was established.

A roar from more than 50 men representing the baseball commissioner's office, the National and American league staffs, and all 20 major-league clubs filled the air. Finally, proceedings were called to order, and attention was focused on the New York Mets, who were called to make the first selection. George Weiss, the Mets' general manager, breathed a name into the phone. A corresponding identification number was read aloud in the meeting room, followed by the name of the first player chosen: "Steven Lynn Chilcott, catcher, Antelope Valley High School in Lancaster, California."

Several minutes later the Kansas City Athletics announced that they had selected Reggie Jackson from Arizona State. "We were ready to take Chilcott, even though we are already stocked with two young catchers," confessed the Athletics' general manager, Eddie Lopat. "Our reports rate them comparable."

Chilcott celebrated the news with his family. Reporters phoned for comments. "I'm kind of excited but glad it's over so I won't have to worry anymore," the teen told *The Los Angeles Times*. "It's an honor to even be mentioned in the first round, and I'm real satisfied that I'm with the Mets." In New York, Bing Devine told reporters that Chilcott and Jackson were rated, "even up." He explained that, "We went for Chilcott because we thought that catching was our greatest need."

Following the draft, Devine went to each of the other 19 tables. Curious, he asked the clubs' representatives which player they had rated number one on their draft list. Ten said Reggie Jackson. The other nine replied that Chilcott was at the top of their list.

The Mets had to wait ten days for Chilcott to graduate from high school before they could begin negotiations. The team assigned responsibility for negotiations to their head California area scout Nelson Burbrink, who took Casey Stengel along on his initial visit to the Chilcott family. Burbrink and the family met three more times before the player's father, Robert, asked the Mets' representatives for a few days so the family could retreat "to the mountains to think things over."

On a Thursday afternoon, just over two weeks after he had been chosen by the team, Chilcott signed his name to a New York Mets contract.

8. The Whole Package

"I'm really happy it's over. I'm anxious to play ball," the catcher told Marshall Klein of the *Los Angeles Times*. The player's high school coach told reporters that with makeable incentives, Chilcott's signing bonus exceeded $100,000. With the ink on the paper barely dry, the prized prospect was dispatched across the country to launch his professional career.

The 22 professional baseball rookies who arrived in Marion, Virginia, to launch their careers were a blend of the confident, the curious, and the overwhelmed. Most were just out of high school and away from home for the very first time. Many the players were directed to a local boarding house, where they would spend the season in a room with two beds and a dresser and nurtured by an understanding couple. Homesickness would drive at least one player off. Reputation and expectation preceded Steve Chilcott's arrival in Marion. Both were delivered by countless newspaper articles and rite-ups in *The Sporting News*. When the team began preseason workouts in their small ballpark, it was a given that the first player chosen in the entire draft would be the best player on the Marion Mets.

The first thing that impressed was a "linebacker's body." Once the prized prospect stepped into the batting cage, he displayed a powerful left-handed swing. During infield drills the catcher whistled throws to second base quicker than his teammates had ever seen. But once the Appalachian League season began, however, Chilcott was more mortal than Superman. In fact, the play of the number one pick raised concern within the Mets front office. Through his first 14 games Chilcott managed just seven hits in 36 trips to the plate. He had shown none of the power that the Mets' west coast scouts had marveled at. The teen's batting average was a paltry .226.

Johnny Murphy, who ran the Mets' farm system, blamed conditions in the Appalachian League. He railed at the "poor" lighting in ballparks around the league. Players nodded in agreement when they read Murphy's comments in *The Sporting News*. Murphy criticized the plethora of night games in a league filled with players "who have done practically all of their previous playing in daylight." Specifically, about his team's number one pick, Murphy snapped that "batting practice in these games takes place before darkness. At that time Chilcott ... would rifle shots over the fence. But when the game began ... his entire swing was out of kilter, and he would be hitting bloopers in the opposite direction."

The Mets quickly got Chilcott out of Marion and the Appalachian League and to another of their farm clubs, the Auburn, New York, Mets in the Class A New York-Pennsylvania League. "The company might be tougher," Murphy said, "but the lights were somewhat better." With his new club, Chilcott got a taste of the major leagues. The Mets played the New York Yankees' Binghamton farm club in Yankee Stadium. With Mets executives watching, the rookie lined a ground-rule double into the right-field seats and deftly caught his teammate Jerry Koosman in an Auburn Mets victory.

Awe accompanied reputation and expectation when Chilcott joined up with the Winter Haven Mets for the 1967 season. The New York brass assigned the touted prospect to spend his first full season of minor-league ball with their Class A farm club in the Florida State League. It was a league stocked with talented prospects. Those with the Winter Haven Mets may have been a cut above. Ken Singleton was being mentioned in the same breath with Mickey Mantle. Mike Jorgenson was ticketed for a rapid rise through the farm system. First- and second-round draft picks dotted the roster. The most gifted player of the bunch was Steve Chilcott.

The first time Fred Nori positioned himself at the second-base bag to take a throw from Chilcott, he watched with amazement as the ball appeared headed for the pitching rubber then rose steadily until it smacked with searing intensity into his glove. More than one Met noted Chilcott's "linebacker build." Teammates marveled at their catcher's tools. "A lot of pulling power," admired Dick Noe. The ball sounds different coming off his bat," said Nori. "He's the whole package."

Chilcott settled into a rented house with three teammates: Dick Noe, Ed Lindblad, and Mike Gerich. When he learned the area's famous Chain O' Lakes were well stocked with largemouth bass, the Mets' starting catcher and Noe secured use of a boat and regularly went out at the crack of dawn in quest. Noe, a Pennsylvanian, knew Florida from previous spring trainings. He insisted on one hard-and-fast rule when fishing with the Californian. Regardless of how well the fish were biting, they had to be off the water by 8:30, or else they'd "be eaten alive by mosquitos."

Over the first two weeks of the season, the Winter Haven Mets were the first team in the Florida State League to tally 10 wins. A month in, they had won 22 games. The club was playing at a .710 clip and sat comfortably in first place. Chilcott turned heads with his power. Teammates kidded that he led the league in home runs that were hooked foul. Many were hit jaw-dropping distances. It wasn't long before opposing pitchers began to intentionally walk the heralded prospect. Chilcott became frustrated. While Chilcott's hitting was among the reasons for his team's success, so too was his play behind the plate. Catching an eclectic pitching staff that was comprised of hard throwers such as Ronnie Paul, a curveball specialist, Jerry Bark, and Noe, who primarily threw a hard-breaking slider,

Chilcott had both the fewest errors and among the least passed balls of any starting catcher in the league. If other catchers had more impressive assist totals, it was because opponents knew full well that the heralded number one pick had a powerful throwing arm, and they elected not to attempt stolen bases when he was behind the plate.

A lot of young catchers in the minor leagues don't like to call for the breaking pitch. The pitchers, especially at the lower levels, don't always control their curveball or their slider very well. There are catchers who worry that they might look bad when the balls skip in the dirt and go to the backstop. The last thing they want is for their manager to turn in a less-than-favorable report about their catching, so they won't call for the curveball. When I saw Chilcott, he wasn't like that at all. He didn't have any problem calling for the curveball.

Winter Haven was a baseball classroom, and for Chilcott, one of his professors was his roommate, Dick Noe. A relief pitcher, Noe had spent three seasons in the Baltimore Orioles' farm system before joining the Mets organization as the player to be named later in a trade. He shared with his roommate the lessons he had learned from managers such as George Bamberger and Cal Ripken in the Orioles' system. During a game, Noe wouldn't hesitate to call "time" and beckon his catcher to the mound. "You've got to put down some dummy signs," he implored during one such conference. "You can't just call for the fastball. When the hitter sees me nod, right away he'll know what's coming. You've got to put down some fake signs and let me shake off a few so it'll confuse him." He would suggest to Chilcott that if he noticed a hitter leaning over the plate as if he were looking for a slider, the catcher should call for a fastball to move the hitter off the plate. He shared Cal Ripken's lesson that if Chilcott were to ever notice a batter peeking and trying to steal the sign or catch a glimpse of where the catcher was setting up to figure out what pitch was coming, you hit him. If you want to hit a batter, you aim at his rear end because you "can't move your rear end fast enough." On the other hand, if you need to send a hitter a message, "throw at the head. Because they can duck, they can dive, they can get out of the way."

The Winter Haven Mets traversed the Florida State League in a dilapidated old bus. Long treks to Miami or Cocoa made players pray that their manager wouldn't order afternoon batting practice, and they could get a couple of extra hours of sleep. The league was a wide-ranging collection of both towns and ballparks. In Miami, the team played in a 13,000-seat stadium that had once been home to class AAA baseball. When

Chilcott and the Mets came to town, the legendary Hall of Fame slugger, Jimmie Foxx, was among the large crowd that turned up to see the heralded prospect. In the tiny ballpark in Cocoa, a light failure interrupted a no-hit effort. No destination was more loathed than games in Leesburg. "The worst," grimaced Ronnie Paul, "real bad mosquitos." In fact, almost every afternoon batting practice would be interrupted by the drone of an approaching bi-plane. Players would hurry into the clubhouse or under the stands while the plane sprayed the ballpark and surrounding area with an oily substance meant to kill mosquito larvae.

When the Mets traveled to posh West Palm Beach to play the Braves' farm team, a mischievous idea came over Chilcott and his three roommates. The four ballplayers clad in denim jeans strolled into a Rolls Royce dealership. A salesman in a black suit approached. "Are you guys lost?" he asked. "Tell us a little about your new model," Chilcott replied. When the man tried to find a diplomatic way of saying that the car was out of the 18-year old's price range, Chilcott whipped out his checkbook and displayed the balance—over $60,000. "Do you know, some of those zeroes are wrong," the man shot back. Teammates chuckled. "His name is Steve Chilcott," one of the ballplayers chortled then explained to the puzzled salesman that their teammate had been the first pick in the baseball draft and signed with the New York Mets for over $100,000.

A similar reaction happened when Chilcott attempted to write a check to pay for groceries in Winter Haven. The checker's eyes bulged when she noticed the balance in the ballplayer's checkbook. "Son, do you have some of those zeroes wrong?"

By the middle of July, Chilcott was second in the league in batting. His .292 average was topped only by Orlando's Herman Hill, who had vaulted to the top of the statistical charts, courtesy of a 26-game hitting streak. Then came a game on July 23 that would change the course of Steve Chilcott's career and his life. The Winter Haven slugger was on second base. The opposing pitcher, believing that he could pick Chilcott off, spun and quickly threw toward the bag. Chilcott dove headfirst to try to beat the tag. The play was close. Chilcott was convinced that he saw the umpire raise his right arm to signal that he was out, so he began to jog toward his team's dugout. Five feet from the bag he realized his mistake; he was not out. The Winter Haven star turned and dove toward second base. As Chilcott reached for the bag with his right arm, the opposing second baseman lost his balance and fell on top of the heralded prospect's right shoulder. Pain shot through the joint. Not only could he not complete the game, but the injury left the Winter Haven catcher unable to play for the remainder of the season.

8. The Whole Package

Chilcott had finished the season with a .290 batting average, 20 doubles, 6 home runs and 45 runs batted in while playing 79 games. Yet while he sat out injured, a firestorm ignited. In Kansas City, Reggie Jackson was promoted to the major leagues. The contrast between the top two 1966 draft picks brought barbs from provocative columnists that provoked ire among Mets fans, long frustrated by their team's losing ways and questioning their team's draft decision.

The following spring, "Did you hear about Chilcott?" was a common refrain around the Mets camp. Enthusiasm about the catcher's prospects began to wane. Over the next two years the shoulder injury and military commitments limited Chilcott to just 26 games. It took cortisone shots to relieve the pain and allow him to play. Fourteen times the catcher suffered semi-dislocations of his right shoulder. The injury had reduced to mediocrity the throwing arm that had evoked fear on high school football fields and awe on the baseball diamond.

During the fall of 1968 season, Chilcott entered the Army. He was stationed at Fort Ord on the Central California coast. While taking part in a drill that involved crawling on his elbows, Chilcott felt his right shoulder painfully pop. He said nothing until he had been discharged and then reported the injury to the Mets. Arrangements were made for the catcher to be examined by Dr. Robert Kerlan in Los Angeles. The noted physician recommended surgery. Chilcott was flown to New York for a second opinion by the Mets' team doctor. After a two-day examination, Dr. Peter La Motte told the team that their talented prospect had suffered a partial subluxation of the right shoulder. The only way to avoid surgery, the doctor advised, was to switch Chilcott to another position that involved less throwing.

In early March, Chilcott reported to the Mets' spring training complex for tutoring on playing first base. One month later he was among 22 players who arrived in Visalia in Central California to play for the Mets' Class A farm club in the California League. "Catching is out," the club's manager, Roy McMillan, told the *Visalia Times Delta* sports editor, Mike Novin. "But we think he can help us at first base."

On Meet the Team Night, Chilcott wowed the crowd with long batting-practice home runs that sailed well beyond the Recreation Park fences. When the season began, the Visalia first baseman hit safely in each of his team's first six games. Pain was a part of every inning and each at-bat. Finally, after going hitless in a game against San Jose, Chilcott's pain reached a level that made the Mets bring him to New York for another examination.

On May 9 Chilcott surrendered to the surgeon's scalpel. In an extensive procedure, damage was repaired to the ballplayer's right shoulder. He spent ten days in New York's Roosevelt Hospital recovering. The *Visalia Times Delta* published the hospital's mailing address so Visalia Mets fans could send get-well cards and letters.

Recovery was slow. A month after the surgery, Chilcott returned to Central California and watched from the stands in Fresno as his teammates played the Giants' farmhands. "The season is over for me," the player told the *Times Delta*'s Novin, adding that he was considering taking real estate classes, "so at least I can accomplish something by going to school."

That fall, as Chilcott continued to recover from surgery, a half dozen of his former minor-league teammates helped the Mets win the World Series and cap an amazing turnaround for the once-woeful franchise.

During spring in 1970, a photograph made it into the newspapers that gave ominous notice to Steve Chilcott's future. A topless Chilcott sat on a table in the Mets' training room. Joe Deer, the team's trainer, had both hands on Chilcott's right shoulder and was manipulating the joint. Grabbing the attention of the reader was a six-inch, L-shaped scar that ran from the top of Steve Chilcott's throwing shoulder over the deltoid and hooked at a 45-degree angle toward the under arm. The once-pristine hope of a franchise was now damaged goods. The bright forecasts and projections for a successful future were shrouded in doubt.

Chilcott had shown enough in spring training to convince the Mets he could to return to catching. While he began the season with the Mets' Class AA farm club, it was quickly clear to scouts and baseball observers that the injury had slowed Chilcott's throwing release, and his swing wasn't the same. He struggled with the bat. Still, when an injury raised the need for a catcher at the Mets' top farm club, it was Chilcott who got the call-up, even though he was only hitting .209. The move rankled other catchers on his own team and in the organization. "First time I've seen money talk," one groused. "Who says there aren't politics in baseball."

By the spring of 1971, 15 catchers in the New York Mets organization regularly scoured *The Sporting News* to study what the others were doing. It was all part of the competition for advancement that permeates the minor leagues. Each of the 15 catchers had been selected in the draft and signed by the Mets in the three years since Steve Chilcott had suffered his debilitating shoulder injury.

During a spring game of golf, Joe Frazier decided that Steve Chilcott would no longer be part of that competition. The sometimes-volatile Visalia

8. The Whole Package

Mets manager had been assigned the former number one pick. Even though Chilcott had finished the 1970 season with the Mets' top farm club, Frazier regarded someone else as better—another of the recently-drafted catchers, Joe Nolan.

While Chilcott was privately frustrated to be back in the low minors, he didn't let it affect his game. He got the season off to a positive start with a long first-inning home run into the pine trees beyond the right field wall in Recreation Park to help Visalia defeat Reno, 11–7. Two nights later, the once-prized prospect drove in five runs with a two-run double and a three-run home run. Three weeks into the season, Chilcott led the California League in home runs with five.

The celebrated draft pick's torrid hitting to begin the season climaxed with a six-RBI night against San Jose in the middle of May. In that game Chilcott had four hits, including a two-run home run in the first inning and a three-run home run in the fifth inning. On the fifth anniversary of his milestone selection in the amateur draft, Steve Chilcott smashed a game-winning three-run home run to leave Visalia sitting in first place in the California League standings.

In mid–May, Frazier learned that the Mets were planning to release a first baseman who was struggling at class AA, George Theodore. In perhaps the clearest signal of Steve Chilcott's standing in the Mets organization, Frazier asked that Theodore be assigned to Visalia. Between Nolan's strong play and the arrival of Theodore, Steve Chilcott was relegated to the bench and occasional starts in the outfield.

Waiting for a teammate to fail in order to gain a second chance was futile. Theodore went on a hitting tear. He averaged a home run every other game and was soon challenging for the league lead in both home runs and batting average. When he wasn't fretting about his wife and daughter being in a rental house from which the owner dealt drugs, Nolan played solid defense. He was topped only by celebrated number one pick, Mike Ivie, in assists by catchers in the California League, and he flirted with a .300 batting average.

The Visalia Mets spent the summer chasing both a pennant and a new California League home-run record. Driven by winning, crowds flocked to watch the Mets play in spite of the searing Central California summer heat. Despite sporadic playing time, Chilcott was a significant contributor to the team's home-run tally. In mid–July Chilcott aroused the excitement of a packed house when he came off the bench to hit a game-winning pinch-hit home run. The next night his grand slam was the highlight of an 11–6 win over Fresno.

With Theodore entrenched at first and Nolan secure behind the plate, Frazier began to give Chilcott more playing time in right field. Through the first two weeks of August, the Mets won 11 of 13 games. The torrid streak helped them to open a five-game league lead. While fun and exuberance enveloped the Visalia Mets, misfortune once again struck Steve Chilcott. During a game in Reno he was tracking a fly ball in right field. As he followed the path of the descending baseball, Chilcott stepped in a sprinkler hole. He split his knee cap. The next time his teammates saw Steve Chilcott, his leg was in a cast.

Little did Steve Chilcott know that the game in which he was injured would be the last he would play in the New York Mets organization. His teammates went on to win Visalia's first-ever California League title. Chilcott finished the year with his best home-run tally, 17, the most runs batted in he had produced in pro ball, 68, as well as nine doubles and a .265 batting average. All of this was achieved while playing in barely over half of his team's games. Yet the Mets determined that at age 22 Chilcott was no longer a prospect. He was outrighted from the team's 40-man, major-league roster then shortly after the season traded to the New York Yankees, who one month into the 1972 season released him and ended his career.

A few years after Chilcott's career ended, some scouts were talking and one said that a lot of finger-pointing went on in the Mets front office after he was traded. The Mets took a lot of criticism from the press for taking the kid ahead of Reggie Jackson. A lot of it was unfair. As we heard it, Casey Stengel got blamed for the pick. He did have a lot of influence. One of the Mets' scouts said, "That's what happens when you let a guy with no scouting experience make that sort of a pick."

Like the annual March return of the swallows to San Juan Capistrano or the arrival of harvesters in cornfields in the Midwest every September, someone somewhere each June for five decades has written of Steve Chilcott's place in baseball history as the only position player ever chosen first in the draft that failed to reach the major leagues. "That's just terrible," Chilcott's former teammate, Fred Nori, groused. One day when he heard criticism of the Mets' decision to draft Chilcott, Nori had enough. "Listen, I played with Steve Chilcott," he said. "He was *not* a flop. Steve Chilcott had a gun for an arm. He could hit for power. He was the whole package." Then Nori trailed off and said, "If only that guy hadn't fallen on his shoulder."

9

CRACKED BY THE WHIP

His is a name that few 21st-century baseball fans know of. In the world of autograph collectors, however, Nestor Chavez is spoken of with reverence. One of the leading Web sites for baseball player autographs calls Chavez's "the crowning jewel of rare signatures." One seasoned collector calls the former pitcher's signature "the Holy Grail" of autographs. The immense value for the signature of Nestor Chavez is a reflection of both the stardom he was on the cusp of and the tragedy that prevented him from reaching it.

In 1963 I was managing Caracas in the Venezuelan winter league. My older brother Chick was the Latin American scout for the San Francisco Giants. He asked if I could arrange for him to hold a tryout camp in our ballpark. On the day of the tryout camp in late September, boys came from all over. Baseball was big in Venezuela. Everyone wanted to be like Alex or Chico Carrasquel or Luis Aparicio, the local heroes who had become big stars in America. There were even boys who came out of the jungle. When we saw them, I looked at Chick and said, "Some of these boys are not human!" At the end of the tryout camp there was one boy, in particular, who stood out. He was just 16. Chick signed him and I added him to my ballclub. The other boys called him *Latigo*, which meant "The Whip!" He was Nestor Chavez.

The teenaged pitcher was the youngest player in the Venezuelan winter league, a league dotted with both local standouts and major-league veterans. During the 50-game season, the pennant was hotly contested. Despite Chavez's young age, his manager did not shy from using him in tense situations.

My pitching staff had some big-league veterans who were pretty good: Eli Grba, Mel Nelson. The veteran players offered the boy pointers. Grba

taught him the slider. I worked with him on his curveball, and I showed him how to throw a changeup. I pitched him out of the bullpen. He didn't pitch a whole lot for me, but he pitched well when he was called upon. When Mel Nelson went home because of an injury, I gave Chavez a start. After the game one of my American players said to me, "The kid's got great poise for someone so young." You could see he had a lot of potential.

Spring training in 1964 was like every other. Rookies come into camp filled with both enthusiasm and a bit of apprehension. The enthusiasm of that first week in professional baseball saw its first signs of wane early in Dick Davey. The rookie catcher had grown weary from having to chase the errant fastballs flung by a hard-throwing young prospect. Amazement from being in the same spring training confines as his baseball heroes, Juan Marichal, Willie Mays, and Willie McCovey, faded into the reality of the sport as business as Davey dropped into the catcher's crouch to handle the next pitcher in the morning bullpen session.

As the 6-foot-3-inch Davey turned his black Giants cap backwards then tugged the catcher's mask over his face, he was momentarily taken aback. Sixty feet, six inches away was a skinny Latin American whom Davey figured was far too young to belong in this complex of professionals. When the boy raised his arms to initiate his windup, turned his torso slightly to the right, kicked his left leg high into the air, and then fired his first pitch in Davey's direction, the college product was in awe. From the first pitch to the last, every ball that flung from the pitcher's index and middle fingers smacked the palm of Davey's mitt. Fastballs, curveballs, sliders, changeups, and even what were clearly experimental offerings of a screwball were all thrown with remarkable accuracy. "He's the best pitcher I ever caught," Davey said with awe. "I never had to move my glove. Great control!" Later in the day, Davey would be dumbfounded to learn that the pitcher with the remarkable control was just 16 years old. He would not forget the boy's name: Nestor Chavez.

Chavez was quiet, serious, and focused his attention on improving his skills. His age helped. The Venezuelan was too young to accompany teammates to the local watering hole, Quick Draws, and that kept him away from the pool hustlers and the cowboys who were keen to make trouble with any ballplayers who drew the attentions of the local girls away from them.

By mid–April, when minor-league teams packed up and left Casa Grande, Arizona, for their summer destinations, Chavez was on his way to the Midwest. He was assigned to the Giants' Class D farm club, the Decatur Commodores. It was a higher classification than most players started their professional careers, and the teen offered several challenges for the Decatur manager, Richie Klaus.

First was the matter of communication. The low minors were for teaching, and Chavez knew barely any English. He certainly couldn't understand what "Old Abe," the stovepipe-hat- wearing, über Commodores fan, shouted from the stands, let alone the instructions of his manager. Next was Chavez's build. He wasn't gangly; he was reed thin. If he was to improve his fastball and endure the five-and-a-half-month season, he would have to put on weight. Then there was the rookie's age. At just 16, Nestor Chavez was not only five years younger than many of his teammates, he was the youngest player in all of professional baseball.

Nestor Chavez battles in spring training for a spot on the San Francisco Giants. At the end of the season he would be in the big leagues. One year later Chavez would die in a horrific plane crash. (Dan Taylor)

Klaus was an easy-going man who was quick to laugh and liked to make the game fun for his players. He paired Chavez up with another Spanish speaker on the team, Miguel Sanchez. The two would be roommates, and Sanchez helped as Chavez's interpreter. Klaus elected to ease Chavez into pro ball and use him mostly out of the bullpen as a long reliever in non-pressure situations. And for the matter of putting on weight, Chavez was instructed to drink milkshakes, lots of them, and to eat plenty of cheeseburgers. The one matter Klaus couldn't do anything about was one that Chavez struggled with privately—homesickness. "He misses his family very much," Sanchez told teammates.

While other boys his age in Decatur were spending their summer handling paper routes, working at filling stations, or stocking store shelves,

Nestor Chavez was challenging some of the best young hitting prospects in baseball—Rick Reichardt, Reggie Smith, and Dave May—and having success. Klaus was particularly impressed with the young pitcher's poise. "Nothing seems to bother him. He's a natural," the manager told a reporter for the local newspaper.

As the summer progressed, the teenaged Venezuelan became a model in maturity. Klaus' confidence in Chavez grew, and he gave the young prospect several starts. By June he held a 5–1 record and an earned-run average of 3.00. Stamina, however, was the rookie's Achilles' heel. In several of his starts Chavez pitched well for five or six innings, only to run out of steam, get hit hard, and have to come out of the game. By season's end Chavez had earned six wins, tossed three complete games, and made more pitching appearances than all but two of his teammates.

Klaus took Chavez back to Decatur for the 1965 season, and this time there was no question about either Chavez's role on the pitching staff nor who "Old Abe" was leading cheers for. Nestor Chavez was the ace. The cheers on nights that he pitched were undeniably for him. Within three months the teenager would grow in both mound dominance and regard. Chavez pitched his way into the Midwest League record books with performances that would evoke marvel for decades.

Chavez pitched a four-hit shutout in his first start of the season, but his ascension to renown began in May on the Memorial Day weekend, he went the distance to beat Cedar Rapids in the first game of a doubleheader. Over the next three months the league's youngest player pitched 18 consecutive complete games. Chavez's streak was snapped on August 23, but only after he had thrown 13 innings in a game that Decatur lost an inning later, 5–4.

One-third of the wins during the streak were shutouts. During the month of July, he pitched three in succession—a five-hit, 12-strikeout blanking of Clinton, followed by a four-hitter with 10 strikeouts to beat Quad Cities, and finally a two-hit gem in which Chavez fanned 11 Waterloo batters. During the three-month-long streak, Chavez amassed a 1.99 earned run average. "Outstanding," Klaus gushed to a sportswriter after one of Chavez's wins. "If he walks a man, you can bet the last pitch could have been called either way."

The success drew a reward. A day after the streak was snapped, Chavez was promoted to the Giants' Class AA farm club. He concluded his season with 13 wins, 12 at Decatur and one for Springfield. His 20 overall complete games and seven total shutouts were the best tallies in the Midwest League, while his 2.15 earned-run average was the best among all pitchers who made at least 20 starts.

9. Cracked by the Whip

In the Giants Candlestick Park offices, the player who had previously been mentioned in the same breath as Juan Marichal only because of his higher-than-usual leg kick now drew comparisons to the San Francisco pitching ace because of his makeup, pitches, and success. Not long after Chavez arrived home in Venezuela, he received more spoils from his record-setting season—a contract from the Giants that called for promotion to San Francisco's top farm club for 1966.

The offseason was no vacation for Nestor Chavez. He pitched for Magallanes in the Venezuelan winter league, where he won five games and helped his team to the semifinals of the playoffs. Swelling enthusiasm at being one rung on the minor-league ladder away from the big leagues would soon be deflated by two men, Bill Werle and Rosy Ryan.

Werle, the Phoenix manager, ignored Chavez's Midwest League records and declared that the 18-year-old would pitch out of the bullpen. "He won't blow the game by walking someone," was the manager's explanation. Ryan, on the other hand, was less head-scratching paradox and more out-and-out road block.

Rosy Ryan ran our Triple A club, and he had an old-school arrangement with Horace Stoneham. Horace let him handle all of the player moves for his ballclub. Jack Schwarz used to say to me, "Carl [Hubbell] and I run the farm system up to Triple A. Rosy handles it from there." Rosy wasn't about development. He made a lot of decisions that were either for business reasons, came from his emotions, or were about winning. If he didn't like you, that could be it for you. He killed a lot of careers.

The Pacific Coast League was in its first season in Phoenix in 1966, and naysayers protested that the club would never draw enough fans to survive. The summer was too hot and the population too small. Ryan tried to counter the first problem by having 42 evaporative coolers installed around Municipal Stadium. He instituted gimmicks that he hoped would boost attendance. Then, when that didn't generate the results he wanted, Ryan turned to his roster and signed veterans such as former Yankees star Don Larsen, whom he thought would be a drawing card.

It was only three weeks into the season that Chavez made Bill Werle rethink the decision to use the prospect solely in relief. The manager had summoned Chavez in the sixth inning of a game against Oklahoma City, and the pitcher responded by retiring all 12 batters that he faced. "His fastball was hopping," the manager told a local sportswriter. After another strong outing two nights later in Tulsa, Werle moved Chavez into his starting rotation.

In his first start, Chavez pitched Phoenix to a win over Indianapolis that snapped a five-game losing streak. Five nights later he opened a game with Oklahoma City by flinging three scoreless innings. In the fourth inning, however, came a play that would change the course of his season. Chavez gave up two singles then surrendered a walk to load the bases. He registered a strikeout for the first out of the inning then turned his attention to retiring a top Houston Astros prospect, Aaron Pointer. Chavez got the result he wanted but made a decision that had both Werle and Ryan tearing at their hair. Pointer topped a one-hopper right back to Chavez, but instead of throwing the ball to his catcher for the force out at home, he spun and fired it toward second base.

Rather than initiate a double play, Chavez's throw sailed into center field. Two runners scored, and Oklahoma City went on to win, 4–1. Ryan was fit to be tied and in days had Chavez demoted to the Giants' Class AA club in Waterbury, Connecticut.

When Chavez joined his new club, he stepped into a welcoming environment. The manager, Andy Gilbert, had played a big part in guiding Juan Marichal toward stardom and was happy to have Chavez on his club. Gilbert spoke Spanish and invested time in tutoring his Spanish-speaking players in their own language. Chavez found familiar faces in the clubhouse, particularly a fellow Venezuelan, Damaso Blanco. Julio Linares was infectiously enthusiastic. "Luck will change. Luck will change," he liked to say to teammates after losses. Jose Morales caught when he wasn't battling injuries.

Not everyone was entirely welcoming. Bruce Nichols was one of the catchers on the ballclub. He had played against Chavez in the Midwest League, where he "hated to face him." Chavez frequently frustrated Nichols, who would trudge back to the dugout after at-bats against the young prospect muttering to himself, "Why am I always off balance against this guy?" Nichols had heard his teammates refer to Chavez as "the next Juan Marichal." He soon came to understand why. Nichols became impressed with the 18-year-old's array of pitches and impeccable control. "He's not afraid to throw any of his pitches, and I'm not afraid to call them," Nichols said. "Catching him is easy, like having a night off." Gilbert used Chavez primarily as a starting pitcher. During the month of August, he started six games, completed four of them, and won three. By the time the season ended, Bruce Nichols had come to relish being on the other end of Chavez's dispensation of frustration, and catcher and pitcher were fast friends.

While the statistics and press clippings didn't generate the regard of

9. Cracked by the Whip

the previous season, those that counted within the Giants organization were impressed with Chavez's performances. After discussions in early October, the decision was made to place the young pitcher on the major-league team's 40-man roster. Chavez would get a crack at pitching his way onto the big-league club in spring training.

Home in Venezuela, stardom began to unfold. Chavez celebrated news of his promotion by pitching eight shutout innings for Magallanes in their winter-league game against Cardinals. Days later he blanked Aragua on a two-hitter. During the latter half of the season, Chavez locked up with a pair of big-league hurlers in tense pitchers' duels. He lost both, 1–0, falling to Mel Queen and Aragua then Jim McGlothlin and Valencia. The highlight of the winter for Chavez didn't take place on the diamond, however. A month before he departed for spring training, he married Carmen Elena Von der Belje.

After a spring audition under the watchful gaze of the San Francisco Giants' hierarchy, Chavez was assigned to pitch for Phoenix. His stay lasted just two weeks. Rosy Ryan again wanted the 38-year-old ex-Yankee, Don Larsen, on his club for the box office appeal. Once Larsen was in shape and ready to pitch, Chavez was demoted to Class AA Waterbury.

If Chavez was angry with Ryan, he didn't articulate it but instead tried to prove his value on the field. In almost no time Chavez established himself as the most dominant pitcher in the Eastern League. He won his first three starts by shutout then dealt Readings' Dallas Green his first defeat of the season for his fourth consecutive victory. Now it was his pitching and not just the high leg kick that drew comparisons with the San Francisco ace, Juan Marichal. "He isn't in Marichal's class right now. But he's at the same stage of development Marichal was when I had him at Springfield," Andy Gilbert explained to a reporter.

Friendship grew with a young outfielder, Bobby Bonds, and his wife, Pat. Bruce Nichols and his wife tried to help Chavez's young bride become comfortable in the U.S. The Nichols were especially thrilled when Nestor and Carmen revealed that they were expecting a baby. Appreciation for the friendship heightened one night when the Nichols had to rush the expectant mother to the hospital with premature labor pains.

On July 7, the day after his 20th birthday, Chavez became the first pitcher in the league to win 10 games. Three weeks later Ryan called. Phoenix needed pitching help, and the team's general manager wanted Chavez. With 12 wins to his credit, a league-leading 15 complete games, seven shutouts, and an earned-run average of 1.79 that trailed only Mets prospect Jim McAndrew, Nestor Chavez packed his bags for Phoenix.

Chavez won six more games for Phoenix, and after earning his 18th win of the season, he got the news that he was going to the big leagues. When the young pitcher stepped into the home team's clubhouse at Candlestick Park, he heard, "*Bienvenido a las grandes ligas*," and turned to see Juan Marichal and other Latin players welcome him to the major leagues. Eddie Logan, the equipment manager, pointed Chavez to a locker where he found a bright white Giants jersey with the number 32 hanging.

Four days later on Saturday, September 9, Chavez saw his first big-league action. Herman Franks sent the young sensation on in relief to start the seventh inning against the Chicago Cubs. The game had reached the latter hours of the afternoon. Wind kicked up off of San Francisco Bay. Hot dog wrappers and a few empty popcorn boxes blew about the park. Loud cheers from a crowd of more than 25,000 fans had been quelled by a 6–1 Cubs lead. The first three hitters that Nestor Chavez would face in the major leagues were the best in the Cubs lineup—Billy Williams, Ron Santo, and Ernie Banks. It was a daunting challenge for a rookie.

From the press box, the Giants' statistician, Art Santo Domingo, did a double take at the young pitcher's similarity to Marichal. Chavez induced Williams to ground out. Santo walked, then Banks lofted a lazy fly ball to Willie Mays in center field for the second out of the inning. As many a young pitcher learns, the bottom half of a big-league batting order can hurt you just as much as the fearful middle hitters. That was the lesson Nestor Chavez took away from his debut.

Randy Hundley drove a single to left field that suddenly created potential for a rally. Chavez remained calm and focused. When Bob Raudman topped a breaking ball toward the shortstop, everyone in the ballpark felt relief that the Giants would escape trouble. Hal Lanier, however, made an errant throw that allowed Santo to score. Adolfo Phillips followed Raudman with a single to left field that brought Hundley chugging home with the Cubs' second run of the inning, which made the score 8–1. Groans and catcalls from the stands were short-lived. Chavez struck out the Cubs' pitcher, Rich Nye, to end the inning and his first taste of action in the major leagues.

With the Giants in a battle with the Cubs and Cincinnati Reds for second place in the National League, Chavez became an observer. He used the opportunity to talk pitching with Marichal and study Mike McCormick, Bob Bolin, and Gaylord Perry.

On the final weekend of the season, Chavez got into his second game. It came during a Saturday doubleheader with Philadelphia. The Giants had won the first game, 3–2, to clinch second place. After three innings of the second game, Herman Franks handed the ball to Chavez. The 20-year-old pitched four innings and was dazzling. He struck out the first batter that he faced, Gary Sutherland, then retired the next six in a row. When he came out of the game after the seventh inning, he had allowed just two hits and only walked two, one of which was intentional. His teammates had scored the only run of the game while Nestor was in the lineup, thus earning him the win, his first in the major leagues and the 19th of the season at the three levels at which he had pitched.

Chavez carried the surge of momentum into the Venezuelan winter season. He opened the season by pitching a four-hit shutout to beat La Guaira and went on to win five games for Magallanes. In January the regular-season champions, Caracas Leones, recruited Chavez to join their club for the playoffs. Leones had a powerful pitching staff that featured Luis Tiant and Diego Segui. The playoffs began with a nine-game, round-robin tournament. In game four, Chavez was handed the ball to pitch and produced one of the greatest performances in Venezuelan winter-league history. Against Valencia, Chavez retired the first two batters in the game before Gus Gil beat out a slow roller on the infield for a single. Gil was the last Valencia batter who would reach base in the game. Chavez retired the next 25 batters in a row, a Venezuelan League playoff record. Fans spilled onto the field to mob their hero. So overwhelming was Chavez that he permitted only five balls to be hit out of the infield in the 3–0 one-hitter.

Exhilaration reached an even loftier height for Nestor Chavez six days later, when Carmen gave birth to a son. The couple christened the boy Nestor Junior.

As January turned to February, Caracas had stormed through the round-robin tournament and into the semifinals. In the final game of the semifinal series, Leones needed a win to advance to the title series. When the starting pitcher struggled during the first two innings, the Leones manager, Reggie Otero, turned to Nestor Chavez for help. Over the next six and one-third innings, Chavez mowed down the rival batting order. Leones rallied to win and advanced to the title series. The championship and record-setting performance placed a fitting exclamation mark on a brilliant season for the 21-year-old, who was knocking at stardom's door.

Optimism that his brilliant summer and record-setting winter ball season would vault Nestor Chavez onto the San Francisco Giants' 1968 pitching staff was tempered by the picture of reality when the young Venezuelan arrived for spring training. All around him in the Giants' Casa Grande, Arizona, camp were veterans who had held firm roles during the previous season. The one slim possibility that a rookie might crack the pitching staff involved Lindy McDaniel. The stellar relief specialist had been plagued by a sore arm the previous summer. In the event that McDaniel would not be ready for the start of the season, Chavez and two other rookies would be auditioned for his role.

Chavez pitched an impressive three innings against the Cubs in one of the Giants' first exhibition games. He didn't walk a man nor allow a run. It was a week later before he pitched again. In an inning against Cleveland he was tagged for two runs. In one of the final days of camp, however, Chavez was sent to the minor leagues. He would once again pitch for Phoenix.

As outstanding as the 1967 season had been for Chavez, the 1968 season was calamitous. In the second game of the season, the pitcher endured a rocky third inning then settled down to retire the next seven Oklahoma City batters in a row. In the bottom of the fifth inning, Chavez walked then promptly raced for third base when Tito Fuentes doubled. As the pitcher slid into the third-base bag, he rolled his right ankle and shouted out in pain. The team's trainer, Harry Jordan, and the manager, Clyde King, ran to the young prospect's aid and helped Chavez to the training room. Jordan made arrangements for Chavez to go to the hospital for X-rays. King was worried that the pitcher may have broken his ankle. Jordan told a sportswriter later that night that the X-rays didn't show a break, and it was likely a strained tendon in the ankle.

It was more than a month before Chavez pitched again. King used him only in relief for the next three weeks. Once he resumed his place in the pitching rotation in mid-June, the bad luck that soured the start of the season was followed by bad breaks over a series of starts. He had strong starts against Portland and Denver then lost pitchers' duels with Seattle, Vancouver, and Indianapolis.

After being hammered in a start in late July, Chavez complained of a problem to Harry Jordan. Discomfort in the pitcher's right elbow had grown into a sharp pain. A doctor diagnosed calcium deposits and recommended surgery to remove them. The diagnosis put Chavez on the disabled list and brought an end to his 1968 season.

For the first time in five years, Chavez was unable to pitch in winter ball. He stirred while he recovered from elbow surgery. The pitcher spent the winter months spectating winter-league games. He traveled to the Dominican Republic to help Juan Marichal with a baseball camp. The bright moments came from playing with Nestor Jr., and spending time with Carmen.

9. Cracked by the Whip

In the middle of March, Chavez was due in Arizona for a physical and to receive rehabilitation instructions for his injured elbow. On the date of the examination, however, the pitcher did not show up. Teammates began to wonder. As each day passed and Chavez failed to appear at the Giants' complex, friends such as Bonds and Nichols would ask their manager if the organization had gotten any word about the player's whereabouts. "Where is he?" teammates asked. It was completely out of character for Chavez to be late.

Several days after Chavez's scheduled arrival date, the Giants received dreadful news from Venezuela. A horrifying plane crash there had been on page one of all the American newspapers and led evening newscasts on television. Everyone on the plane had been killed. The Giants learned that one of the passengers on board that fateful flight was Nestor Chavez. The Giants' spring training complex became awash in shock. Bruce Nichols slumped into a chair and sobbed. Bobby Bonds shook his head in silent dismay.

It was unbelievable, really. Just terrible. I hadn't had much contact with him since I became a scout, but I followed his progress. He was such a great kid. He was doing great, and he had a great future. You felt awful for his family, his young wife. Everyone around the complex there in Casa Grande was kinda shook up.

It was a Sunday afternoon, March 16, that Nestor Chavez had boarded the DC-9 for a flight from Maracaibo to Miami. From there he would catch another flight to Phoenix, where he would report for spring training. In the airport Chavez had recognized another ballplayer, Carlos Santeliz, and smiled when the Atlanta Braves' minor-league first baseman said he was on the same flight. Family members accompanied their loved ones onto the tarmac and waved as the stewardess pulled the door shut, and the plane began to taxi toward the runway. Many shielded their eyes from the sun as the plane, after a short pause, began down the runway, building up speed along the way. Several of the onlookers, though, became alarmed. They felt the plane was not moving as fast as it should. It had passed the normal takeoff point and appeared to be struggling to get off the ground. Houses and several rows of apartments lay at the end of the runway. Onlookers began to run toward the plane, convinced that a catastrophe was about to happen. Women screamed and men shouted in horror as the plane slowly lifted off the ground near the runway's end. Its wheels clipped a power line then struck a building, which sent the 91,000-pound aircraft hurtling to the ground. In a split second the air was filled with tragedy.

More than five miles away people heard what they thought was a loud explosion. It was the sound of the plane, full of fuel for the scheduled 1,200-mile flight, bursting into flames on impact. Everyone on board, the 74 passengers, 10 members of the crew, as well as 71 on the ground were killed. Television, radio, and newspaper reports around the world called it the worst aviation disaster the world had seen to that date.

The country suffered under a morose pall. Venezuelans were plunged into deep shock and mourning by the catastrophe. In the town of Barinas, Rosa Ines Chavez consoled her 14-year-old grandson, Hugo. Nestor Chavez was the boy's hero, and he vowed to his grandmother that one day he would pitch in the major leagues just like *El Latigo*. Throughout the weeks and months that followed the crash, tributes were paid to Chavez around the country. In October, when the 1969 Venezuelan winter league season commenced play, a solemn ceremony was held in Estadio José Bernardo Pérez in Valencia. Before a near-capacity crowd, the local ballclub, Navegantes del Magallanes, announced that no Magallanes player would ever again wear the number 23, which had belonged to Nestor Chavez.

By the late 1980s the late pitcher's son, Nestor Chavez, Jr., had carried his father's passion for baseball into success as an amateur ballplayer, although he would never play professionally. Thirty years after the fatal crash, the adolescent boy who had grieved his hero's death had changed career paths and ascended to the Presidency of Venezuela. During his 14 years in office, Hugo Chavez never tired of telling people that his hero was Nestor Isaias Chavez.

Four decades after the crash, the number 23 remains proudly on display at Estadio José Bernardo Pérez in Valencia. It reminds every fan that attends a Magallanes game of euphoria and grief, the greatness and the legacy of Nestor Isaias Chavez.

10

THE MAN AMONG BOYS

The banquet room in the Las Vegas hotel was awash in laughter. Many of the men in the room hadn't seen one another in decades. They were brought together by a reunion. Three of the attendees reminisced and swapped stories in one area of the room. Al Strane laughed about a time in college ball when a powerful left-handed hitter ripped a line drive so hard that it left not just the imprint of the ball's stitches on his brother Bert's chest but the logo of the manufacturer as well. The story made Mick Babler somber. "I never saw a left-handed hitter like Bill Seinsoth," the one-time pitcher remembered. "It didn't matter what I threw or what arm angle I threw from. He hit some rockets!" Reminded of their former teammate, the Strane brothers grew silent and nodded in agreement.

Everybody in Southern California back in the '60s knew about Bill Seinsoth. I went out to see him when he was in high school. What talent. He was mostly a pitcher for his high school team. Nobody could beat him. You could see when it was his turn to bat that he had tremendous power. Every scout in the area followed him. He was definitely a number one.

Bill Seinsoth was a baseball prodigy who had begun to attract the attention of college coaches and impressed pro players with his swing from the age of seven. His father, Bill Sr., had pitched in the minor leagues for 13 seasons. He won 24 games during his best year. In 1944 he broke spring training with the St. Louis Browns but was drafted into the military before he could get into a major-league game.

Bill Seinsoth, Sr., had an unabashed love of baseball. A burly man who threw left-handed, the senior Seinsoth pitched for semipro clubs around Southern California into his fifties. Everybody knew him as "Big Bill." Afternoons he could be found at Arcadia County Park pitching batting practice to pro players who were getting ready for spring training. He welcomed young high school players who offered to shag fly balls and let them grab a bat and take some swings themselves when the pros were finished. Some who watched the father-son relationship might say Seinsoth Sr. encouraged the boy, while others would label it pushing. Bill Seinsoth, Sr., was neither pushy nor overbearing, and his son relished being on the ball field.

The dad was a friend of mine. He had an amateur team like I did, and he used to call me up looking for games. He'd been a pretty good pitcher in the minor leagues. Bill Sr. was a big, strong guy who even in his fifties liked to get on the mound and throw a few innings. He really loved the game, and he passed it on to his son, who was a real chip off the old block.

By the time Bill Seinsoth joined the varsity at Arcadia High School, he was already a local sensation. He raised that reputation by going 11–2 and pitching seven consecutive complete games with a streak of 28 straight scoreless innings to drive his team to the league title. His earned-run average was 0.97. Seinsoth pitched and won all four playoff games to help Arcadia reach the Southern California 3A title game. Before 3,000 fans at Blair Field in Long Beach, however, Seinsoth became mortal. Arcadia lost to Lynwood High, 7–1. Still, his junior season had impressed scouts, foes, and rival coaches. Seinsoth was named first-team all-Pacific League and the only junior selected to the first team all-Southern California team.

When the spring of 1965 arrived, Bill Seinsoth's skills sent every pro scout and college baseball coach in Southern California to Arcadia. Seinsoth's pitching helped his team blitz through their league rivals to claim a second consecutive title. By the time Arcadia High had reached the Southern California title game, Seinsoth had been the winning pitcher in 14 of his team's 20 wins. In the title game, Seinsoth tossed a three-hit shutout, and Arcadia High earned its first-ever region championship. It was no surprise when he was named the Southern California Player of the Year.

Nineteen sixty-five was the first year of the draft. I had Bill as a number one, but you had to be sure you could sign a boy. Bill and his father made it very clear that the boy was going to college. No amount of money was going to change that. Watching him wasn't a waste of my time, though. By scouting Seinsoth, I saw his teammate, Chris Arnold. I liked his arm, and we got him in the draft that year. Chris played six years in the big leagues for the Giants.

The Houston Astros gambled. They used a 15th-round pick in the June 1965 draft to select Seinsoth, but the Astros' scout learned that Bill

10. The Man Among Boys

could not be swayed from his plan to attend college. Once Seinsoth arrived on the USC campus, he expressed another conviction to his new coach, Rod Dedeaux. He no longer wanted to pitch. Bill Seinsoth wanted to play every day. The pronouncement got no argument from Dedeaux. The former Brooklyn Dodgers shortstop had been watching Seinsoth for more than ten years. Dedeaux admired the standout's swing, knew that Seinsoth had hit over .400 every year that he was in high school, and had little doubt he would be a success.

Seinsoth's freshman year was restricted to playing for the USC junior varsity by an NCAA rule that forbid freshman from playing varsity sports. His schooling and preparation for varsity competition began in earnest during the summer of 1966 in, of all places, Fairbanks, Alaska. Like the coaches at most top collegiate baseball programs, Rod Dedeaux arranged for many of his players to play in summer amateur leagues. Top collegians from west coast schools played in the Alaska Summer League, where players lived with host families and, in some cases, received pay from cushy jobs. Seinsoth was second among the Goldpanners' regulars, with a .315 batting average, which trailed only Stanford freshman Bob Boone's .382 mark.

The following summer was an impactful one for the Southern Californian. Hours after he and his teammates arrived in Fairbanks, the city was struck by a massive earthquake. The team's owner and head coach, "Red" Boucher, had his hands full calming frightened, anxious players who wanted nothing more than to be on the first plane out of Fairbanks. The coach's efforts succeeded, and the team went on to put together one of the greatest seasons in Goldpanners history. Seinsoth was its catalyst. With the power-hitting first baseman batting .382, hitting a dozen home runs, and driving in 50 runs, the Goldpanners reached the National Baseball Congress World Series. After winning their first four games, the Goldpanners lost twice and finished fourth. Seinsoth was voted the best professional prospect in the tournament.

During his final year with the Goldpanners, Seinsoth had established himself as the undisputed team leader. The first baseman was also a stickler for fundamentals. One teammate's sloppiness sent the Southern Californian into a rage in the middle of a game. Dan Pastorini, a two-sport standout and future NFL quarterback from Santa Clara University, was the right fielder on the 1968 Goldpanners. During a game, Pastorini overthrew the cutoff man, and Seinsoth verbally admonished the college freshman from his position at first base. Pastorini snapped back, and in an instant the two had to be separated in shallow right field by their teammates.

Throughout the summer, teammates were in awe of one another's skills. Fellow infielders Boone and brothers Al and Bert Stane, who were standouts at Santa Clara University, marveled at Seinsoth's soft hands. "If we get the ball in his area, he's going to turn it into an out," said Bert Stane. Brent Strom marveled at how Seinsoth would, "drop to a knee to take a pickoff throw to be able to pick the runner off." Players were also impressed with Seinsoth's unique approach at the plate. Asked by Al Strane why he took so many pitches, Seinsoth replied that he wasn't just looking for a pitch to hit. "I'm looking for a pitch I can hit hard," he explained. By the time he had completed his three-summer stint with the Goldpanners, he held team records for home runs with 23 and runs batted in with 182.

His father's advice planted not just a talented ballplayer but a serious student on the USC campus. Bill Seinsoth told the pro scouts he was committed to spending four years at USC and might even consider graduate school beyond that. As a freshman, Seinsoth was confined by NCAA rules to the Trojans' junior varsity team and could only watch as the Trojan varsity reached the College World Series. By the spring of 1967, however, the first baseman had launched his own varsity career in an impressive fashion. With Big Bill and his wife Jane fixtures at USC home games, the sophomore first baseman led the Trojans in hitting with a .327 average. "A man among boys," the Trojans' center fielder, Jay Jaffe, noted. Teammates found the sophomore to be serious but likeable and quick to enjoy a good laugh. The hitting of the big first baseman helped the Trojans streak through the schedule with a 29–8 record until a late-season collapse hit. Losses in four of their final seven games dropped the Trojans to third place in the Pac-8 and kept them home when the playoffs began.

Dedeaux always had good teams. He was a good teacher. Their games were always on my list to see. I followed Tom Seaver when he pitched there, and in 1968 USC had Seinsoth, Jim Barr, and Bill Lee. The scouts were all there. They liked those guys a lot.

By the time Bill Seinsoth was a junior, he was considered to be among the top college players in the country. He confirmed that with aplomb during a February exhibition game against a team of Los Angeles Dodgers prospects. Seinsoth slugged a three-run home run to highlight a 4–1 USC triumph. Weeks later, however, Seinsoth's promising season soured when he was hit by a pitch and suffered a broken hand. While the injury had calamitous effect on the first half of USC's season, it proved fortuitous for Seinsoth. He had been playing almost nonstop for three years. A sense of monotony had developed. Now, unable to play and with his hand in a cast, a yearning for the game stirred within. Bill Seinsoth missed baseball and came to appreciate how much the sport meant to him.

Once the doctors removed the cast from his hand and gave clearance to play again, Bill Seinsoth's season resumed with a vengeance. In one of his first games back in the USC lineup, he clobbered a home run against the Trojans' arch rival, UCLA. Six days later, Seinsoth's home run made the Trojans a 4–3 winner over Stanford. Fueled in part by Seinsoth's hitting, USC went on a tear. They won 24 of their last 28 games, claimed the Pac-8 title, and earned a national ranking of number two. Seinsoth finished the regular season as the Pac-8 Conference batting champ with a .429 average.

USC brushed aside Cal State Los Angeles in the District 8 regionals to advance to the College World Series. In Omaha the Trojans were handed a challenging schedule. Their side of the bracket was stacked. In their opening game, BYU held them to just two hits. Seinsoth had one of them in the first inning. BYU errors, however, would hand USC a 5–3 win. The next night, Seinsoth doubled and singled to help the Trojans defeat St. John's, 7–6. When USC took the field against North Carolina State, the Trojans knew that a win would send them into the national championship game. Again, Seinsoth rose to the occasion with two hits and a run batted in to highlight a 2–0 USC win.

The 1968 college baseball championship came down to a battle between USC and Southern Illinois. The Salukis had advanced impressively through the loser's bracket, winning three straight lose-and-go-home games, and they quickly jumped out to a 2–0 lead on USC by the fourth inning. It was then that Bill Seinsoth ended the Trojans fans' worries. The slugger clouted a two-run home run that electrified the crowd and evened the score. With two outs in the ninth inning, USC rallied to win, 4–3, and claim the national championship. Bill Seinsoth, who had hit .389 during the tournament, was named the Most Outstanding Player of the College World Series. *The Sporting News* named Seinsoth to its All-America team.

While Seinsoth and his teammates celebrated winning the national championship, the Los Angeles Dodgers hoped they could lure the slugger into pro ball. They used their fifth-round pick in the June 1968 draft to select the USC standout. Seinsoth's coach was hardly surprised. "He has major-league power, and he can play major-league defense," Rod Dedeaux told the *Los Angeles Times*. While most players routinely take advantage of the bargaining power that exists following their junior season and sign pro contracts, Seinsoth did not. His father had stressed education, and Bill had come to appreciate the wisdom of the advice. "I figure playing here is like playing double A ball," he explained to Dwight Chapin of the *Los Angeles Times*, "If you make it through four years of school at most universities, the odds are you're going to do pretty well."

Seinsoth returned to USC for his senior season. He launched the campaign with a home run against Pepperdine. Days later he hit two in a win over BYU. The afternoon following the his two-home-run game, the Trojans' first baseman and captain doubled twice against the Cougars. Seinsoth's torrid hitting continued at the Riverside Tournament with a home run to highlight a 9–2 win over Delaware and another in an 11–3 win over UCLA.

The third week of April sent the Trojans into Pac-8 conference play. The defending league champs made a statement with a 9–0 conference-opening win over Washington State in which Seinsoth belted a grand slam. Two days later USC faced Oregon State. Seinsoth hit a two-run home run in the first inning to give his team the lead. Later in the game, however, an errant fastball struck Seinsoth just above the right eye. He was hurried across campus to the USC medical center, where doctors used nine stitches to close a gash above the eye. The beaning also left Seinsoth with a badly swollen face and blurred vision that would bother him for several months.

With Seinsoth out, USC's title hopes came crashing to earth. Their rival, UCLA, roared past the Trojans to grab the Pac-8 crown. Having missed a considerable stretch of the season, Seinsoth was named to the all-league second team behind UCLA's standout first baseman, Chris Chambliss.

As the college baseball season concluded, major-league baseball teams huddled to craft their plans for the June draft. Within the Los Angeles Dodgers hierarchy there was considerable discussion about Bill Seinsoth. By returning to USC, Seinsoth was thrown back into the draft pool. Al Campanis, the Dodgers' scouting director, was a close friend of Dedeaux, the USC head coach, and was enamored with Seinsoth. Among the scouts who had evaluated Seinsoth, at least one raised concern. "His defense is okay. He's a pretty good first baseman," the scout said. "But the bat's a bit slow. He anticipates the fastball, and that gives him trouble with the slider." Ben Wade had followed Seinsoth extensively ever since a bird-dog had tipped him off to the teenaged talent several years before. The former big-league pitcher was unflinching in his belief in Seinsoth and recommended the team grab him. When the Dodgers' turn came up in the draft, they made Seinsoth their first-round pick—the eighth overall pick in the 1969 draft. Four days later Wade and Seinsoth agreed on a deal that paid a $40,000 bonus.

10. The Man Among Boys

By the middle of June, the Bakersfield Dodgers were a baseball dichotomy. Despite having three of the best hitters in the Class A California League—Ron Cey, Joe Dodder, and Tom Paciorek—the club was fighting to stay out of last place. In the early afternoon of June 9, Dodder arrived at Sam Lynn Park. As he passed the doorway to the manager's office, he heard "Ducky" LeJohn summon him inside. "Got an outfielder's glove?" the manager asked. Dodder was puzzled. "I can get one," he answered. "Good," LeJohn said as he turned in his chair. "Got a new kid. He's a first baseman. Name's Seinsoth. You'll be playing left field from now on."

The news sent Dodder into a bad mood that didn't change once he had met Seinsoth. Dodder, an Iowan, considered his new teammate to be arrogant, but on reflection thought that all the college players he played with had a chip on their shoulder. Dodder's bad mood grew when he looked at the lineup card for that night's game against Lodi. He was no longer the team's clean-up hitter. Bill Seinsoth was.

The arrival of the newest "B-Dodger" was given fanfare by the local media. "He will be an important run producer and should also help at the gate," wrote columnist Larry Press in the *Bakersfield Californian*. It took Seinsoth a few games, however, to get acclimated to the new level of play and his new home ballpark. Sam Lynn Park in Bakersfield was the only park in minor-league baseball built to face west. That configuration put the setting sun in a left-handed hitter's eyes during the first several innings of a night game. Once the sun went down, a left-handed batter's troubles still weren't over. A prevailing wind kicked up and made it a challenge for left-handed hitters to pull home runs.

It was not until the B-Dodgers reached Stockton that Seinsoth managed his first professional hit. In Visalia four nights later, he hammered two hits in the first game of the series then concluded the set with his first professional home run.

Consistency was not a companion of the Bakersfield Dodgers throughout the summer of 1969. The team would rip off a few consecutive wins then fall into an even longer streak of defeats. Seinsoth too struggled to find consistency. He was seeing far more sliders than he had in college ball, and pitchers who threw the breaking pitch well gave Seinsoth trouble. "The quality in the minors is much more consistent than it is in college," he told Vic Marin of the *Bakersfield Californian*. "You face good pitchers every day, and the pitchers have good sliders. They've mastered their pitches and control."

In early July the rookie confided to a teammate that he was tired. The college season and the intense central California heat had worn on him.

The rookie told the *Californian's* Marin, "I need a month's vacation." The late-night hours and road trips were a change from college life. At USC the Trojans flew to most of their road games. The Bakersfield Dodgers traveled on an old bus, chugging three and a half hours to Stockton, four hours to San Jose, and almost six hours to Reno. What also weighed on Seinsoth was something he confided to few aside from the team's trainer. He continued to struggle with bouts of double vision, which was a lingering effect of the beaning he suffered at USC back in mid–April.

Fatigue and frustrations erupted into fury during a game in early August in Visalia. Seinsoth was drilled with a fastball thrown by the Mets' pitcher. He stood at home plate and shouted in ire at the pitcher. The hurler stomped off the mound and with both words and gestures challenged Seinsoth to take action. In an instant, a bat was dropped and a glove thrown to the ground. The two charged at each other as the Visalia catcher and home-plate umpire scrambled to successfully intercede before punches could be thrown.

Over the final two weeks of the season, Ducky LeJohn made a move that ignited Seinsoth's bat. The manager wrote the former college sensation into the third slot in the batting order ahead of Cey, Paciorek, and Dodder. Seinsoth saw fewer sliders and more fastballs and quickly went on a tear. He hammered out two hits to open a series against the Fresno Giants then had three more hits in a game two nights later. The next night in Modesto, Seinsoth had another three-hit game, and he drove in two runs while also scoring twice. During the final week of the season, Seinsoth homered and rapped out two doubles in a win in Lodi. When the Dodgers returned home for a series with Visalia, Seinsoth's two-hit game highlighted an 11–10 win in the opener. The next night he had two more hits off of Mets pitching prospect Charlie Williams. Then in his team's final home game, Seinsoth had two hits, scored twice, and drove in two runs.

When the team finished their season on September 4 in Reno, Bill Seinsoth had finished strong. For his first 80 games in professional baseball he had a .276 batting average, ten home runs, 37 runs batted in, along with 14 doubles, two triples and four stolen bases. In Los Angeles, the Dodgers were pleased. Ben Wade was heard to call Seinsoth a potential heir to the team's first baseman, Wes Parker, who was about to turn 30.

After the game in Reno, teammates packed their belongings. They talked about winter plans and bid one another goodbye. Within hours the Bakersfield Dodgers would be splintered for another year, each player on the road, and headed for home. It would be six months before the players would see one another again on the first day of spring training. In the case of one teammate, the night would be the last time his teammates and friends would ever see him.

Jay Jaffe was waiting for his girlfriend, Denise, to drop by his parents' home on Sunday morning, when the phone rang with news that left him staggered. Al and Bert Strane were packing up their apartment in Clinton, Iowa. Their season with the Seattle Pilots' farm club had just ended. A teammate dropped by to ask if they had heard the news. Joe Dodder had stayed behind in Bakersfield for a job managing an apartment complex and to attend college at Cal State. It was a day later, on Monday, September 8, that he opened the *Bakersfield Californian*. Like Jaffe had when he answered the phone and the Strane's when they learned from a teammate, Dodder gasped when he saw the headline on page 17. "Star Dodger Rookie Dies in Accident." He stared at the words in disbelief.

On the night of September 6, 1969, tragedy had intersected fate. It occurred on a lonely stretch of Interstate 15, the highway that connects Las Vegas with Southern California. Friends say Seinsoth had gone to Las Vegas after the season to "blow off some steam." The ballplayer's mother was expecting him home on Saturday night. Her son planned to attend the Los Angeles Rams' exhibition game that night at the Coliseum. He had wanted to see his friend from USC, O. J. Simpson, play for the visiting Buffalo Bills.

Seinsoth was motoring through the desolate landscape in his green Volkswagen. He was about 20 minutes from reaching the town of Barstow when his car suddenly veered out of control and overturned. Seinsoth's seatbelt broke. He was thrown from the vehicle. The 22-year-old star athlete was gravely injured with severe head and spinal cord trauma. In spite of his injuries, Seinsoth somehow managed to summon the strength to crawl toward the highway. A motorist noticed the overturned green Volkswagen, stopped and ran to the stricken ballplayer's aid. An ambulance was summoned, and Seinsoth was rushed to the closest hospital in Barstow. Almost immediately doctors realized he needed more care than they were equipped to give, and Seinsoth was hurried to a larger, better-equipped hospital 70 miles away in San Bernardino. From there he was transferred again to Harbor General in Los Angeles. When his parents arrived, they found their son on life-support with little hope of survival. The next day, Bill Seinsoth succumbed to severe head trauma.

Almost immediately after hanging up the telephone, Jay Jaffe and his girlfriend had dashed to Harbor General Hospital. As the couple hurried toward the entrance, they saw Big Bill and Jane Seinsoth. The couple was despondent. In their despair, they shared that they had given consent for their son's corneas and kidneys to be donated. Men in New Orleans and Southern California each received one of the kidneys.

In the days that followed, the California Highway Patrol said there were no witnesses to the accident. An investigation was never able to determine why the car had gone out of control. Dodgers executives told employees and questioners that Seinsoth had probably fallen asleep at the wheel.

For many of Seinsoth's former USC teammates, stepping into the Arcadia Presbyterian Church was the first time they had attended a funeral. Their initial shock had by now turned to disbelief and grief. The throng that turned out to pay respects both at the church and at Rose Hills Memorial Park in Whittier, where Bill Seinsoth was buried, was massive.

Had he lived, I have no doubt Bill would have been a very good major-league ballplayer. He had great talent and most of all, he had a real love of the game. You felt bad for the family, for everyone. He was a great kid. His death was a terrible tragedy.

In the decades since his passing, Bill Seinsoth remains an influence on many of his former teammates. Jay Jaffe became a prominent criminal defense lawyer in Los Angeles. "Bill's death made me focus more on what's really important in life," he said. Seinsoth's former teammates have never wavered in their conviction that greatness was on the horizon. "Had Bill not been killed," Bert Stane pondered, "nobody would have heard of Steve Garvey." Stane's brother Al added, "Bill would have been up there hitting home runs for the Dodgers for a long time."

11

Aloha Means "Goodbye"

Three scouts sat in the bleachers watching a high school baseball showcase. Eighty-degree fall weather made the men loathe the idea of returning home. When one felt raindrops, another looked up. Hank Jones of the Los Angeles Dodgers laughed, "This must be the 17th rain shower since I've been here." The men were in Hawaii, a place that was not a common destination for scouts over the years.

The island's baseball landscape has changed, however. Many in professional baseball point to the late 1970s as the time when Hawaii's garden of baseball talent was watered by a remarkable team and its star, a pitcher who was pegged as a can't-miss, major-league standout—Derek Tatsuno.

Hawaii was part of my territory, but I rarely went over. Aside from some guys back in the '30s, Hawaii had only produced a couple of major leaguers [Mike Lum, 1967, and John Matias, 1970]. Not many teams bothered to scout the islands. The Dodgers had a guy on Maui, Iron Maehara. He was a friend of the O'Malleys. Al Zarilla was a former ballplayer who retired over there and worked for the scouting bureau. There weren't a lot of prospects over there. I had a guy giving me information. Then one day he said, "There's a boy over here who must be seen. He's a left-handed pitcher." I got on a plane and went over, and what I saw was a pitcher with a pretty good arm. He had a lot of ability!

Honolulu was abuzz. Fans pressed through the turnstiles into Aloha Stadium like never before for a college baseball game. Never mind that the seasonal rain showers fell on the large stadium; nothing would dampen the enthusiasm of the fans who settled into the seats.

That the NCAA regionals had come to the island was indicative of the explosion the University of Hawaii had made into college baseball prominence in 1977. Seven years after the school's baseball program had been brought back to life, it had gone from being fodder for teams from military bases around the island to the host of college baseball powers: USC, Fresno State, and Cal State Los Angeles. The winner of the regional championship would earn a trip to the College World Series.

Further magnitude of the significance of the event was its host venue, 50,000-seat Aloha Stadium, and the turnout. As the University of Hawaii prepared to play USC, the largest crowd for an NCAA regional—14,006—settled into their seats. "Great. Absolutely great," marveled the Fresno State coach, Bob Bennett, to a sportswriter. "The turnout is just tremendous."

As Bennett scanned the crowd, the match that had lit the spark that propelled the University of Hawaii to baseball prominence strode to the pitcher's mound: a 5-foot-10-inch tall, 18-year-old freshman by the name of Derek Tatsuno.

He had a live arm. He reminded me of Ron Guidry; his fastball got on you quick. He was fearless out there on the mound, the kind of a pitcher you want to play behind. The success the university had at that time got people excited about baseball over there. The school drew big crowds, and more and more kids started playing ball.

Les Murakami was a man with a vision. In 1971 with no equipment, no field, and no scholarships, Murakami revived a dormant baseball program at the University of Hawaii. In its first two seasons the program played just four NCAA games, eight in its third season. While toiling to convince administrators to provide greater resources, Murakami dreamed of running a full-fledged NCAA Division 1 baseball program. Finally, in 1975 he achieved his goal, receiving the funding to offer scholarships and play a 38-game schedule. All the while Murakami envisioned more—a program that basked in national prominence. In the spring of 1976, the significant piece that could bring the puzzle into focus was pitching for a high school 11 miles from Murakami's campus office.

Derek Tatsuno was a phenom. "Gotta watch him," Ron Nomura's father said after his son's team had lost a PONY League game to the young sensation. Stories of the young Tatsuno were legendary in the Hawaiian amateur baseball ranks. Parents and opposing players talked with admiration of his crackling, darting fastball. At an age when most adolescents are just learning how to throw a curve ball, Tatsuno could throw one with unhittable ferocity. In one game his tight-spinning curve ball caught the front lip of home plate and, possessed with so much speed, it caromed clear over a backstop. By the time Derek Tatsuno completed his senior season at 'Aiea High School, he had amassed a 27–1 pitching record and helped his team win the state championship.

Success locked Tatsuno's focus on playing Division 1 college baseball, but there was little interest. College baseball's reigning national champions, the University of Arizona, suggested he attend a junior college. The University of Oregon offered a partial scholarship. The University of Hawaii and its small school schedule held little interest until, that is, Tatsuno learned of Les Murakami's plan to bring many top powers to the island. He enrolled at UH, and in the spring of 1977 a college sensation was born.

Tatsuno's college debut came in celebrated fashion. He opposed Vanderbilt University's coveted pro prospect, Scott Sanderson, who had spent the previous summer pitching for the U.S. National Team. With a fastball that clocked from the low- to mid-90s and what his catcher called a "nasty curve," Tatsuno struck out ten Vanderbilt batters and didn't walk a man. Hawaii prevailed, 7–5, and the win helped to ignite a fervor on the island of Oahu.

As the season progressed, crowds swelled. Where a hundred fans or less had once made up the crowd for Hawaii games, now the campus ballpark's aluminum bleachers were filled to its 2,500-fan capacity. Hours before games, players would exit the athletic department locker room for the walk to the ballpark for batting practice and be startled to see long lines of fans waiting to buy tickets. Fans tabbed Tatsuno "The Franchise." Employees in the University's athletic department called him "Pied Piper," while his coach called the pitcher "special."

Tatsuno mowed through his first season of college competition, winning 11 of the 12 games that he started. He pitched a one-hitter to beat Hawaii-Hilo. The hard thrower led the nation with 146 strikeouts and pitched 11 complete games, four of which resulted in shutouts. His only regular-season loss came to the tenth-ranked team in the country, USC. The season culminated with the school's first trip to the NCAA regionals and a magical night, when an NCAA record crowd saw Tatsuno pitch in Aloha Stadium.

The pitcher's first-season success brought an invitation to pitch for the U.S. National Team in a July series against the top collegiate players from Japan. Particular attention was focused on Tatsuno for becoming the first Japanese American to pitch for the U.S. In the first game of the series, Tatsuno was thrust into the spotlight. He opposed the top collegiate pitcher in Japan, Suguro Egawa, who had turned down a $100,000-offer to play professionally in order to attend college, where he had amassed an 8–0 record during the 1977 season. Tatsuno retired the first 11 batters that he faced. Egawa didn't allow a hit through five innings. In the fourth inning Tatsuno allowed two singles. An error let the first Japanese run score, and an ensuing triple plated the second. The U.S. roared back to tie the game in the bottom of the sixth inning. Tatsuno then exited the duel having allowed just four hits, one walk, and striking out ten. In the bottom of the eighth inning, the U.S. rallied to score the go-ahead run and won, 4–3. Five nights later Tatsuno pitched the U.S. to a 2–1 victory, throwing a complete game in which he allowed four hits and struck out 12. News of Tatsuno's skills gained great attention in Japan.

Through the marvel, Les Murakami studied his pitcher with an objective eye. He felt there was room for improvement and that his standout needed to add another pitch to his arsenal. He taught Tatsuno how to throw a changeup. In two weeks' time the pupil had mastered the pitch with devastating effect. As a sophomore, Tatsuno improved on his freshman strikeout tally, whiffing 161. Twenty came in a single game against the University of Oregon. He threw 12 complete games and his earned-run average was a minuscule 1.45. With success came recognition; Tatsuno was named a third-team All-America.

Teammates came to both revere and loathe Tatsuno. Days when he pitched were electric. When he pitched batting practice to his teammates, however, his fellow players regarded the drill akin to having a root canal. "The ball never comes in straight," one lamented. The pitcher's former youth-league foe, Ron Nomura, was now his UH battery mate, a role that evoked both pain and awe. The movement on Tatsuno's fastball almost always made the ball smack an unprotected part of the catcher's glove and leave Nomura's left thumb painfully sore and bruised. In time, it became a burden the catcher learned to live with. Nomura frequently found himself in amazement at the pitcher. On days when Hawaii's games were dotted by the island's frequent rains, the catcher was spellbound by the odd sound made when the ferociously spinning ball cut through raindrops and streaked through the heavy damp air.

Following his sophomore season, Tatsuno was lured by an offer to pitch in a talent-laden summer collegiate league, the Jayhawk Baseball League. When he learned of the invitation, Les Murakami had reservations. He felt his pitcher should decline it and rest his arm. Tatsuno listened but lived to play baseball and was soon on a plane bound for Kansas to join the Liberal BeeJays. The pitcher helped his team to a 19–3 record and the Jayhawk Baseball League championship. The title launched the BeeJays into amateur baseball's prestigious National Baseball Congress championship tournament. Liberal entered play as the number one seed and Tatsuno got the tournament going with an impressive pitching performance to beat Charleston Pro Sports, 7–1. In the second round, Tatsuno flung a three-hitter and struck out eight as Liberal beat Kankakee, 13–3. The semifinal round matched the BeeJays and the tournament's number two seed, Rapid City. The game was tied, 1–1, in the ninth inning, when Tatsuno was tagged for a three-run home run that sent Liberal to defeat and elimination.

Two weeks after the tournament, Tatsuno was back in classes and soon immersed in Hawaii's fall preseason program. Success had brought celebrity. Tatsuno was often approached in restaurants and recognized while shopping. Carnivals banned him, fearful that his pitching acumen could wreak disastrous prize payouts. As the 1979 college baseball season drew near, scouts stepped up their treks to Hawaii.

Every summer I would take my daughter Kathy on a scouting trip with me. I'd let her bring a friend, and we'd make a vacation of it. We might go to the Connie Mack World Series in Farmington, New Mexico, or to Idaho for an American Legion tournament. I guess by the time she was a teenager she didn't find these places all that much fun because one afternoon she came home from school, and I told her I had picked the place for our summer vacation trip. In a sarcastic tone, she said, "Oh where are we going this year, Hawaii?" When I said, "Yup!" she went from disbelief to excitement in about two seconds. The Giants were having me go over to take a look at Derek Tatsuno.

Entering his junior season, Tatsuno drew acclaim. "I rate him as one of the best college pitchers in the country," Oregon State coach, Mel Krause, told the *Los Angeles Times*. Al Zarilla, a scout and former major-league outfielder, told reporters that Tatsuno was a likely first-round draft pick. Fueled by their pitching ace, the University of Hawaii began the season on a tear. They won their first 11 games. By the latter part of March, they had won 23 of 24. That's when it happened. "My thumb doesn't hurt anymore," Ron Nomura told his coach. Indeed, the zip on Tatsuno's fastball that had frequently left his catcher's thumb bruised wasn't there anymore. The pitcher insisted he wasn't injured. His coach chalked it up to fatigue. "What's the issue?" a reporter asked. "He needs to rest," Murakami answered.

Having continued to recruit talented players into his program, Murakami now enjoyed the luxury of a bullpen. He often used it, removing Tatsuno from games in the late innings. Regardless, the pitcher was still highly productive. He struck out 18 in a win over Oregon State, 17 when

Hawaii beat Nebraska. By the end of March, Hawaii was in the midst of a 23-game winning streak and had soared to number one in the college baseball polls.

Buoyed by the success, the school turned in a bid to host the NCAA regionals. It was thwarted, however, when United Airlines employees went on strike, limiting travel options from the mainland.

In the final weeks of the regular season, Tatsuno was zeroing in on some of the biggest records in college baseball. The mark that drew the most attention was the 20-win mark. No college pitcher had ever won 20 games in a season. With fervor rising like never before and Tatsuno projected to pitch Hawaii's final home game against Nevada-Las Vegas, the university arranged for the game to be played in Aloha Stadium. In what would likely be the last home game Tatsuno would pitch, 18,348 fans turned out for the game. They cheered wildly as the pitcher struck out 12 and won, 5–3, for Tatsuno's 17th win of the season. That string of 17 consecutive wins by the pitcher was snapped the following week, when Hawaii lost to eventual national champion, Cal State Fullerton.

The approach of the Memorial Day weekend at the end of May saw major-league teams step up their draft preparations. By now, Tatsuno's performances had made him a lock to be chosen in the first round. In the days before the June 5 draft, as teams sought to learn what sort of bonus offer it would take to secure Tatsuno's signature on a contract, alarm broke out. There was talk making the rounds in Hawaii that Derek Tatsuno was considering playing his professional baseball not in the United States but in Japan.

While still in high school, Tatsuno met Wally Yonamine, a legendary Hawaiian, who in 1951 became the first American to play professional baseball in Japan. Yonamine, manager of the Chunichi Dragons in Japan's Central League, dropped by the Tatsuno home while on a visit to Hawaii. "Would you be interested in playing professionally in Japan?" he asked. The question planted a seed.

Major-league teams that had targeted Tatsuno with their first-round selection were thrown into disarray. Scouts were dispatched to learn the validity of the rumor. In Arizona, where the University of Hawaii was preparing to play in the NCAA regionals, Tatsuno was coy. "I'm going to wait until the playoffs are over," he told reporters. "I want to see who drafts me and what kind of contract I'll get."

On May 25, one week before the draft, Derek Tatsuno pitched his way into the college baseball record books. He defeated Indiana State, 4–3, to become the first pitcher in college baseball history to win 20 games in a season. He increased his single-season strikeout record by 73 over his sophomore year tally of 161. The figure, added to his two prior seasons, eclipsed Eddie Bane's career strikeout record of 505 with 541. Derek Tatsuno was named a first team All-America.

With teams unable to get a clear picture of Tatsuno's professional plans, the Hawaiian fell out of the first round of the draft. The San Diego Padres gambled and used their second-round selection, the 40th pick overall, to grab Tatsuno. "We are handling him as though he were a first-round draft choice because we think he was a first-round candidate," Padres general manager, Bob Fontaine, Sr., told reporters. Fontaine flew to Hawaii to meet with the pitcher. Once the meeting broke up, rumors swirled that Tatsuno had received the richest bonus offer in Padres history. "Contract-wise," the pitcher said, "Mr. Fontaine said he would give me a six-figure bonus." If true, the amount would exceed the $60,000 Seattle had given to the first player chosen in the draft. When reached by reporters, Fontaine was noncommittal. "We feel we can reach a satisfactory agreement. We'll be in the ballpark."

Team USA extended an offer to Tatsuno as well to pitch once again for the U.S. National Team in another seven-game series against Japan. This, however, would take place in Japan and during the height of contract negotiations.

Ten days after being chosen by the Padres, Tatsuno boarded a plane for Japan. At the airport in Tokyo, sight of the Japanese American pitching sensation with his collar-length black hair sent fans shrieking and dozens of flash bulbs popping. It was a scene reminiscent of an arrival by an iconic entertainer such as Elvis or The Beatles. "Japanese teams look for foreign players who will adapt to Japanese baseball," longtime Tokyo baseball fan, Jin Hisa, explained. "Many foreign players do not adapt. Tatsuno was Japanese. There was a good chance he would." What further stoked the flames of excitement in Japan was the idea that the best collegiate pitcher in America would elect to play in their country rather than the major leagues.

Newspapers reported that Tatsuno would announce his decision on July 5, four days after the all-star series had concluded. Behind the scenes, a Tokyo business magnate was hard at work. Japanese conglomerate Kokudo Keikaku had added the Seibu Lions to its stable of more than 100 companies that included a railroad and upscale hotels. Its chairman, Yoshiaki Tsutsumi, sought to end the team's decade of mediocrity and make the Lions into a powerhouse of Japanese professional baseball. The excitement over Derek Tatsuno convinced Tsutsumi that he must secure the pitcher for his ballclub.

For days reporters from Tokyo's seven daily sports newspapers followed Tatsuno in hopes of landing a scoop. They were at practices, social functions, and the games. Tatsuno got the start in game two of the series. Before 25,000 fans he struck out nine, scattered just five hits, and shutout the Japanese rivals, 3–0. In the fifth game of the series, Tatsuno won again, this time with six strikeouts and no walks.

Away from the stadium, negotiations intensified. The Padres extended a firm $100,000 bonus offer and proposed that Tatsuno begin his pro career with their top farm club, the Hawaii Islanders of the Pacific Coast League. The offer paled against that of Tsutsumi.

On July 5 more than 60 reporters gathered at one of Tsutsumi's hotels, the Shinegawa Prince in southern Tokyo. In an electric news conference, Derek Tatsuno announced that he would play in Japan. The bonus he was offered was three times that of the Padres and included a management job after his career at a hotel that Tsutsumi was building in Hawaii. "It's too bad you're not here to see the magnetism this boy has here in Japan," his college coach told the *Los Angeles Times* from Tokyo. "If you were here, you could see why he couldn't play anyplace else."

Before the excitement could wane, however, a technicality arose. It stemmed from an agreement that had been reached decades earlier between the commissioners of professional baseball in Japan and the United States. The pact would prevent Derek Tatsuno from playing for the Seibu Lions.

I'm afraid I had something to do with that. In 1955 I was in Mexico, and I signed a young catcher for the Pirates. The owner of one of the ballclubs down there got upset. He claimed the player belonged to his club. He filed kidnapping charges against me because I took the catcher to his home so his parents could sign the contract. I had to flee the country. The commissioner of the Mexican League complained to the commissioner of Major League Baseball, so they came up with a rule. Amateur players were property of the club in their home country that owned their rights. If you wanted to sign that player, you had to negotiate with the club that owned their rights. Several years later that same rule was applied to players in Japan, Taiwan, and South Korea.

Tatsuno was assigned to pitch for a semi-pro team in Japan's Industrial League, which was owned by Tsutsumi's Prince Hotels chain. During the pitcher's first season in Japan, the country was host to the Baseball World Cup. An exhibition game was arranged between the Prince Hotels Industrial League team and the Cuban National team. "I want to pitch," Tatsuno urged his manager. For seven innings, the 21-year-old held the reigning world champions to just two hits while striking out 12. He left with the game a 1–1 tie.

Hitters in Japan weren't the only ones baffled by the wicked movement of Derek Tatsuno's fastball, however. His catchers struggled to handle the American sensation's fastball, and soon the pitcher learned that different ideas existed in the Japanese game. "That's not a fastball," coaches would bark when he would unleash a rocket. In Japan, it was explained, a fastball was to be clean and devoid of movement. Catchers must be able to frame pitches. "You must throw the ball where it can be caught," he was instructed. Trickery was reserved for breaking pitches. Tatsuno protested. To ensure that he complied, his mechanics were changed.

Prior to Tatsuno's second season in Japan, Price Hotels sent their team to Hawaii to train and play exhibition games against the University of Hawaii. Many of Tatsuno's former teammates, such as shortstop Thad Reece, were "really nervous" at the prospect of facing their former ace. Once the game began the Hawaii players were, to a man, surprised by what they saw. "They've changed everything," Reece exclaimed. Indeed, Tatsuno's leg kick was altered and the arm angle on his delivery was changed from a three-quarter slot to straight over the top. His pitches had little movement, and the velocity was down. Tatsuno struggled and was hit hard. Ron Nomura sensed that his friend was frustrated and lacked confidence.

Branch Rickey told his managers and coaches to never change a player. He'd say, "Only change them if they come to you first." He never wanted us to be the ones to go and change a player's mechanics. When I'd see a player who had become frustrated and struggled because he'd been changed, I felt bad.

By the end of his second season in Japan, the frustration consumed Tatsuno. In America, teams had continued to select him in the draft—the White Sox, Mets and Reds—blocking hope of pitching in Japan's professional league. The altered mechanics and intense training methods had diminished his once overwhelming fastball. On December 1, 1981, Tatsuno packed his things to travel home to Hawaii. "I'm not coming back," he told his team and terminated his contract.

Once home, Tatsuno ran into a scout for the Milwaukee Brewers. "Tell them I'm interested. If they draft me, I'll sign," the pitcher said. Just two weeks later, in the January 1982 draft, the Brewers made Tatsuno their first-round selection. He promptly signed with the ballclub.

For the bulk of the 1982 season, the onetime sensation pitched for the Brewers' Class AA farm club in El Paso. He was no longer the sensation scouts had flocked to evaluate at the University of Hawaii. Tatsuno was used primarily in relief and finished the year with a 7–2 record and 6.42 earned-run average. The following season he returned to a starting role but in Class A ball. Tatsuno won ten games and lost six, but it was clear that his days as a prized prospect were over.

There are a lot more ballplayers coming out of Hawaii now. Ever since those great Hawaii teams of the late '70s and early '80s, more kids over there are playing baseball. We signed Sid Fernandez and Shane Victorino with the Dodgers. Those players should be real proud. Their success made others want to follow in their footsteps, and the kids that do, like Kolten Wong, are getting a chance to play pro ball and becoming pretty good ballplayers.

Eight years after Derek Tatsuno pitched his last game for the school, the University of Hawaii retired his number, 16. *Collegiate Baseball Newspaper* named him its Co-Player of the Century. Tatsuno was also named to *Baseball America* magazine's All-Century team and All-Time College All-Star team. In 2007 Tatsuno was inducted into College Baseball's Hall of Fame. Decades later, his former teammates still marvel at his skills and success. "To this day, he's still the very best that I've seen," said Thad Reece, who ascended to the Oakland Athletics 40-man roster during his professional career. "I've seen a lot of good pitchers here in Hawaii," Ron Nomura reflected. "Sid Fernandez, he pitched 15 years in the big leagues. But Sid Fernandez couldn't compare with Derek Tatsuno."

12

THE BLUE MOON

They dot his desktop in greater numbers than the normal business executives' phone messages and coffee stains. Each of the business plans, research charts, and proposals promises success and rapid returns. In Eric Hardgrave's world—venture capital—there are no fat fastballs like the ones he used to hammer in batting practice at Stanford and in pro ball. Identifying a company worth investing in is akin to determining what pitch he wanted to swing at in the summer of 1985, when he hit 29 home runs. It involves talent, study, experience, and discipline.

On rare occasions within the wording of a business plan is terminology that projects can't-miss or high potential for success. It will make the former Stanford first baseman pause and ponder the one true certain success that he was ever associated with—a baseball teammate at Stanford, John Elway.

In the spring of 1979, there was a lot of talent in Southern California. Tim Leary and Steve Buechele looked like premium picks. I liked Chris Brown over at Crenshaw High School. The guys in the class behind them were really something—Darryl Strawberry, Eric Davis, Glenn Braggs, Jessie Reid, Darnell Coles, Rick Renteria—and over at UCLA you had Matt Young and Don Slaught. The player I really liked, though, was that boy Elway over at Granada Hills. He could run. You could see he had the makings of a power bat, and what an arm!

During the winter of 1976, the middling football program at Cal State Northridge sought to attain acclaim when it selected an ambitious assistant football coach from the state of Idaho, Jack Elway, to takes its reigns. The job lured Jack Elway's family, his wife Jan, two daughters, and teenaged son to Granada Hills, north of Los Angeles. While father sought to rebuild the Northridge football program, it would be his 16-year-old son, John, who would create the bigger sports stir. It was no secret that the teen was a gifted quarterback, one of the most coveted in the nation. What would surprise pro baseball scouts was that the younger Elway possessed covetous baseball talent as well.

John Elway stepped into one of the best baseball programs in the state. Prior to his arrival, Granada Hills High, in Southern California's San Fernando Valley, had won Southern California titles in both 1975 and '76. They did it with a style of play that was employed to make up for a lack of raw talent. Unlike their crosstown rival, Kennedy High, who was sending two to three players a year into professional baseball, not a single player from either of Granada Hills High School's title teams was chosen in the draft.

The coach there liked to play what they'd call "small ball." Other coaches would say, "He's a tricky guy," to describe him because he liked to use the bunt and play station-to-station baseball. That's good for a program that doesn't have a lot of talent. It wasn't the good old-fashioned hardball that I was brought up playing, but he got great results.

The Granada Hills High class of 1979 would change that reputation. A group of talented players matriculated to the varsity, and the undisputed standout among the team's talented players was John Elway. During his junior season, Elway hit over .500 and helped the program win 21 of 22 games to claim its third Southern California title in four years. When post-season honors were announced, Elway was not only named to the all-league team, he was its Most Valuable Player and earned a place on the all-city team as well.

Once the season had ended, Elway's baseball gear went on the shelf. His focus from then on was strictly on football and his senior season. College recruiters swarmed to Granada Hills from all over the country. They considered Elway to be the top high school quarterback in the land. Baseball scouts in the region held the high school junior in almost equally high regard. While the focus of the football talent chasers was on which university he would agree to attend, the baseball scouts held their breath that Elway would come through his final high school football season uninjured and that they might persuade him into their sport with a lucrative financial offer.

My father was an immigrant from Italy. The first time he ever saw a game of football he laid down the law to my brothers and me. Times were tough. This was during the Great Depression. "I barely make enough money to feed you kids," he hollered. "I don't have the money for a doctor if you get hurt playing football. If you get hurt playing football, I'll hurt you worse! No football! Got it?!"

12. The Blue Moon

John Elway (back row, left) with Stanford teammates Vince Sakowski (center) and Eric Hardgrave (right), Mike Aldrete (bottom left) and Steve Buechele (bottom right). Teammates still marvel at Elway's baseball talent. (Eric Hardgrave)

The injury worries manifested during the fourth week of the season. In a heavily-hyped game against Banning High School, Elway suffered a bruised collarbone. One week later in a route of Bell High, the quarterback injured the collarbone again. Elway played on, but four weeks later injury bit again. During the second quarter of a game against San Fernando High School, Elway took off on a run. He planted his left leg to try to cut by a defender when he felt a pop in the knee. The school's trainer taped up his knee, and Elway completed the game. A later diagnosis, however, determined that he had torn cartilage, and his football season was over.

By the time the Granada Hills High baseball season got underway, Elway's knee had recovered. He had also signed a letter of intent to play football at Stanford University. In doing so, the quarterback had made clear to the Stanford football coaches that he also wanted to play baseball.

Professional baseball scouts were made frenetic by a bevy of talent that played on high school diamonds around Southern California during the spring of 1979. Few regions anywhere had ever produced the number of highly-talented players as Southern California had that year. Once April turned into May and the playoffs loomed, two forces had energized. In the suburbs of the San Fernando Valley north of downtown Los Angeles was John Elway and his Granada Hills High teammates. At Crenshaw High in inner city Los Angeles, Darryl Strawberry and Chris Brown were racking up wins aplenty with their play and attracting scouts in droves.

In the quarterfinal round, savvy baserunning by Elway helped Granada Hills advance with a 2–0 win. Home runs by Strawberry and Brown pushed Crenshaw into the semifinals as well.

Brown, Strawberry, Eric Davis at Fremont High, and Jessie Reid at Lynwood, who was emerging as a prospective first-round draft pick, were friends. By their senior year, they had heard tales about the standout from the valley and became curious to see John Elway play. Reid was in the stands when Elway hammered out four hits and drove in six runs to power Granada Hills into the championship game. "I thought *I* was good," the power-hitting outfielder told a friend after seeing Elway play. "This guy is one great athlete. He is on another planet!"

Elway's skills would be showcased in the region's championship game in marquee fashion. Granada Hills would face off with talent-laden Crenshaw High. Chris Brown's 11th home run and two runs batted in by Darryl Strawberry had highlighted the Cougars' semifinal victory. Led by its dynamic duo, Crenshaw had averaged 11 runs a game in the postseason.

The title game was played in Dodger Stadium, and the matchup drew a crowd of over 5,000. In the first inning, Elway singled in the game's first run. He then stole second base and scored on a teammate's single. In the third inning, Elway singled and later scored another run. One inning later with Granada Hills leading 4–1, Crenshaw High threatened. Daryl Stroh, the Granada Hills coach, marched to the pitcher's mound. Just before he reached the mound, he decided to change pitchers. When the umpire asked

12. The Blue Moon

whom he wanted, the coach pointed to his third baseman. John Elway jogged to the mound.

Elway had not pitched in six weeks but promptly retired the first five Crenshaw batters that he faced. With one out in the ninth inning, Darryl Strawberry and Chris Brown stood between Elway and a win. Firing a fastball in the low to mid–90s, the two-sport sensation whiffed first Strawberry and then the future big-leaguer Brown, and Granada Hills earned its fourth Southern California title in five years.

Elway was awarded the Most Valuable Player Award for the playoffs. He batted .692 in the postseason games. Days later he was named the Los Angeles City Most Valuable Player. His season batting average was .491, and his earned-run average from the games that he pitched was 1.03.

I had Elway number one on my draft list. But I had to hear from him what he wanted to do. One day we talked. He said, "Mr. Genovese, I appreciate the consideration, but please don't draft me. I'm definitely going to go to Stanford to play football."

The Kansas City Royals took a flyer and selected Elway in the 18th round of the draft. "Most scouts told me had he not been going to college, he would have been the first or second player taken," his coach, Daryl Stroh, told the *Los Angeles Times*. Stroh said that a club asked Elway if he would sign if offered $130,000, and the two-sport talent said no. The coach claimed Kansas City had told Elway to name his price. Elway replied that he was not interested.

Elway started nine games at quarterback during his freshman season at Stanford then became part of a celebrated class of recruits to join the baseball team. Mark Marquess was working to rebuild a program that hadn't been to the postseason in 15 years. He had persuaded high school standouts Mike Aldrete, Steve Buechele, Mike Dotterer, and Eric Hardgrave to come to Stanford. Whatever egos they brought disappeared once they saw the fifth member of their freshman class perform.

Thirty seconds into Elway's first batting practice session, Dave Meier turned to a Stanford teammate and exclaimed "This dude is better than me, and baseball isn't even his primary sport!" As the Cardinal shortstop continued to watch, he made mental notes about his new teammate. *The most beautiful left-handed swing, perfect leverage, and perfect timing. Power to all fields. A polished five-tool talent. No weaknesses.* Of the 6-foot-4-inch, 205-pounder, Hardgrave was more blunt when he said to a teammate, "Guy can run for a big fuck!"

The 1980 Cardinal team was young. On many nights five of the starting nine were freshmen. On March 6 the team was presented with a unique opportunity. Only six months earlier, an all-sports cable channel called ESPN had launched. The new channel arranged to carry Stanford's game with perennial national power Arizona State. Optimism was quickly crushed, and so were the Cardinal. A nationwide audience watched them get humiliated by the mighty Sun Devils, 34–2.

The thrashing wasn't all that left some of the Cardinal frustrated. Even though his .269 batting average was 20 points higher than the other freshman, Elway wasn't happy. He talked it over with his coach and came back the following year to help change the fortunes of the Stanford program. During the fall, Elway had a stellar football season. He was named Pac-10 Conference Player of the Year as just a sophomore. Once baseball season began, he helped to end the Cardinal postseason drought.

The Cardinal won their first 10 games and rocketed to number one in the national rankings. Scouts became a constant presence at games and even practices. Elway exhibited power. He hiked his batting average by almost .100 points. As impressed as opponents and fans were, their awe was nothing compared to that of his teammates. Hardgrave, his roommate, marveled that Elway was "the best athlete I've ever seen in my life, bar none!" Meier noted to the small number of critics that Elway devoted little time to baseball. "He missed the fall season because of football. In March he's playing spring ball then running over to suit up and play in our games at night. In the summer he's working football camps and not playing in a summer league. Just think what he could do if he were to focus on baseball."

In May Arizona State came to Stanford. The Sun Devils were 23–1. Motivated by the thrashing on ESPN the year before, the Cardinal swept the series winning by scores of 18–3, 9–6, and 16–4. To put an exclamation mark on the sweep, Elway made a play that his teammates continue to marvel at decades later.

Arizona State had the speedy Ricky Nelson at second base. A fly ball was launched toward right center field. Elway raced to his right and caught the ball on the warning track. With a quarter turn of his upper body, he unleashed a powerful throw. The ball streaked through the air and into the mitt of Steve Buechele at third base without bouncing once. Nelson was still eight feet from the bag when it got to Buechele, and the Arizona State runner was easily tagged out.

Two weeks later with Stanford in hot pursuit of a playoff spot, Elway told the football coaches that he wanted to travel with the baseball team to its final regular-season series in Seattle against the University of Washington.

Elway was given the green light to play, and the annual spring football game was called off.

The Cardinal had won eight of their last nine games going into the final game of the regular season. They beat the Huskies, 10–6, with a three-run home run by Elway among the highlights. The win sealed a second-place finish in the Pac-10 and earned Stanford its first trip to the NCAA regionals since 1967.

The Cardinal were placed in the Central Regional at the University of Texas, joining BYU, Lamar, and the host Longhorns in the field. The football-savvy local fans made sport of heckling Elway. Those same fans, though, rose in a standing ovation to throws Elway made from the warning track to the infield during pregame practice.

An opening night 6–5 loss to Lamar knocked Stanford into the loser's bracket. But the Cardinal stormed back. They beat BYU in a pitchers' duel then avenged the loss to Lamar to setup a must-win game with the University of Texas. Lose, and the season was over. Texas would go to the College World Series. Win, and the two teams would play once more, with a trip to the College World Series to the victor. More than 6,000 fans packed the campus ballpark. Five hundred more were turned away. The atmosphere was electric, and the source of ionic charge in the game was Stanford's right fielder, John Elway. Early in the game Elway made the defensive play of the tournament—a running, over-the-shoulder catch with his back to the infield that robbed a Texas player of an extra base hit. Texas had hoped their standout pitcher, Calvin Schiraldi, would shut the Cardinal down, but Elway, among others, thwarted the plan. The two-sport sensation hammered out four hits—his four-for-four game helped propel Stanford to a regional title showdown with a 9–8 win.

An electrical storm and flooding in the Austin area pushed the title test from Sunday night to Memorial Day, Monday. The delay didn't dull the excitement of area fans, many of whom waited more than two hours for the games to be thrown open. By first pitch, every seat in the stands was filled. As sportswriters settled into the press box at Disch-Falk Field, many were convinced that Elway, with eight hits in his 15 at-bats, would be the tournament's Most Valuable Player. But in the crucial title game, the Stanford bats were kept silent after an early outburst. Elway went hitless, and Texas won, 10–2. Stanford's players trudged home and were left to wonder what-if when their league rival, Arizona State, won the College World Series.

Elway finished his sophomore season with a vastly-improved .361 batting average. He hit nine home runs. In the 49 games that he played, Elway drove in 50 runs. Proof of the havoc his remarkable throwing arm wreaked, the two-sport talent tallied 45 outfield assists. His sophomore season play was recognized far beyond the inner-circle of the Stanford baseball program. Elway was selected to play on the U.S. National Team, which would spend part of the summer touring Asia. He had also impressed a very powerful man at the highest level of the game.

During Stanford's late-season surge, George Steinbrenner, the owner of the New York Yankees, had become enamored with the young talent. Steinbrenner gleaned unique insight into Elway. "Dutch" Dotterer, a Yankees scout, was the grandfather of Stanford's left fielder, Mike Dotterer. Gary Hughes, one of the Yankees' top scouts, filed glowing reports on Elway. "He has a well-above-average, major-league arm. He runs well, makes contact, and this year he started hitting for power," Hughes told his boss and a few reporters.

The baseball draft arrived one week after Stanford had been eliminated in the regional playoffs. Many noted that Elway was only a sophomore, and that in most cases college sophomores were not eligible to be selected. The Yankees, however, had recognized a loophole in the draft rules. To be eligible for selection the player had to be either a high school senior, a junior college player, or a player at a four-year university within 45 days of their 21st birthday. Elway would turn 21 three weeks after the 1981 draft.

When the Yankees' first selection came up, the 52nd pick overall in the second round, the name they announced over the speaker phone to the commissioner's office surprised almost everyone in the game—John Elway. "It caught everyone off guard," Stanford's sports information director, Bob Rose, told the *Los Angeles Times*. "Even John. He's really surprised he was drafted that high and by the Yankees. They hadn't contacted him before the draft."

Few in the game thought the Yankees could succeed in signing the Stanford standout. Most felt that Elway was on a path to play pro football. "We tend to operate on the theory that no one is unsignable," a Yankees scout told a sportswriter. In late September, with an understanding that playing for them would not interfere with football, Elway signed with the Yankees and received a bonus of $140,000. The amount was $40,000 more than what the first pick in the draft was paid.

The college student invested most of his windfall but held a bit back to splurge and buy something for himself—a new car. His campus buddies, who had long before pinned him with the nickname "Woody," heaped good-natured ribbing on Elway when he showed up one day driving a sleek black Nissan 280-z. The joshing intensified once the car bore a specially-ordered license plate: 007.

During Elway's spring break, the Yankees invited him to their minor-league training complex in Florida. He suited up and took batting practice. When he clubbed the third pitch that he saw over the right-field wall, Steinbrenner gushed to reporters, "Right then I knew, he will be a great outfielder for me in the tradition of Mantle, Maris, DiMaggio, and all the others."

The Yankees assigned Elway to play for their farm team in the New York-Penn League, the Oneonta Yankees. The club was near the bottom rung of the Yankees' minor-league ladder, lower than where some organizations might choose to send an accomplished college player, but Elway didn't mind. "I'd been away from it [baseball] for a while," he said to a reporter. "I didn't want to go to a league where I'd be so overmatched that the experience would leave a bad taste."

The New York-Penn League played a 76-game season that spanned from late June through the first week of September. As the season drew near, both the interest in Elway's professional debut and expectations for his play soared. Both concerned his college coach. Mark Marquess explained to the *New York Times* that his former right fielder is, "not going to give the Yankees a true indication of what he can do in six weeks, unless he works out for two months solid before he heads east. But he's not. He's going to be playing spring football and not working out for baseball. He may hit in the cage, but it's not the same as live pitching." Marquess' words would become prophetic. Elway struggled. Through his first two weeks of pro ball, the ballyhooed Yankees prospect managed only two hits in his first 22 plate appearances.

Long telephone conversations with his father and extra batting practice sessions with his manager, Ken Berry, would soon flick the on-switch to the player's immense baseball talent. Three weeks into the season, Elway went on a tear. A home run on July 1 at Batavia got his average above .200. "Hitting a homer is a much greater thrill than throwing a touchdown pass," he said. Over a 17-game stretch Elway would add three more homers to his tally, bat .361, and help his team to win 15 of those games.

Whenever Elway had multiple-hit games, the news was flashed on the message board in Yankee Stadium. Notes about Elway's performances were regularly distributed by the Yankees to the New York sportswriters.

In almost every city and town in the New York-Penn League, larger than usual crowds turned up when Oneonta arrived. Media flocked. *Time Magazine*, *Newsweek*, the *Los Angeles Times*, almost all the New York newspapers as well as local television and network crews trekked to upstate New York to feature Elway and his baseball progress. Teammates seized on the occasional media frenzy, phoning Elway's hotel room with disguised voices while claiming to be a reporter from a major newspaper. Elway fit in with his teammates. They found him to be humble and "one of the guys."

Elway played hard. He was aggressive on the bases, didn't hesitate to use a headfirst slide. His foot speed surprised many. The rookie successfully swiped 13 bases. Everyone was in awe of his throwing arm. Berry, himself a standout outfielder during his major-league career, marveled at its strength.

By the time Elway had to pack up and leave the team to participate in a prearranged college football promotional tour on August 1, he was batting .318. In 42 games Elway hit four home runs, six doubles, two triples, and drove in 25 runs. His powerful throwing arm tallied eight outfield assists. The Yankees were impressed. "We envision him playing right field for the Yankees in just a couple of years," the team's vice president, Bill Bergesch, told sportswriters.

As impressive as Elway was over two months in Oneonta, he was sensational during his senior football season at Stanford. The rocket-armed talent threw 24 touchdown passes and finished second in voting for the Heisman Trophy. A duel was on for the talented player's services.

One week before the NFL draft was to take place, Elway and his parents visited the Yankees. Over several days, Steinbrenner, Bergesch, and the team's manager, Billy Martin, put on an aggressive sales pitch. Elway's agent, Marvin Demoff, and Bergesch went back and forth on contract ideas. On Saturday, April 23, Demoff indicated to the Elways that an agreement had been reached with the Yankees on a five-year contract worth $2,500,000. The news was met with incredulity around baseball by men who didn't share the Yankees' regard for Elway's baseball skills. "The craziest thing he's done yet," the Seattle Mariners' scouting director, Jeff Scott, said about Steinbrenner. "Our scouting reports were that Elway wasn't the caliber of a first-round choice," said Calvin Griffith, who owned the Minnesota Twins. "We wouldn't give him any big money to sign."

Three nights later Elway was made the number one pick in the NFL draft by the Baltimore Colts. There had been whispers around the league for days that Elway did not want to play for the team. During a sometimes-tense press conference near the Stanford campus, the two-sport standout confirmed the rumor. "As I stand now, it's going to be baseball," he said. Frank Kush, the Colts' coach, confirmed to reporters that Elway had told him he had no desire to play for the Colts and would play for the Yankees

12. The Blue Moon

instead. Few felt Elway was serious, that he was using baseball as leverage to force the Colts to trade him.

The Yankees became oddly quiet. Many took it as a sign of defeat. Demoff had no additional discussions with Bergesch or Steinbrenner. Six days after his selection, Elway was traded to the Denver Broncos and almost immediately signed a six-year contract worth $12,700,000, which ended any idea of him playing professional baseball.

Elway's football career was every bit as sterling as experts predicted. He played 16 seasons with Denver, made five Super Bowl appearances, and won the title game twice. His career excellence brought induction into the Pro Football Hall of Fame. There are those in baseball left to wonder, however, what might have been.

When I watch Mike Trout, I think of Elway. That's who he reminds me of. His build was similar, and he had similar tools. A lot of people who saw Elway play in Oneonta say he was right to go with football, that he wouldn't have been a good baseball player. He could play. If he had stuck with the game, the power would have come. Elway would have been a very good baseball player.

Elway's former Stanford teammate, Dave Meier, spent seven seasons in the major leagues. During that time he sought to learn the ingredients of greatness. Meier would tap the knowledge of teammates such as Kirby Puckett and Ruben Sierra. He made a point to jog alongside George Brett and pepper the superstar with questions. It left him with a strong belief. "Once in a blue moon," Meier explained, "God decides, 'I'm going to give someone the whole package.' He definitely gave it to John."

13

Upping the Ante

While driving to his physical therapy class, Tyrone Culver chuckles as he admits that some of his Palmdale High classmates still can't get over the path his life took. "I was always a baseball guy," he explains. While fellow players from Palmdale High's 2000 team have expressed surprise that Culver went on to be an all-conference college football player, spend five seasons in the NFL, intercept Drew Brees and almost take it back for a touchdown, his is only the second biggest surprise from their team. That Matt Harrington never made it remains something none of his teammates can get over.

Harrington had a great arm. I went out to Palmdale to look at him a couple of times, and he was definitely a number one. He needed work. Some of his pitches weren't where they needed to be. Everybody came to see him, though. It was hard not to like that arm.

It was the summer of 1998 that Matt Harrington first burst onto the radar of professional baseball scouts. The United States was to host the World Youth Baseball Championships, and two dozen of the country's best high school sophomores were assembled with the goal of winning the gold medal.

Harrington initially stood out because at almost 6-feet-4-inches tall, he was bigger than most of the other players. Once he got on the pitcher's mound during workouts, he quickly stood out because of his skill. *What a great arm*, thought Chris Patrick, the team's third baseman. Teammates found the small-town pitcher to be a bit of an outcast. One labeled him "goofy." The team's catcher had trouble remembering Harrington's name and took to calling him "Ferringworth."

Once Matt Harrington took the mound for Team USA, however, everyone remembered his name. During a game against the Czech Republic in the pool-play portion of the tournament, Harrington put on a pitching performance that left observers in awe. The teenager overwhelmed the

13. Upping the Ante

opposition with an electric fastball. He pitched a complete game and racked up a record 16 strikeouts. Within 24 hours of the game, word of Harrington's sensational performance got back to the scouting departments of every major-league club, and Harrington was a target of every scout evaluating talent for the 2000 draft.

The city of Palmdale rests in the Mojave Desert, separated from Los Angeles by a 40-mile-wide mountain range and 70 miles of highway. During the 1990s its population almost doubled to 100,000 as the lure of affordable housing acted as a magnet to draw young families from higher-priced communities around Los Angeles. In the spring of 2000, Matt Harrington was the lure that coaxed professional baseball scouts, cross checkers, and in some cases, general managers from all 30 teams to the area.

Harrington was the hardest worker on a team with talent. He rose early to run every morning, was on the field before teammates arrived for practice, and stuck around after others had gone. "A hard worker and such a great guy," his teammate Tyrone Culver said.

Dozens of scouts dotted the bleachers to watch the Palmdale High School senior in the season-opening *Daily News* Tournament the first week of March. "A circus," Culver called it. "I don't know how Matt can concentrate with 20 radar guns pointed at him on every pitch." What the scouts witnessed was a pitcher who had added 15 pounds to his frame and threw a fastball that was on average four miles an hour faster than the year before. Some radar guns would catch its top speed at an eye-popping 97 or 98 miles an hour. On a more consistent basis, Harrington's four-seam fastball was clocked between 92 and 94.

Harrington used his fastball to pitch aggressively. "Basically, my philosophy is to go right after

Matt Harrington was considered the best pitching prospect in the 2000 draft. Contentious contract negotiations sent his path to stardom awry. (St. Paul Saints)

hitters," he told Gerry Gittelson of the *Los Angeles Daily News*. "If it's a real good hitter, I might throw a couple of extra sliders, but that's about it." Harrington's aggressiveness helped him tear through his high school competition, winning all 11 decisions while striking out a staggering 126 batters in 65 innings. By the season's end, the hard thrower sported a microscopic 0.54 earned-run average to go with his 11–0 record.

Evenings after Harrington's performances, the scouts would sit in motel rooms or home offices to fill out their evaluation of the pitcher. There was unanimity in admiration for his high-velocity fastball. A scrutinous few wished for more movement from the pitch. While some evaluators liked the tall, right-handed pitcher's breaking ball, others graded it as so-so, and many felt that his changeup needed work. Still, there was plenty of talent to be excited about. In the end, almost all of the evaluators noted that Harrington was young, just a high school pitcher with an ability to learn and improve from experience.

By April reality had set in. It brought the once-steady stream of evaluators that followed Harrington to a trickle. Five clubs with picks at the top of the 2000 draft intensified their efforts toward the Palmdale senior. Each ordered their Southern California area scout to "sit on" the pitcher in a clear indication that Harrington was the target of their first-round pick. Murmur over Harrington was blown into an electric buzz.

Once you have evaluated the player, signability becomes important. With a premium pick like those at the top of the first round, you want to be certain you can sign the boy. This is where baseball has changed. It used to be that the scout handled everything. Now negotiations with premium picks are taken out of the scout's hands. The scouting director and sometimes the general manager take over, especially when you're talking about millions of dollars. You just can't afford to make a mistake.

In mid to late May with the draft three weeks away, scouts were replaced in the stands by general managers. Dave Dombrowski of the Marlins, Ed Lynch of the Cubs, Kevin Towers of the Padres, and Kevin Malone of the Dodgers were among those who came to get a firsthand look at Harrington. Kansas City Royals vice president, George Brett, was beseeched by autograph seekers when he attended games. When Brett learned one autograph seeker played softball, he urged the girl to "hit a home run." The next time the Royals area scout visited Palmdale High School, the girl's mother approached. "Tell Mr. Brett my daughter didn't hit that home run," the woman stated. "She hit three of them, and she's never hit a home run before!" Brett beamed when he learned the news.

13. Upping the Ante

Rumors grew that the Marlins had told the Harringtons that Matt was on their short list to be the number one overall pick. *The Sporting News* called the Palmdale High sensation "the favorite to be the number one pick in the draft." In the ensuing weeks, *USA Today* named Harrington its national high school player of the year.

The baseball men who paid visits to the Harrington home were taken aback by the economic struggles that enveloped the family. A half dozen neighboring homes were abandoned. Their owners had become unable to maintain payments and walked away. The pitcher's parents, Bill and Sue Harrington, were gracious hosts. Bill worked as an appraiser for a swimming pool repair company. Sue worked at a nearby big-box discount store. Together they raised five children. Matt was their middle child. A team that happened to visit on a particularly hot Mojave Desert day would receive an apology from Bill Harrington, who would explain that the family could not afford to turn on the air conditioning. The meeting would proceed with the visitors sweating, sometimes profusely, throughout the discussions.

While some of the visits ended with an assurance that signing wouldn't be a problem, a volatile cat-and-mouse game was about to break out. The Harringtons retained the services of an experienced agent, Tommy Tanzer. The 50-year-old had been a player agent for 16 years. Five of his clients were taken in the first round of the 1998 draft. Tanzer had several major-league clients, was well regarded within his profession, and considered honest by several baseball executives. During the final week before the draft, Tanzer took the lead in the Harringtons' signability talks with teams.

Handicapping of the 2000 draft was largely based upon money. Major League Baseball was urging teams to pay signing bonuses based upon the round and the pick number in which the player was chosen. Agents, however, continued to wheel and deal for far more. Tanzer was no different than his brethren in developing a financial demand, finding a team willing to pay it, then scaring off other clubs who held higher picks in the first round with news of his client's price and a willing suitor.

The Marlins held the draft's first pick. One year earlier, they had taken Josh Beckett in the first round, the second overall selection, and spent $7,000,000 to sign the hard-throwing pitcher. Now, Marlins executives let it be known that after much consideration they would not spend such an exorbitant amount to sign their first-round choice in the 2000 draft. A signing bonus closer to the 1999 first-round average of $1,800,000 was likely what they had in mind. Many speculated that their declaration ruled Matt Harrington out of consideration.

The Minnesota Twins held the second pick in the 2000 draft and made no secret that it was Harrington they wanted. The Twins' general manager, Terry Ryan, was perturbed when he learned the price tag that Tanzer had affixed to the pitcher—$4.9 million. The agent had arrived at this asking price by using the $3.96 million signing bonus given to 1999's number one pick, Josh Hamilton, by the Tampa Bay Devil Rays and tacking an additional 25 percent onto it. The figure was almost twice what Ryan wanted to spend. The night before the draft, Ryan spoke to the Harringtons by phone for close to two hours. When it became clear that neither side would budge from their positions, Matt Harrington requested that the Twins not select him.

Tanzer was convinced that the team selecting seventh would meet his asking price. Josh Byrnes, the Colorado Rockies' assistant general manager, had told Tanzer that Harrington "will not get past our pick." In less than a week, however, any perceived understanding between the two men would explode in a fury of contemptuous acrimony.

Since being made to realize that he had been blessed with a supreme pitching gift, Matt Harrington had dreamt of playing professional baseball. Conversations and actions throughout his senior season at Palmdale High had pointed toward the June amateur draft. Days before the draft Harrington told Steve Henson of the *Los Angeles Times*, "This is one of the most exciting things you can go through; I'm not nervous." A gathering was assembled at his parents' house to await the call from the selecting team. "It's funny," Matt Harrington told the *Times*' Henson, "I always want to get out of going to school, and on a day I *could* stay home, I want to go because I want to be with my friends."

The Marlins opened the draft by selecting San Diego-area high school first baseman, Adrian Gonzalez, whom they would quickly come to agreement with on a $2 million signing bonus. Minnesota, selecting second, chose Cal State Fullerton pitcher Adam Johnson, and the two struck a deal for a bonus reported to be in the neighborhood of $2.5 million. It was shortly before 10:30 on the morning of June 5 when the phone rang at the Harrington home. The Colorado Rockies were calling with news that they had selected Matt with the seventh pick in the first round. Jubilation erupted. Bill and Sue Harrington hurried to Palmdale High School to share the news with their son. An announcement was made over the school intercom letting the entire study body know of Matt's selection in the baseball draft.

Within the Rockies offices, executives were ecstatic to have nabbed the talented pitcher. "We didn't think he would be on the board when we picked," Bill Schmidt, the Rockies' scouting director, told the *Denver Post*. "He was the best player on the board when our pick came around. We made some progress today." Harrington was happy with the news. "I want to get on my way as soon as possible," he told the *Times*' Henson. "I think the Rockies will pay me what I'm worth."

Three nights later Schmidt, Josh Byrnes, and two Rockies scouts traveled to Palmdale and met with the Harringtons. Compliments and pleasantries flowed. The next day Byrnes told Tanzer the Rockies would not meet his $4.95 million asking price. According to several accounts, the agent became angry. He railed at Byrnes, claiming the Rockies' executive was reneging on a predraft agreement. Byrnes vehemently denied making any such deal. The team's first offer, $2.2 million, was rejected out of hand.

For almost six weeks the two camps were mostly silent. The Rockies turned their attention to signing other players they had chosen in the draft. They inked a stellar draft crop that included Jason Young, Garret Atkins, Clint Barmes, Brad Hawpe, Scott Dohman, and Darren Clarke. The Harringtons followed Tanzer's counsel and remained patient. At times, it was challenging. Around Palmdale, the word "greed" was loosely bandied about. Local media criticized the Harringtons. *Los Angeles Times* columnist Eric Sondheim wrote, "Sign, Matt, sign. There are many more millions to be made in the major leagues. But first, you have to get there." When such criticism reached the eyes and ears of Matt, Bill, or Susan Harrington, it made them angry and upset.

Six weeks after the draft the Rockies extended a larger offer of $3.2 million. The total was higher than the signing bonus the Marlins had given to the first player chosen, Adrian Gonzalez. The offer was rejected. Four weeks later the Rockies proposed a multi-year deal that, when totaled, equaled the $4.9 million Tanzer had demanded.

By this point in the summer, the Chicago White Sox shook up the negotiations. The White Sox had agreed to a $5.3 million multi-year deal with their first-round draft pick, Joe Borchard. Tanzer changed his stance. He countered the Rockies $4.9 million package with a demand for $5.835 million—a figure derived from the total of Borchard's deal plus 10 percent. The amount would ensure that Matt Harrington received the largest signing bonus of any 2000 draftee. There was also an additional new twist to Tanzer's demands—a guaranteed major-league call-up by the end of the 2002 season. This presented an entirely new sticking point.

The demand pushed negotiations into a new realm. From simple dickering over the amount of a signing bonus, talks would now involve the complexities of labor agreements, future major-league budgets, and club makeup. Looking at the demand from a development perspective, the insistence could push Harrington to the big leagues before he was ready. Financially, a guaranteed 2002 major-league call-up would hasten the pitcher's eligibility to participate in the salary arbitration process and to gain free agency. Competitively, his hastened eligibility for free agency could cause the Rockies to lose Harrington at an age when statistics show that players are entering the three prime years of their career. Tanzer told Alan Schwarz of *Baseball America* he sought the guaranteed call-up "so they [wouldn't] leave him down in the minors to rot."

In early September Dan O'Dowd, the Rockies' general manager, was brought into the negotiations. The Rockies were to travel to Los Angeles for a series with the Dodgers, and O'Dowd invited the Harringtons to meet at Dodger Stadium. Tanzer answered for them, saying they would only meet if it were with Jerry McMorris, the Rockies' co-owner. The meeting did not happen.

Two weeks later the Harringtons received a letter from O'Dowd that contained two offers. The first was a proposal similar to Borchard's, an eight-year contract worth $5.3 million. The *Los Angeles Times* reported that the offer contained incentives that could triple the contract's value once met. It involved major-league contracts that bought out several years of arbitration eligibility. O'Dowd's second proposal was a straight signing bonus of $3.7 million spread over two years. Both offers were rejected.

O'Dowd and Byrnes were frustrated. Tanzer spewed rancor and laced negotiating sessions with profanity. The general manager and his assistant had grown to believe that the agent was the lone obstacle to a deal. They accused Tanzer of trying to promote himself at the expense of his client. Tanzer stuck to his guns that a pre-draft agreement had been breached, and he would not settle for anything less.

The Harringtons were angry. Matt Harrington called the Rockies liars. Bill Harrington believed the team's executives were trying to take advantage of his family's economic situation. Rival agents phoned the family to try to pry them away from Tanzer. Matt Harrington spoke of loyalty and refused to be swayed. The Harringtons remained confident that their agent would come through with the sort of deal they wanted for their son.

At games during that summer and in the fall, a lot of scouts talked about the Harrington situation. Everyone was really puzzled over what was going on. You'd hear guys ask, "What's wrong with these people?" A scout might answer, "Not the smartest bear in the woods." Everyone in the game was talking about it and nobody could believe it was dragging on.

13. Upping the Ante

Frustration became disbelief in the Colorado Rockies front office. Dan O'Dowd thought that a face-to-face sit-down with the Harringtons might resolve matters once and for all. He had not been a part of earlier meetings between the family and his assistant and scouting director. O'Dowd invited the Harringtons to come to Coors Field, the Rockies ballpark, but he was insistent that they come without their agent. Bill Harrington was equally adamant that Tommy Tanzer had to be part of the meeting. When the Harringtons refused to change their stance, the Rockies cancelled the family's plane tickets on the morning of the meeting.

In early October Tanzer made three proposals to the Rockies—$5.3 million over seven years, $4.95 million over two years, and a third option that called for $4.5 million with a major-league call-up in 2002. In addition, the agent insisted that Harrington retain his arbitration rights. The Rockies said no to each.

The four months following the draft filled with bitterness and anger. Tanzer and Matt Harrington began to explore the option to prepare for to the 2001 draft. The agent arranged a $5 million insurance policy to guard against a career-threatening injury. Harrington wanted to play, and there were two avenues to do so and be eligible for the 2001 draft. First was to attend and play for a junior college. The pitcher met with coaches at Pierce College, a two-year junior college in Woodland Hills, an hour from his home. His second option was to pitch for an unaffiliated independent club. This was a strategy that had been used successfully by the agent Scott Boras to leverage larger contracts for two of his clients, Jason Varitek and J.D. Drew.

Playing for an independent club would pit Harrington against players with previous professional, even major-league, experience. It would offer a stronger level of competition than he had previously faced. On the down side, independent leagues didn't begin until mid–May, which would only give Harrington three weeks to showcase his skills before the 2001 draft took place.

Tanzer cast about for an independent club for his client. When one of the top such clubs in the country, the St. Paul Saints, expressed interest, Harrington agreed to a deal worth $800 per month.

In January the Rockies and Harringtons made one last attempt to strike a deal. The pitcher and his parents traveled to Denver and met with the Rockies' owners, Jerry McMorris and Richard and Charles Monfort. "Class people all the way," Bill Harrington told reporters. The meeting was strictly get-to-know-you. Money and contracts were never discussed. McMorris and the Monforts sought to sweep aside the acrimony and create a fresh start. Everything seemed to go well.

The meeting left Tanzer and the Harringtons optimistic that they could strike a deal with the Rockies. One week after their trip to Denver, the Harringtons received another offer. The letter came prefaced with explanation that the Rockies had signed two veteran major-league free agents, Denny Neagle and Mike Hampton, to big contracts. The deals had altered the team's budget. In light of the expenditures, the best the Rockies were able to offer Harrington was a $4 million signing bonus spread over eight years. The total amount would still be the largest ever given to a right-handed pitcher in the history of the baseball draft. Tanzer replied with a request that the $4 million be paid out over five years. When O'Dowd took Tanzer's request to McMorris, the owner gave thumbs down and ordered an end to all future negotiations with the Harringtons.

With the door now slammed shut to a deal with the Rockies, Harrington turned his focus to showcasing his talent with the St. Paul Saints. While the pitcher and his agent were confident that a strong showing would net the kind of deal they wanted, naysayers were in abundance. Sportswriters pointed out that the 2001 draft would be far deeper in pitching talent than the 2000 draft was. Veteran baseball scouts and executives had concerns, too. They noted that Harrington would have gone almost a full year without pitching in a competitive game when he finally pitched for St. Paul. Training outside the structure of a team would be difficult, scouts reasoned. Conditioning would suffer. Such a long competitive layoff could also throw off a pitcher's mechanics, which would adversely affect the velocity of his fastball and the sharpness of his breaking pitches.

During a workout in February, Harrington felt tightness in his right elbow. A specialist ordered him to stop throwing and rest the joint for several weeks. It was in April when the pitcher got the "all clear" to resume his training. No sooner had Harrington received the good news, however, when he was felled by the flu. Once that cleared, he contracted an ear infection.

When Harrington joined the St. Paul Saints in early May, he was part of a club with a half dozen players who had major-league experience. Several on the Saints roster had played at the highest levels of minor-league ball. Harrington, on the other hand, was two years younger than any other player in the entire Northern League and had no prior professional experience. His talent impressed his teammates, while the young pitcher's actions left some of them bemused. "Big, strong kid with good stuff," the Saints' center fielder Keith Williams said to an acquaintance. "It's a no-brainer why he was taken high in the draft."

Veteran players were quick to notice Harrington's professional naiveté, though. "Doesn't have a regimen," noted Williams, who had played in the big leagues with the Giants and Pirates. "The experienced guys have a regimen. They know how to prepare for a game. He doesn't. He seems to do what he thinks he needs to do." Some Saints players were rubbed the wrong way by Harrington. Many had a determination to get back to either the big leagues or a high level of minor-league ball. They didn't like that Harrington was using their team as a showcase and felt the pitcher came off, as one Saints player said, like a high school kid "excited to get $500 a month to play ball."

Harrington's debut attracted a sellout crowd on a wet, cold Friday night. A dozen major-league scouts came to watch. Radar guns noted a fastball velocity that was down from what he had clocked in high school. It ranged from 86 to 89 miles an hour. Scouts jotted in their notebooks that there was little break to Harrington's curve. Four days before the 2001 draft, Harrington made his final start for the Saints. Heads nodded when the digital readout on the scouts' radar guns displayed 95 miles an hour after Harrington fired fastballs. His control was erratic, and he left the game trailing 4–0. The pitcher told a reporter he was focusing on his fastball, trying to show the scouts that his high velocity was still there. While that became evident during the game, Harrington's stay with the Saints was far from overwhelming. The prospect hurled 19 innings, allowed 18 hits, surrendered 20 runs, walked 18 batters, and struck out 17.

Entering the 2001 draft, Matt Harrington was a young man shrouded in question marks. Outwardly, scouts and their bosses wondered how the long layoff from baseball had affected the now 19-year-old's pitching skills. Internally, teams wondered about Harrington as a person and wondered if they too would be subjected to prickly negotiations should they draft the pitcher. Tanzer's reputation did not escape the previous year unscathed either. It was reported that he was having difficulty attracting new clients because of the difficult negotiations with the Colorado Rockies.

On June 5 Harrington logged onto the Internet to listen to a feed of the major-league draft. One year after he was regarded as the best pitcher in the draft, he hears seven of the first nine picks go to pitchers. He is not one of them. When the first round and the sandwich round of supplemental picks concludes, 24 of the 44 players selected have been pitchers. Matt Harrington's name has yet to be called. It is only in the middle of the second round, when the San Diego Padres announce the 58th selection, that Matt Harrington hears his name called.

The Padres' general manager, Kevin Towers, heaped praise on Harrington. "When he was in high school, he was one of the best I ever saw." Towers and the Padres are careful, however, that their praise be packaged in the past tense, for they have concerns. They are well aware that Harrington suffered shoulder soreness when he pitched with St. Paul. The team's first offer to the pitcher is one made merely to meet baseball requirements for retaining a player's rights. It is for only $850.

By the summer of 2001 the Harringtons' frustrations reached a breaking point. They fired Tommy Tanzer as their son's agent. In his stead, the family hired the renowned super-agent, Scott Boras. Throughout the summer there is little discussion between the Padres and Harringtons. It is a full eight months after they selected Matt Harrington that the Padres begin to take serious action. Convinced that the pitcher's shoulder is now healed, the Padres invite Harrington to their spring training complex in Peoria, Arizona. They want to see the onetime sensation pitch under live game conditions. Against a group of tryout hopefuls who were seeking a minor-league contract, Harrington pitched three innings. He retired all nine batters that he faced. His fastball tops out at 91 miles an hour.

Six weeks later the Padres extend a significant offer. It is for $1.25 million. The proposal calls for the money to be paid out over five years. Upon signing, $300,000 will be paid. The family's new agent, Scott Boras, turned the offer down. Several publications reported, without attribution, that Boras sought double what the Padres had offered.

Within days the Padres withdrew their offer. They wanted to evaluate Harrington further. For a second time, the pitcher decided to use an independent ballclub as his showcase, but rather than return to St. Paul, Harrington joined the Long Beach Breakers. The team was managed by former Los Angeles Dodgers catcher, Steve Yeager. John Curtis, a former major-league pitcher, was the pitching coach.

In Harrington's first game with the Breakers, he pitched five innings. He allowed six hits, walked two, gave up four runs, and was charged with four wild pitches. San Diego's scouting director, Bill Gayton, watched the performance. While he offered favorable news that Harrington had hit 93 on the radar gun, Gayton said he felt Harrington had poor command of his pitches and had regressed. "Based on where he was at," Gayton told the *Long Beach Press Telegram*, "we told him to re-enter the draft."

While the Padres chose not to pursue Harrington, another ballclub was deciding they would take a chance. The only other scout at Harrington's debut performance with the Breakers had been a scout for the Tampa Bay Devil Rays.

The 2002 draft was a startling picture of how far Harrington's stock had fallen. Through 12 rounds, not a single team bothered to select the pitcher until Tampa Bay picked Harrington in the 13th round. When asked about the risk of taking a player who had twice turned down seven-figure offers, Tampa Bay's scouting director, Dan Jennings, said, "If he's going to be a major-leaguer somewhere, at some point he's going to have to open the door and jump in." The Tampa Bay offer was less than $100,000.

Harrington continued to pitch for Long Beach. Scouts who turned up to watch were surprised by his added weight. "He's been sitting on the couch eating potato chips," one exclaimed. With each performance, Harrington's manager became more fed up with the pitcher. The onetime phenom walked eight in five innings against Solano, five in four innings against Chico. Against Yuma, Harrington surrendered six hits and five runs in just one inning. When the pitcher was tagged for nine hits and six runs a week later against Yuma, Yeager had had enough. "He has no business being here. He can't pitch here," Yeager groused to Blair Lovern of the *Long Beach Press Telegram*. Harrington was released soon after.

The pitcher's downward slide continued. He joined another independent club, the Ft. Worth Cats, but pitched poorly. Negotiations with Tampa Bay never became serious, and Harrington entered the draft for a fourth time.

The Cincinnati Reds took a chance on Harrington, selecting him in the 24th round of the 2003 draft, but talks between the two parties amounted to nothing. In 2004 the New York Yankees picked the pitcher in the 36th round but soon after the draft learned that Harrington was to have shoulder surgery to repair minor rotator cuff damage. The team notified the pitcher it was not interested in signing him.

During the summer of 2002, a year after they had fired him, the Harringtons filed a lawsuit against Tommy Tanzer for negligence. In March of 2004 Boras directed the family to drop the suit. Instead, Boras urged the Harringtons to focus, instead, on collecting on the $5 million insurance policy they had taken out in 2000 to guard against a career-damaging injury to their son. The Harringtons and the insurance company agreed to mediation and settled for $2.5 million.

In May of 2005, recovered from shoulder surgery, Matt Harrington showed up to the Ft. Worth Cats preseason camp weighing 250 pounds, almost 65 pounds more than his high school playing weight. Throughout the season, Harrington struggled to get his fastball above 87 miles an hour. His pitching coach, Dan Smith, implored Harrington that his chances and time in baseball were running out. The two discussed a workout and nutrition plan which Harrington adopted. When the pitcher reported for the 2006 season, he had lost more than 30 pounds. Used as a relief pitcher,

Harrington recorded a 6–1 win-loss record. His fastball velocity came back, and he consistently registered between 92 and 93 miles an hour on the radar guns. Scouting reports convinced the Chicago Cubs to take a chance. The Cubs offer Harrington a contract. This time, Harrington quickly agreed. He received a signing bonus of $1,000.

In February 2007 Matt Harrington reported to the Cubs minor-league spring training complex in Arizona. He was 25, the age when the Colorado Rockies had feared the accelerated big-league promotion might make the pitcher a coveted major-league free agent. Now, Matt Harrington was a guy looking for was a chance—a chance to make the Cubs' Class A farm club. Three weeks into spring training and two weeks before minor-league teams were to break camp and begin their season, Matt Harrington was released.

I saw the boy's father one afternoon at a game, and I asked him what happened. He shrugged his shoulders. I felt bad for him. I felt bad for the kid. He had such a good arm. Whenever I talked to a kid I'd ask him, "Do you want to be a [pro] ballplayer?" If they'd say, "Yes, Mr. Genovese," then I was interested in them. If they'd say, "Well, maybe," or "if the money's right," then I wasn't so interested. You've got to have passion to be successful. It carries you through the tough times. Besides, the big money is in the big leagues. Harrington loved baseball. It's just a shame what happened to him. He had the tools.

Years later his high school teammates still talk with amazement of the skills Matt Harrington displayed. They remain disappointed that their teammate was unable to fulfill the stardom that beckoned. "It's a crazy thing," Tyrone Culver recalled. "The movement. The velocity. He's the best high school pitcher I've ever seen. We all talk that it's a shame people never got to see what Matt could do."

INDEX

Adenhardt, Nick 3
Alexander, Grover Cleveland 55
Alexander, Hugh 3
Allyson, June 5, 25
Alou, Jesus 2
Alston, Walter 41, 42
Appling, Luke 13, 17, 18
Arnold 168
Averill, Earl 11

Baker, Dr. Lenox 126
Bamberger, George 149
Barbao, Kenny 114
Bark, Jerry 148
Bavasi, E.J. "Buzzy" 41, 43, 44
Baxes, Jim 28–45
Beiden, Pete 56
Bennett, Bob 178
Bennett, Dr. George 63, 127
Berger, Boze 13
Bergesch, Bill 196
Berra, Yogi 86
Berry, Ken 195
Bishop, Bob 128–140
Bishop, Harry 128, 129, 131
Bonds, Bobby 161, 165
Boone, Bob 169, 170
Boras, Scott 205, 208, 209
Brett, George 200
Bridges, Tommy 14
Brown, Chris 189–191
Buhl, Bob 41
Bunning, Jim 43
Burwell, Bill 63, 64, 115
Byrnes, Josh 202, 203

Campanis, Al 172

Cardenal, Jose 2
Carey, Tom 11
Carr, Rex 129
Cereghino, Ed 73–96
Cey, Ron 193
Chandler, Happy 55
Chapman, Ben 9
Chavez, Hugo 166
Chavez, Nestor 4, 155–166
Chilcott, Steve 141–154
Clark, Jack 2
Coates, Jim 105
Cobb, Bob 31, 38, 39
Cobb, Ty 2, 30, 82
Cochrane, Mickey 7
Coleman, Ed 11
Comiskey, Grace 27
Comiskey, J. Louis 7, 16, 17, 21
Cox, Billy 16
Crosby, Bing 55, 81
Crosetti, Frank 15
Culver, Tyrone 198, 199, 210
Curtis, John 208

Davey, Dick 156
Dean, Dizzy 23, 112, 118
Dedeaux, Rod 169
Deer, Joe 152
DeRosa, Alex 112
Detore, George 113–118
Devine, Bing 145, 146
Devine, Joe 74, 76–78
Dickey, Bill 15
Dickson, Murray 116
DiMaggio, Joe 11, 15, 86
Donatelli, Augie 68
Dotterer, Dutch 194

Index

Dougherty, Bill 97
Dunlap, Harry 116, 118, 119, 127
Dykes, Jimmy 7, 9, 11, 12, 13, 16, 17, 21, 23, 24

Easter, Luke 36
Egaway, Euguro 179
Elway, Jack 187
Elway, John 187–197
Erautt, Eddie 90
Evans, Billy 9

Fagan, Paul 78
Farrell, Wes 14, 113
Feller, bob 16, 18
Fernandez, Sid 186
Fontaine, Bob, Sr. 183
Fox, Charlie 134
Foxx, Jimmie 10, 19, 150
Franks, Herman 162
Frazier, Joe 152, 153

Galindo, Al 103
Ganss, Bobby 64
Garagiola, Joe 116, 120, 121
Garcia, Dave 134, 139
Gehrig, Lou 9, 15, 18
Gehringer, Charlie 8
Gibson, Bob 42
Gil, Gus 163
Gilbert, Andy 160
Gilhousen, Rosie 49
Gilliam, Junior 41, 42
Gomez, Lefty 16, 113
Gonzalez, Adrian 202
Gordon, Joe 43, 44, 85
Gorman, Lou 131, 132
Goslin, Goose 8
Grabiner, Harry 20, 24
Gray, Dick 41, 42
Grba, Eli 156
Greenberg, Hank 8
Griffith, Calvin 196
Grimm, Charlie 11, 23
Grove, Lefty 14

Haas, Bert 130–132
Hamey, Roy 36, 54, 55, 57, 63, 65
Haney, Fred 29, 31, 37–40, 67, 68
Harder, Mel 14
Hardgrave, Eric 187, 191, 192
Harrington, Matt 198–210
Harris, Bucky 1, 3

Hartnett, Gaby 23
Hayes, Jackie 10
Henley, Gail 71
Henricks, Tommy 18
Herman, Babe 57, 65
High, Andy 41
Hisa, Jin 183
Hope, Bob 35
Hopper, Hedda 26
Hornsby, Rogers 82, 84, 123
Hubbell, Carl 2, 130, 132, 134, 136, 159
Hughes, Howard 38
Hundley, Randy 2, 162

Jackson, Larry 46
Jackson, Reggie 141, 143, 145, 146, 150
Jaffe, Jay 170, 175, 176
Jennings, Dan 209
Jennings, Howie 4, 97–110
Johnson, Adam 202
Johnson, Tom 57
Johnson, Van 25
Jones, Hank 177
Jordan, Harry 164

Keltner, Ken 18
Kerlan, Dr. Robert 151
Kerr, Buddy 135, 137
King, Clyde 164
Klaus, Richie 157, 158
Kluszewski, Ted
Koehler, Ray 7
Koosman, Jerry 148
Koufax, Sandy 4, 72
Kush, Frank 196

Labruzzo, Duke 99, 100, 104
LaMotte, Dr. Peter 151
Lane, Frank 43, 44, 76
Lanier, Hal 136
Lanier, Max 132. 133
Largent, Ray 7, 22
Larson, Don 159, 161
Lary, Lyn 11, 18
Lau, Charlie 104
Law, Vernon 58, 64
LeJohn, Don 173, 174
Lillis, Bob 41
Logan, Eddie 162
Lopat, Eddie 94, 146
Lotshaw, Andy 21
Luby, Hal 58, 60–63
Lyons, Ted 21, 23

Index

Maehorn, Iron 177
Marichal, Juan 4, 156, 159, 160, 161, 162
Marquess, Mark 191, 195
Martin, Billy 56, 120, 121
Mathews, Eddie 64
Mathis, Red 62
May, Lee 131
Mays, Willie 129, 1567, 162
McCarthy, Joe 14, 15
McCovey, Willie 1, 129, 156, 164
McCullough, Clyde 65, 116, 123
McDaniel, Lindy 164
McDowell, Sam 131
McGlothlin, Jim 161
McMillan, Roy 151
McMorris, Jerry 204, 205
McPhail, Lee 93–96
Meier, Dave 191, 192, 197
Meyer, Billy 56, 120, 121
Mick, Bunny 101, 105
Milberger, Ethel 9
Millican, Fred 45
Mitchell, Jim 107, 108
Morrison, deLessups 94
Morrow, Douglas 25, 26
Moses, Wally 13, 16
Murakami, Les 178–181
Murphy, Johnny 147
Murtaugh, Danny 142
Muse, Charlie 113, 114
Musial, Stan 122

Necciai, Ron 111–127
Nelson, Mel 155, 156
Nelson, Ricky 182
Nichols, Bruce 160, 161, 165
Noe, Dick 148, 149
Nolan, Joe 153, 154
Nomura, Ron 178, 180, 181, 185
Noren, Irv 28, 34, 38
Nori, Fred 141, 148, 154

O'Doul, Lefty 28–80, 83, 86
O'Dowd, Dan 204, 205
Orengo, Joe 78
Orsino, John 179
Otero, Reggie 163
Owen, Marv 18

Paciorek, Tom 173
Pastorini, Dan 169
Patrick, Chris 198
Paul, Ronnie 148, 150

Payton, Barbara 35, 39, 40
Pearson, Monte 18
Perry, Gaylord 162
Petrocelli, Rico 136
Pettit, George 47, 54
Pettit, Paul 4, 46–72
Piet, Tony 13, 23
Pivar, Sonny 99, 101, 106, 108
Porter, J.W. 75
Powell, Bill 15
Purkey, Bob 57, 58, 60, 64

Queen, Mel 161

Raffensberger, Ken 120
Raft, George 35, 49
Reagan, Ronald 25
Reece, Thad 185
Reichardt, Rick 3, 118
Reid, Jesse 190
Richards, Paul 142, 145
Rickey, Branch 3, 31–33, 51, 65–69, 76, 97, 98, 100, 102, 112, 115–120, 122, 124–127
Rickey, Branch, Jr. 29, 36, 39, 40, 70, 102, 105, 19, 115
Ripken, Cal 149
Rivera, Jim 82
Roberts, Robin 121
Roettger, Harold 100, 102, 109, 117
Rojas, Minervino 2
Ross, Don 31, 32
Ruel, Muddy 8
Ryan, Blondy 10
Ryan, Rosy 159, 161
Ryan, Terry 202

Santo Domingo, Art 162
Schwarz, Jack 1, 2, 130–132, 134, 136, 159
Seinsoth, Bill 167–176
Seinsoth, Bill Sr. 167, 175
Selkirk, George 9, 10, 89, 89
Sewell, Rip 115
Shallock, Art 34
Shea, Marvin 11
Singleton, Ken 148
Sisler, George 98, 105, 109
Slaigh, Fred 55
Spink, J.G. Taylor 27
Sprinz, Joe 83, 84
Steinbrenner, George 194, 195, 197
Stengel, Casey 88, 92, 93, 143, 145, 146
Stephani, Frederick 53–55
Stevens, R.C. 99, 101–103, 107

Index

Stewart, Jimmy 5, 25
Stoneham, Horace 2
Strane, Al 167, 170, 175, 176
Strane, Bert 167, 175, 176
Stratton, Ethel 19–23, 25
Stratton, Hardin 20
Stratton, Monty 5–28
Stratton, Roland 20
Strawberry, Darryl 189–191
Stubing, Moose 130
Sturdivant, Tom 92, 93
Swartz, Art 47–49
Swartz, Bud 48

Tanzer, Tommy 201, 203–206, 208, 209
Taormina, Sal 130
Tate, Jude 6
Tatsuno, Derek 177–186
Tavares, Oscar 6
Theodore, George 153, 154
Thomas, Frank 59, 124
Thomasson, Dr. Arthur 20, 21
Tincup, Ben 58, 60
Towers, Kevin 207
Traynor, Pie 32, 109

Truman, Harry S. 92
Turner, Jim 88

Upright, Dixie 60

Veeck, Bill 36

Wade, Ben 172, 174
Ward, Arch 14
Webb, Billy 21
Webb, Del 34
Weiss, George 77, 90, 93, 146
Werber, Billy 13
Werle, Bill 159
White, Jo-Jo 8
Williams, Keith 206
Wills, Maury 4, 103, 104, 106, 108
Wrigley, Phillip K. 21
Wynn, Jimmy 131

Yeager, Steve 208, 209
Yonamine, Wally 182

Zarilla, Al 177, 181

www.ingramcontent.com/pod-product-compliance
Ingram Content Group UK Ltd.
Pitfield, Milton Keynes, MK11 3LW, UK
UKHW041956140426
5217IPUK00015B/829